Cosmopolitanism and Culture

For John Berger

Cosmopolitanism and Culture

Nikos Papastergiadis

polity

First published in 2012 by Polity Press

Polity Press
65 Bridge Street
Cambridge CB2 1UR, UK

Polity Press
350 Main Street
Malden, MA 02148, USA

ISBN-13: 978-0-7456-5382-2
ISBN-13: 978-0-7456-5383-9 (pb)

A catalogue record for this book is available from the British Library.

Typeset in 10.5 on 12 pt Times New Roman MT
by Servis Filmsetting Ltd, Stockport, Cheshire
Printed and bound in Great Britain by MPG Books Group Limited, Bodmin, Cornwall

The publisher has used its best endeavours to ensure that the URLs for external websites referred to in this book are correct and active at the time of going to press. However, the publisher has no responsibility for the websites and can make no guarantee that a site will remain live or that the content is or will remain appropriate.

Every effort has been made to trace all copyright holders, but if any have been inadvertently overlooked the publisher will be pleased to include any necessary credits in any subsequent reprint or edition.

For further information on Polity, visit our website: www.politybooks.com

Contents

Acknowledgements

This book started with an examination of the artistic reactions and experiments against the politics of fear, and it would not have been possible to keep going if it were not for the prompts, invitations and comments issued by a wide circle of friends and colleagues. At various stages it has been 'held up' – for scrutiny – and vastly improved by the feedback from Carlos Capelan, Maaretta Jaukkuri, Sneja Gunew, Sean Cubitt, Hou Hanru, Okwui Enwezor, Nick Tsoutas, Manray Hsu, David Elliott, Soh Yeong Roh, Kim Hong-Hee, Harald Kleinschmidt, Gerald Raunig, Virginia Perez-Ratton, Björn Frykman, Maja Pojarnowski, Berndt Clavier, Bo Reimer, Jonathan Friedman, Warren Crichlow, Florian Schneider, Nina Montmann, Jean Fisher, Charles Esche, Mike Featherstone, Francis McKee, Pavel Büchler, Paul Carter, Michael Ann Holly, John Frow, Barbara Creed, Ien Ang, Seva Kammer, Vasif Kortum, Anna Kafetsi, Maria Margaroni, Robert Nelson, Mark Cheetham, Scott Lash, John Hutnyk, Gerard Delanty, Jan Verwoert, Jennifer Tee, Lorenzo Romitto, Yanis Varoufakis, Danae Stratou, Alan Cruickshank, Alison Young, Peter Rush, John Cash, Zoe Castoriadis, Suzi Adams, Cesare Pietroiusti, Leon Van Schaik, Daphne Vitali, Louli Michaelidou, Kate Sturge, Keith Jacobs, Martin Flannagan and Marina Fokidis.

I am particularly grateful to Malmö University for offering me the Willy Brandt Guest Professorship at the Institute of Migration and Ethnic Relations in 2005, the Australian Research Council for providing teaching relief and the University of Melbourne for awarding me a sabbatical in 2009. I would also like to express my appreciation for the support of Anthony Giddens and John Thompson.

Without the ongoing care and camaraderie of my dearest friend Scott McQuire and my family John, Helen, Bill Papastergiadis and Betty Alexopoulos, I would have found it difficult to make ends meet. Research assistance provided by Meredith Martin, Victoria Mason, Meg Mundell and Isabelle de Solier has been an invaluable benefit. Of course, the deepest tribute must go to my wife, Victoria Lynn, for all her critical insight, companionship and loving support. And finally, to my darling daughter Maya, thank you for your patience.

Introduction: Waiting for the Barbarians

Just over a hundred years ago Constantin Cavafy wrote the poem 'Waiting for the Barbarians' (Cavafy 1984). Cavafy spent most of his life in the cosmopolitan merchant quarters of the Egyptian port city Alexandria. At various stages his family, like many other foreigners, had been expelled from the city. He kept returning. In this poem we can infer the irony with which Cavafy experienced being a stranger in the city of his birth. It begins with a description of the foreboding that precedes an invasion. There is the suggestion that insecurity originates in the absence of a common language. The Greek city is preparing itself for a siege by foreigners who mutter incomprehensible 'bar-bar-bar' sounds. How will the Greeks know what the barbarians really want? Cavafy then turns to the fears that are spread by rumour. There is a dread and hint of panic that the barbarians' real aim is the devastation of civilization. In readiness for the final battle, the city braces itself for the worst. However, Cavafy does not end his poem with either victory or disaster.

> Night is here but the barbarians
> Have not come
> And some people arrived from the borders,
> And said that there are no longer any barbarians.
> And now what shall become of us without any barbarians?
> Those people were some kind of solution.

After all the waiting, nothing happens: neither conquest nor defeat. Cavafy does not follow this realization with the exhalation of relief:

he intimates that something else has occurred. The city had become dependent on the barbarians. Addicted to the fear they inspire. And its identity could only be affirmed by the desperate stance of defensive hostility. Three times Cavafy underlined the disappearance of the barbarians: 'And some . . . And said . . . And now . . .' The barbarians had served a purpose. They helped bring a focus into the city. By closing up the city, needs could be simplified, loyalties resolved and identities separated. 'Those people' were indeed 'a kind of solution'. The barbarians could be seen as a mirror of the internal fears. We need them to see ourselves. In the immediate aftermath of 9/11, there were repeated calls that the barbarians were closing in and, as Arundati Roy observed, 'ordinary people in the US had been manipulated into imagining that they are a people under siege', and in this state of anxiety they were 'bonded to the state by fear' (Roy 2004, p. 7).

This book commenced as a commentary on two events that occurred in 2001 at opposite ends of the world: the arrival in Australia of the Norwegian container ship *Tampa*, carrying 433 refugees, and the terrorist strikes in the USA. The sight of the Pentagon in flames and the collapse of the twin towers of the World Trade Center in New York exposed the vulnerability of even the most powerful military centre and cancelled any illusion of exemption from global terror. Thousands died, many more were injured and the financial damage was astronomical. When refugees arrive unexpectedly there is also a rupture. Adjustments and special provisions have to be made to determine their right to asylum. The state needs to accommodate new needs. However, the horror of death caused by vicious acts of violence cannot be compared to the inconvenience of interrupting normal administrative procedures in order to facilitate the settlement of a few strangers. Surely the disruption caused by refugees is trivial in comparison to the harm of terrorism. And, yet, these two events were routinely conflated.

One of the first responses of the Bush administration to September 11 was the closure of the airports and the suspension of refugee resettlement programmes. The following month his attorney general, John Ashcroft, went a step further. He warned terrorists that, if they overstayed 'even by one day, we will arrest you' (Meeropol 2005, p. 162). The US government threw out the widest anti-immigration net in the hope of catching terrorists. Although thousands were detained and interrogated, not a single person was charged with terrorist offences. By linking terrorism to breaches in border security, Ashcroft was drawing on a deeper fear that the sources of threat are always from the outside. As Judith Butler argued, rather than taking the moment to reflect on the trauma, the political imaginary of America was dominated by a thrusting hunger for revenge. There was a quick succession of steps that justified 'heightened nationalist discourse, extended surveillance mechanisms, suspended constitutional rights, and developed forms of explicit and implicit censorship' (Butler 2004, p. xi). Even Hollywood was quick to fall in with self-censorship and happy to be part of the defensive. The shooting of catastrophe movies was not only suspended but, between October and November 2001, Hollywood directors were 'recalled' to the Pentagon for advice on future 'unimaginable' scenarios and to help co-ordinate the messages on the 'war on terrorism' (Caterson 2007). Amidst panic, fear spreads, and its sources become more obscure. The Australian and the UK governments took note of the new Patriot Act and responded by passing similar legislation that linked anti-terrorism laws with migration policies. The former Howard government in Australia even went so far as to initiate a series of media campaigns urging all members in the community to 'dob in' invaders. This inspired an obliging citizen to issue a car bumper sticker: 'Help the government. Honk if you are a terrorist!'

Shortly after 9/11 I flew from Melbourne to Helsinki. On board the flight I read an article by Hugo Young (2001) that accurately predicted a new era of boundless warfare. I had been invited to Helsinki to present a lecture in a symposium that celebrated the opening of the exhibition ARS 01.[1] The theme of the exhibition was the hybridization of art and culture in an age of heightened mobility. While viewing the exhibition, I found my attention was captured by the large number of works that addressed fear and insecurity. For instance, in a prescient video installation, *3-Minute Survival Attempt* (2000), Anna Jermolaewa simulated both the destabilizing effects of conflict and the anxiety over the faceless aggressor. The fragile balance in the social order is, in the course of this video installation, played out in the interaction of toys made in the shape of pendulous figures. Accompanied by an ominous soundtrack of jackboots, one piece suddenly swings out of control and falls onto another. This precipitates a cascading effect in which all the pieces begin to tumble into each other and fall in a multitude of directions. As this energy overwhelms the scene it is never clear in which order the toys will ultimately fall. The only certainty is that disaster is imminent. Although each toy is uniform in shape, and at first appears to be stable, their combined movement generates a chaotic fall. The displacement effect is compounded by another unseen force that creates an additional swirling motion. The toys spin and fall into a vortex. The video ends when the surface tilts and everything falls off the edge. But the aggressor who supposedly precipitated the fall remains invisible. The hand and face of the aggressor are never revealed.

This video resonated with Jean-Luc Nancy's earlier claim that 'nowhere, then, is there war, and everywhere there is a tearing apart'

(2000, p. 135). It was also expressive of this new generalized anxiety over terrorists in our midst and refugees on the move.[2] In this context, identifying the figure of dread was not as clear and obvious as previously thought. Irrespective of whether the enemy was from abroad or 'home grown', it was impossible to distinguish them from the ordinary citizen. The old racist practice of denigration and distinction did not work. The fear of these others was not stimulated through any visual signs of ugliness or inferiority, but rather through an imaginary embodiment of values that threatened 'our' security. For a brief period after 9/11 there was an uncertainty as to who the enemy was and where the fight should be staged. Then the wars were waged in Afghanistan and Iraq.

Even before these military battles, the former Australian prime minister John Howard had already commenced a 'war on refugees'. The flashpoint for the refugee crisis took place at sea, some 1,400 kilometres off the Australian coast. In August 2001 a Norwegian container ship, the *Tampa*, loaded with 433 refugees rescued from a sinking Indonesian fishing boat, headed for the nearest port, in the Australian territory of Christmas Island. This conventional maritime rescue triggered an international crisis: the Australian, Norwegian and Indonesian governments refused to accept the refugees, and the Australian government banned the ship from entering Australian waters. The *Tampa* affair unleashed a violent response involving military interception, the redrawing of Australia's borders, the mandatory incarceration of refugees, an aggressive backlash against humanitarian refugee policies, and the so-called Pacific Solution – the forced transportation of refugees to countries such as Papua New Guinea and Nauru, which were paid by the Australian government so that refugees could be incarcerated there in purpose-built detention centres.

Howard's policies on border protection and mandatory detention motivated new levels of public protest and opposition from a wide spectrum of activists, artists, public intellectuals and community groups. People of vastly different political orientation found themselves on a common front that was both *against* the government's dehumanizing policies and *for* a renewal of humanitarian principles.[3] The 'war on refugees' was not fought exclusively on an Australian front. It was another ambient war that had numerous visible and invisible frontiers. Zygmunt Bauman has captured the moral and political dilemmas that became evident as it was fought in the European and North American contexts:

> The present trend to reduce drastically the right to political asylum, accompanied by the stout refusal of entry to 'economic immigrants', signals no

new strategy regarding the refugee phenomenon – only the absence of a strategy, and a wish to avoid a situation in which that absence causes political embarrassment. . . . Increasingly, refugees find themselves in a cross-fire; more exactly, in a double bind. They are expelled by force or frightened into fleeing their native countries, but they are refused entry to any other. They do not *change* places; they *lose* a place on earth, they are catapulted into a nowhere. (Bauman 2002, p. 112)

One of the most significant features of the protest movement was the formation of Kein Mensch ist Illegal (No One is Illegal), which was initially based in Germany but soon inspired synonymous groups in other parts of the world. Elie Wiesel, a Jewish survivor from Nazi Germany, a refugee and a Nobel Prize winner, first used the phrase 'No one is illegal' (NOII). In 1997, a group of media activists, radio practitioners, photographers, filmmakers and artists adopted Wiesel's slogan and published the manifesto 'no one is illegal' as part of an anti-racism project called Cross the Border, which ran for ten days in the Hybrid Workspace at the Documenta X festival in Kassel, Germany.

NOII is now a loose global network of anti-racist groups comprised of localized chapters which blend grassroots political activism with creative arts practice and a strong emphasis on the use of new technologies. They campaign for the total abolition of immigration controls and advocate free movement across borders. NOII has chapters in around ten countries and is affiliated with numerous activist and anti-racist groups all over the world. There is no centralized structure to the global network; chapters differ in their foci and forms of public engagement, but remain united in their opposition to immigration controls and their support of a united, border-free world. Strong anti-war sentiments are another unifying characteristic of the various NOII chapters. Some have a stronger focus on civil disobedience activities; others practise artistic interventions in public spaces or provide legal advocacy to refugees and displaced persons. Some chapters are more strongly arts based than others; several place an emphasis on campaigning for the rights of indigenous and 'colonized' peoples. At one level these collectives publicize the standards of international law and humanitarian principles in order to expose the shortcomings of state practices, but on another level this provides a new stage for opening a debate on human rights, ethical behaviour and responsible citizenship. These collectives thereby take on a dual and paradoxical role; they place themselves as witnesses to events and as mediators of the testimonies of those who are excluded from the public arena.

Assembly of the Invisible – Sea of Chairs, created by the Melbourne chapter of No One is Illegal, is an example of the cross-flows between physical protest and poetic gestures. NOII was actively involved in protest against the mandatory detention of refugees in places like Woomera, but it was also responsible for artistic actions such as the placement of over 200 empty chairs in front of the Melbourne doors of the Department of Immigration and Multicultural Affairs at 8 a.m. on 15 October 2001. On each chair there was a name and a story of exile. In the subsequent exhibition *Borderpanic*,[4] seven chairs were assembled in two semi-circular rows. On each there was a tag with a brief message by a refugee who was being forcefully detained. The message stated the person's name and occupation, and through its form the chair declared their lack of freedom to move and continue their life. The chairs carried a heavy sense of waiting and exuded an agonizing brooding. These tags resemble the tags on our luggage, but they did not confer ownership. Here they addressed abandonment, loss and dislocation.

Opposite the empty chairs were headphones that gave access to a recording by an anonymous refugee. The story was told in two parts. The first part recounted the experience of applying for asylum. A man's voice carefully led us through the bureaucratic machinations of the procedure. He told his story in an abstract and generalized way. It sounded horrendous enough on its own, but we then discovered that his application was rejected. Having lost all hope of legal appeal, he then told his real story to the unknown listeners at the other end of the recording. At this point there was nothing for him to gain. He will never even know if his story will find another form of kindness. The events are so shameful that he could only address them by assuming that he was actually talking to his dead father.

Numerous similar collectives have appeared throughout the world. One notable example is Multiplicity, an Italian-based collective of artists, architects and activists, and in particular their project, *Solid Sea* (2001), on the 'ghost ship' that sank off the coast of Sicily in 1996. This project referred to an incident in which a handful of survivors tried to convince authorities of the tragic circumstances in which many of their fellow refugees drowned. The incident was ignored until fisherman discovered bodies in their nets and the identity papers of the dead began to wash ashore. Multiplicity then began its own investigations. By examining Italian Navy surveillance records and meteorological department satellite footage, the collective demonstrated that the state had callously turned a blind eye to the drowning refugees. The project's title, *Solid Sea*, refers to the blockage of a historical process and the fluid networks that previously enabled coastal Mediterranean populations to share the view that they possess a common sea.

Despite the emergence of these new artistic and political coalitions, the public debates on the Australian, European and North American refugee crisis also revealed to me that the argument could not be won on purely moral appeals to the humanitarian issues, or by remonstration against the abuse of legal conventions (Burnside 2002; Manne with Corlett 2004). During this period not only did public opinion remain unmoved by reasoned arguments in favour of showing hospitality towards refugees but, in the first instance, news polls consistently showed that approval for the government increased alongside the exposure of its heavy-handed tactics (Burchill 2006). The problem in these public debates was not a matter of public indifference or ignorance. The needs of the refugees and the brutal effects of government policies were well documented and widely discussed. It was obvious that members of the public were more fearful of their own security than they were concerned over the human rights of refugees. However, to dismiss these specific fears as simply unfounded and to berate the public for being selfish is to overlook the myriad of ways that fear had already saturated the public imaginary.

Another approach was necessary. In particular, I turned to the ways artists sought to resist the political dogma, as well as to propose new forms of public debate. I had before now been engaged with the diverse ways in which artists had already extended the form of their visual practice to engage with social and political issues and to situate their work in the heart of everyday spaces. My aim was not to draw on art as an expression of the more virtuous side of the national character or the universal condition that binds together all of humanity. These moral appeals, while worthy antidotes to chauvinism, did little to illuminate the complex interplay between the public ideas on global movement and personal feelings of insecurity. A genuine dilemma had become more apparent during this crisis, and it could not be resolved by promoting either the 'goodness' of hospitality or the 'righteousness' of sovereign authority. It required both an acknowledgement of the ambivalence towards the processes of globalization and a more nuanced vision of a cosmopolitan subjectivity. My focus on art is based on the belief that artists can both articulate this social tension and hold together competing, if not conflicting, claims on identity.

One prominent artistic response to the Australian refugee crisis was Juan Davila's *Woomera* (2002), a series of paintings and drawings depicting the asylum seeker's plight through the frontier myths of Australia's colonial history. While the government was seeking to prevent the media from interviewing and photographing the asylum seekers, Davila deliberately depicted their struggle by drawing parallels to the history of Aboriginal displacement, and disrupted the 'monstrous' portrayal of the refugees by presenting them in the physiognomy of the dominant race. In the painting *Detention Place* (2002), two figures dominate a desolate, turbulent and parched landscape. At the centre a middle-aged man is kneeling – perhaps as a sign of penance, or in stunned exhaustion. Behind him is the glow of an industrial city. The atmosphere is dominated by whirling remorseless skies and a wind that has stripped the trees of vegetation. In the foreground is a strong, beautiful and naked woman. There are signs of blood smeared on her arms and thighs. She holds the shutter cable for a camera that faces the viewer. Amidst the scenes of violence the gaze has also turned awry. It points only to the outsider: the one not inside the camp.

Almost three years after this painting was completed, a story emerged of the incarceration of a former Qantas airline crewmember in an Australian immigration detention centre. Cornelia Rau, a German-born Australian citizen, suffered a mental breakdown and became delusional over her origins. Convinced that she was ill, the northern Queensland Aborigines who found her delivered her to the police. She was detained along with the other 'illegals'. After ten months of searching, her family found her in tatters. She was eating dirt, refusing to wear clothes and did not recognize her own sister. The story sparked a national scandal: on the basis of her 'foreign', unco-operative and clearly schizoid testimony, the Australian government had concluded that she was an alien and attempted to deport her to Germany. One commentator noted that this ordeal gripped national attention and provoked unparalleled protest against the detention system – but only when it was revealed that, like the figure in Davila's painting, she turned out to be one of 'us' (Marr 2005).

Contemporary art is usually defined by its critical attitude towards formal and political concerns, and it seemed to me that many artists were not only seeking to expose the fallacies of populist fears but also initiating alternative models for cross-cultural dialogue. The closer I examined these projects, the more I became convinced that they also provided a new grounding for the debates on the politics of globalization, the ethics of hospitality, and the culture of cosmopolitanism. Hence, my aim moved away from a direct critique of the politics of fear and headed towards the representation of mobility and difference in visual art practices, which range from works based on the conventional media of painting, photography and video to those that utilize social encounters such as discussions, meals and journeys as the material basis for the artwork. All of these works address the issues of globalization by 'creating' dialogues in displacement, 'sculpting' out new scenes of hospitality, or initiating 'platforms' for transnational exchanges. Of particular note was the emergence of tactical media.

Since the mid-1990s, artistic groups such as Critical Art Ensemble, RTMark, the Yes Men, and Institute of Applied Autonomy aimed to 'hijack' the new media technologies that had been made accessible by global capitalism and re-route them towards alternate modes of civic generosity, corporate unzipping, public revitalization and general mayhem. Hence, these groups would organize media pranks that mocked the duplicity of universities and art institutions, expose the hypocrisy of politicians, and swarm the websites of major corporations. However, rather than using strategies that called for an outright opposition and confrontation, these collectives developed a new kind of hit-and-run electronic guerrilla tactic. Inspired by the writing of Michel de Certeau on the practices of reclaiming everyday life, these groups organized themselves along a flat hierarchy, rejected the idea that they were visionary leaders that could spearhead the changes to come for the rest of society, and embraced the notion that utopia was an imaginative state that needed to be experienced in the complex layers of 'now time'. With ironic micro-steps and a holisitic vision of human freedom, they proposed that the potential for revolution was already in their everyday relationships rather than in a haughty manifesto for the future. From high-profile interventions by the Yes Men into Union Carbide's reparations for the damages to the people in Bhopal, to the countless acts of everyday resistance, there is, according to Sholette, 'a shadowy productivity that spreads across, rather than sinks deeply, into the broader social firmament' (2011, p. 31).

Although globalization is increasingly identified as a threat, it is equally clear that the desire to stage an open conversation between the local and the global has emerged as a core aim among artists. This broad expression of aesthetic cosmopolitanism is evident in a range of locally grounded and globally oriented artistic tendencies – denationalization, reflexive hospitality, cultural translation, discursivity and the global public sphere. These trends in artistic practice can be traced back to some of the artists' biographic experiences of migration, but in more general terms it can be related to the habitual encounters with 'newness' in everyday life. Indeed, these approaches have led to numerous investigations into the themes of exile and diaspora, as well as establishing a new line of inquiry into the influence of new communication technologies in the production of art. These two strands of research have extended the conceptual basis of art history to sustain a cross-cultural analysis and added new dimensions to the cultural critiques of globalization. However, I believe that the new globally oriented artistic practices are also expressive of a worldview that I refer to as the cosmopolitan imaginary. They all involve a commitment to the process that Anthony Appiah described as the 'imaginative engagement' with the other. Ethical relations with the other, political networks for activating social change, and cultural

platforms for facilitating exchange have become powerful themes that
have informed the practice of many contemporary artists. This fascination with the nexus between art and politics has inspired me to propose
that artists are knowledge partners in the theories of cosmopolitanism
and innovators in the modes of global belonging.

The structure of this book is twofold. Part I examines how the politics of fear have reshaped the social landscape. Part II explores the role
that art has played in reigniting cosmopolitan ideals. The three chapters of Part I explore how the aestheticization of fear, in both formal
political mechanisms and informal social networks, has transformed
the relationship between the global and the local, and thereby altered
the perspective on the status of refugees and human rights. This pre-
liminary investigation into the scenes of fear in everyday life provides
an outline of the social and political context in which contemporary
art operates. The second part of the book focuses on artistic responses
and emergent aesthetic strategies as exemplars of the new modes of
cosmopolitan agency.

The first chapter traces the aestheticization of politics after 9/11 and
examines how the image of fear was dispersed across almost all aspects
of social life. The political rhetoric of the 'war on terror' often stressed
that the enemy was no longer on the other side of a boundary, but pos-
sibly someone who is nearby. In this war we were repeatedly told that
the identity of the enemy was indiscernible, and that the next moment
of threat was unpredictable. I describe the phenomenon where fear is
so widespread that its sources become unlocatable as 'ambient fear'.
In the second chapter I use the concept of ambient fear to address the
shifts in the meaning of mobility and the broader transformational
effects of globalization. Much of the commentary on globalization
also relies on a mechanistic framework for explaining the impact of
mobility. At best, such viewpoints produce an ambivalent perspective
on mobility, and in times of crisis they are manipulated to inflame inse-
curities and 'naturalize' xenophobic attitudes. These approaches not
only perpetuate a deep fear of mobility but also obscure the dynamic
features of social change. In the third chapter I examine the image of
the zombie that appears in many of the contemporary accounts in
which migrants are described, and they themselves describe their experience of migration. Through these grotesque accounts of the fear of
the other, I claim that there is also evidence of renewal of what it means
to be human and a demand for a new framework of equality. This
section closes with the proposal that cosmopolitanism offers a critical
perspective towards both the specific politics of fear and the general
aestheticization of politics.

Part II explores the politicization of art. In particular, I examine artistic practices that have occurred since the 1990s. This period marks a distinctive turn towards collaborative and social forms of artistic practice. Throughout this section I have selected artistic projects that originate from almost every corner of the world and employ a wide variety of media. Despite lacking either formal resemblances or a common cultural tradition, these projects demonstrate a shared consciousness towards global issues such as the war on terror, migration and hospitality. There is a global optic that frames this analysis. However, the basis of my selections rests neither on a geographic claim that the specific choice of artists is representative of a global constituency nor on a formalist claim that a specific style, set of motifs or overarching aesthetic has achieved global influence. While eschewing the conventional taxonomies of art, I do uphold the view that art can 'tell us' something about the global condition. According to David Summers, art makes evident the 'first impulses in which the world is formed and made into a characteristic unity'. This idea that art has a role in both forging a specific knowledge of the world and initiating new modes of being in the world presents a challenge to the conventional modes of social and cultural analysis. In response to this challenge, I have adopted an interdisciplinary methodology that combines a close reading of visual images, participant observation in transnational projects, and contextual theoretical commentary. Where art history once aimed either to place art within an evolutionary story of cultural progress or to provide an overview of how national cultural traits are manifest within specific visual forms, I argue that the methodological challenge for this and many other disciplines is to construct a discourse that enables a cosmopolitan dialogue.

In part II I make the broad claim that the recent shifts in artistic practice have vitalized the concept of cosmopolitanism. What is now at stake is the capacity of art not only to capture a cosmopolitan vision of the world but also to initiate situations in which the artists and public participants are engaged in the mediation of new forms of cosmopolitan agency. This extended role has highlighted a significant shift in the meaning of imagination. Since Kant, the function of the imagination has been understood as the sensorial and pre-purposeful mode by which the mind constitutes its world. While the imaginative process is obviously the basis of all social and political structures, this link has been relatively obscured and ignored in social theory. By highlighting the productive role of the imagination, Arjun Appadurai made a major contribution to the understanding of the cultural landscape of modernity. Further to this, we can now consider the role art has played in re-evaluating the function of imagination in the construction of reality. In particular, I will argue that the artistic combination of a critical attitude towards the forces of globalization and a creative engagement with the forms of spatial belonging ushers forth a cosmopolitan imaginary. Hence, this section has a dual focus on the creative function of art – as a reflector of emergent forms of global change and as a generator of new modes of being and action in the world.

Chapter 4 commences with a critical survey of the classical and contemporary theories of cosmopolitanism and argues that the growing emphasis on the deliberative and moral dimensions has not only overlooked the aesthetic processes but also diminished the scope of the idea. By adopting the concept of aesthetic cosmopolitanism, I seek to provide a new perspective for understanding the significance of globally oriented art practices and their relationship to transnational social movements. Chapter 5 extends this perspective on aesthetic cosmopolitanism by re-examining a series of debates on aesthetics and politics in art history. It is my contention that a cosmopolitan conceptual frame is not only a valid field for grasping the relationship between aesthetics and politics, it is also a more useful paradigm for identifying the emergent tendencies for globally oriented artistic practices that are explored in greater depth in chapter 6.

In chapters 7 and 8 I revisit the concepts of hybridity and cultural translation in order to highlight the role of critical imagination in cross-cultural interactions. I seek to renew these terms by both extending the conceptual reach of hybridity beyond a mere term for describing the effects of cross-cultural exchange and stressing that the communicative function of cultural translation also includes innovation and invention. Hybridity and cultural translation therefore serve as tropes for addressing the relationship between creativity and mobility. Chapter 9 provides a focus on the emergence of collaborative artistic networks and their role in the mediation of new social meanings. By following the shift from the position of the artist as producer to the artist as a collaborator in the construction of social knowledge, I note that artists have sought both to develop consensual social representations and to redistribute agency to all the participants. In chapter 10 I begin by narrating my own experience as a participant in a transnational collaborative art project. This project provided an opportunity to witness the ways artists utilize both personal narratives about global mobility and political discourses on globalization to transform the materiality and form of their visual practices. I argue that these globally oriented artistic practices demand a new conceptual paradigm, a kind of 'deprovincialized' methodology, that is adequate for representing the mobilities and mixtures that constitute the social context of art. The overall objective of this section is to 'rescue' the account of artistic practice from both the formalist accounts that are underpinned by a quasi-mystical universalism and the dogmatic versions of political activism that abrogate the autonomy of creativity.

In the face of these global forces, what can we learn from art? The politics of art is usually determined from the other side of this question. Theorists routinely adopt a variety of approaches from the humanities and the social sciences in order to explain how politics informs and shapes art. For instance, theories of ideology have been used to illuminate the social context of art. Psychoanalytic, semiotic and anthropological concepts have played an invaluable role in clarifying the influence of gender, language and culture. The philosophical frameworks proposed by Deleuze and Rancière have come to prominence in the recent debates on art and politics. However, it is also necessary to turn the question around and ask: What knowledge does art offer? From this position the lessons from art are often framed in terms of its function as a harbinger of forms that have not yet arrived in full. Sociologists have frequently turned to art in order to glimpse the rise of emergent practices and marvelled at the capacity of artists to morph vague ideas into comprehensible forms. Cultural critics have also noted the incontrovertible dynamic by which the margin modifies the centre, and political commentators have observed that the premonitions expressed by artists often point to major institutional shifts. In short, we have become accustomed to examining the influence of social forces on art, and we persist with the vanguardist claim that artists often anticipate social changes.

I have attempted to develop an alternative approach towards art and politics. Art does not proceed as an investigative exposé followed by a judicious declaration of truth. It does not possess a fixed knowledge of things, but rather develops a critical attitude towards the possibilities in and between things. Art begins in curiosity, the sensuous attraction towards difference and connection,[5] and proceeds through a relational mode of thinking that serves simultaneously as an instrument for suspending the existing order of things and as a platform for imagining alternatives (see also Raunig 2008). Thus affects, thinking and practice are transformed through the action of carriage and connection. The artistic strategies of the twentieth century have, in broad terms, been classified under two headings: iconoclasm and redemption. Throughout modern history we can see a common expression of discontent against the existing social order in artistic, political and philosophical statements. All proceed from the shared starting point that human potential is restricted. They may differ in relation to identifying the restrictive forces and articulating the form of human subjectivity, but they all possess the aim to overcome the perceptual and real constraints that are imposed by habits, norms and

rules. Within these diverse aesthetic strategies there is also a singular
vision that I am calling a 'cosmopolitan imaginary'. It is a restless and
dynamic form of mobility that gathers momentum from, rather than
permanently settles into, clusters of like-minded elements. It arises
from the rub and swerve of affects, intellect and practice, rather than
heading towards some utopian space. This process of flow and rupture
has a multiplicity of singularities, and, as numerous commentators
have noted, it is from these instances that there is also a reframing of
both the meaning of human rights and the form of the social (Holmes
2009, p. 14; Negri 2008, p. 28).

Given the radical social changes and significant shifts in artistic
practice, I have sought to situate the operational effects of politics
in art, and extended the contextual parameters *of* art, within a cosmopolitan frame. However, I have also argued that this demands a
critical examination of the interplay between regional forces – the local
and the global – and the epistemic link between mobility and creativity. The dual focus on the creative function of art helps to distinguish
between the substantive and conceptual engagement with politics. In
substantive terms, artists have been engaged with political issues by
reflecting the distorted claims and revealing the flawed means by which
the politics of fear are defined. They have also opposed these divisive
goals by initiating new modes of exchange between strangers and generating alternative conceptual frameworks for organizing collective
action. From modest gestures that interrupt everyday communicational practices, to ambitious projects that seek to revitalize the public
sphere, art has become a medium for reconstituting the social. Art is
now a mode through which cosmopolitan ideals have materialized
both in visual forms and through collective social actions. The normative aspects of cosmopolitan theory gain new dimensions once we bear
witness to the wide range of artistic projects that have engendered an
effective interplay between the ethical issues of hospitality and legal
conceptions of human rights. This shift in the collaborative demands
that we consider not only how art can represent the condition of the
world but also the way it can enable an alternative way of imagining
our participation in the world.

The challenge of cosmopolitanism is paradoxical. It requires a
greater commitment towards openness and an appreciation that differences really matter. This paradox is often explored with vibrant
effect in artistic practices. The projects that are examined in this book
demonstrate the ways that art both reflects the cosmopolitanization of
everyday life and generates new modes of cosmopolitan agency. Art
cannot be reduced to the status of an instrument that illustrates other
forms of knowledge. It is involved in the mediation of new meanings

and the emergence of possibilities. Hence, art is not bound by the constraints of rational calculation and pure logic. Through this wider lens, art gives form to alternate imaginings and emergent systems for making sense of our place in the world. It embraces the classical cosmopolitan maxim 'I am a citizen of the world', and raises it to a platform for both expressing an aesthetic vision of the world and testing the imaginary worlds that are made through art. This conception of art and cosmopolitanism is indebted to Cornelius Castoriadis's theory of the imaginary. Castoriadis stressed that the institutions of society must be imagined in order that they be defined, developed and defended. Thus the work done in the imaginary and the works made in reality are deeply interconnected. And we should recall that if, as claimed by Benedict Anderson, artists were at the forefront of imagining the form of national consciousness that led to the construction of the nation-state, then the post-national forms of belonging and the cosmopolitan imaginaries that are currently being developed by artists also deserve serious consideration.

What are we really afraid of? Who are the barbarians? Just as in Cavafy's time, there are those who think that they lurk outside the city and that they can be seduced, appeased and distracted by shiny jewels. Then there are those who believe that the barbarians resent us so deeply that they scorn every opportunity for dialogue and have an inextinguishable wish to destroy our civilization. And yet, as Cavafy also warned, these figures are not the limits of our fears. Adam Phillips describes an incident at a school of so-called maladjusted students. He was employed as a psychotherapist to help teachers deal with their problems. One of the issues that repeatedly challenged the staff was whether they should lock the classrooms when the children were playing in the yard. There was a growing consensus that an unlocked room was an invitation to theft and vandalism. Most of the teachers believed that the classrooms needed to be locked and that the children should be protected from themselves. Then suddenly one of the teachers asked with innocence: 'But what if one of the kids wants to put something good *into* the classroom?' This produced a moment of stunned silence. Until another question emerged: 'Like what?' And then, as Phillips notes, there was immense relief that no one could think of anything (2001, p. 118). What sort of failure of the imagination is this? The tragedy of 9/11 prompted some critics to make the plea that, in a time of grief, there is the possibility of feeling more connected to a deeper sense of humanity (Butler 2004) rather than reasserting the 'self righteousness about one's own condition, a seeking proof of one's special place in the world, even in victimhood' (Mamdani 2004, p. 10).

Part I

The Aestheticization of Politics

1

Ambient Fears

At the precise midpoint of Gillo Pontecorvo's *The Battle of Algiers* (1966), a scene of colonial revenge is exacted at a cafeteria on rue Michelet. It is late afternoon, and the French colonial middle class has gathered to relax. Couples are having coffee, children are enjoying ice creams and hopeful men are hanging at the bar. A young woman in a white dress enters and approaches the bar. A man moves to the side, offers his seat and smiles. She orders a coke, places a bag beneath her feet. She is sexy and cool. Midway through her drink she gets up. 'Leaving?' he inquires. 'Yes', she replies. 'Pity', he adds. No sooner has she crossed the road than the bar explodes. Within minutes two other bombs are detonated.

Who can you trust? The enemy could be anyone or anywhere. Prior to the explosions, three women met. They removed their veils and burkas. They dyed their hair, dressed like Europeans, assumed an aloof sense of entitlement and subsequently passed every security checkpoint, pausing only either to take nervous breath or to flirt with the soldiers. These scenes play out the colonizer's greatest fear: the invisibility of the intimate enemy. This kind of fear was not immediately apparent after 9/11, but it has come to dominate our political imaginary.

What Changed After 9/11?

In his first public address to the American people after the attacks on 9/11, George Bush declared that these were 'acts of terror'. The following day he added: 'The deliberate and deadly attacks which were carried out yesterday against our country were more than acts of terror. They were acts of war.' In the weeks after 9/11, almost all the world leaders spoke in calm voices but were quick to adopt the new catachrestic phrase: 'war on terror'. Their initial response was couched in a discourse that switched between the apocalyptic and an epiphany. For George Bush it was 'civilization's war against barbarism', and for Tony Blair a 'wake-up call'. The events of September 11 were immediately taken as symbols of the end of a previous world and the beginning of a new and as yet unknown and unnamed world. The headline in the *Washington Post* demanded that Congress should immediately declare war: 'It does not have to name a country.' The *New York Post* followed with equal bloodlust: 'Kill the bastards . . . As for cities or countries that host these worms, bomb them into basketball courts.' The US administration decided that this was the moment to implement in full its foreign policy of unilateralism, while on the domestic front it went into overdrive to redefine the sphere of liberties under the new banner of homeland security, as well as outsourcing fear management to private agencies and 'fear experts' (Lapham 2005; Meeropol 2005; Grey 2006).

In Bush's words: 'To those who scare peace-loving people with phantoms of lost liberty, my message is this: your tactics only aid terrorists, for they erode our national unity and diminish our resolve; they give ammunition to America's enemies and pause to America's friends.' Concerned university professors and civil rights advocates were mocked as either juvenile idealists or anachronistic obscurants that were blind to the fact that the 'world has changed'. By 10 November, Bush had informed the UN of its ultimatum: 'either you are with us, or you are with the terrorists'. The 'war on terror' marked the point at which the Bush administration claimed that the USA was 'compelled' to act outside of the conventions of international rule, and that the urgency of the crisis demanded that there was no time to follow normal democratic procedures and the Geneva conventions.

If the 'war on terror' was the beginning of a new world, then what made that war different from other wars? For instance, Clausewitz's description of war as a symmetrical conflict in an open field made perfect sense during the Napoleonic era. In this period the enemy was sighted and the aim was to destroy their vital organs. As strange as the Cold War was, the identity and location of the adversaries was also never in doubt. They were on the other side of the Iron Curtain. Until the Soviet bloc imploded, it was a war of containment. When Muhammad Ali refused to be drafted into the Vietnam War, he justified his stance by claiming: 'No Vietcong ever called me nigger!' Asked if he even knew where Vietnam was, he replied with quicksilver irony: 'Yes, it's on TV!' In the scene from *The Battle of Algiers* with which I began this chapter, people have the knowledge that the enemy is already in their midst: 'They are everywhere in the Casbah and in the European sectors.' For the French commander, the problem is not where they are, but how to distinguish them. He concedes that their invisibility is a product of the method of parallel recruitment that isolates the different teams from each other. 'The reason we do not know our enemy is because they do not know each other.'

Anonymity and mobility have formed the weapon of the weak throughout guerrilla warfare. However, in the contemporary context of a 'war on terror', the scene of battle and the identity of the enemy are even more complex and elusive. At one level, the origins of the war can be linked to Reagan's policy of the 'rollback' of the 'evil' Soviet empire (McCoy 2003). Kissinger's solution of outsourcing and privatizing the spread of violence – 'Asian boys to fight Asian wars' – seemed to be a convenient short-term solution. However, it also produced the nightmare scenario of training and arming a new transnational warrior elite that would eventually be recruited by Al Qaeda. These new 'homeless' militias that were instrumental in micro-wars became 'blowback' agents of a new kind of transnational war that spread out of control.

After 9/11 the Bush administration argued that 'terrorist' states such as Afghanistan under the Taliban and fanatical movements such as Al Quaeda had no regard for international law, and therefore it was pointless to pursue them within the established legal frameworks. Osama bin Laden had always justified 9/11 as a counter-attack against the invasion, occupation and humiliation of the Islamic holy lands. What one side called terrorist attacks, the other described as a continuation of a war that had begun long before. The violence of terrorism produced its violent responses, including a novel form of infinite retaliation and vigilance against anonymous enemies. Threat, we were warned, no longer takes the form of an invading army, but assumes a covert identity. The image of 'sleepers' in our midst, or an infinite network of terrorists, incites new levels of dread. Killing has become an invisible and irregular business (Mbembe 2003). This moral void, and in particular Bush's moral absolutism and unilateralist stance, turned global public opinion against what was seen as a modern form of cowboy vigilantism (Micklethwait and Wooldridge 2005, p. 222).

The 'war on terror' is a misnomer because terror is not an object that can be attacked. However, what this phrase does signal is an expansion and blurring of the modes of military assault. It represents a departure from the classical warfare, in which the adversaries aimed at each other's body, to a kind of struggle that seeks to violate the realm of the imaginary (Sloterdijk 2009, p. 25). I will argue that the interplay between the unilateralist stance by the Bush administration and the networked terrorism of Al Qaeda also generated an ambiguous and multifaceted form of fear, or what I call ambient fear. This form of fear manifests itself through the dissolution of the conventional means for identification, categorization and classification.

Finding Fear: Its Meaning and Dynamics

Ambient fear is a kind of dread that has become so widespread that its sources appear to be both unlocatable and ubiquitous (Bauman 2006a; see also Buchler and Papastergiadis 1996). It is a force that is experienced viscerally, framing our suspicious glances at our neighbours, and extending into the gleeful approval of the state's use of violence. Cultural critics are quick to debunk the hysteria and prick the balloons of hyperbole that surrounded the political uses of fear, but in the process they overlook the way fear is entangled in a complex web of associations. When they do admit that fear has a social reality, the focus tends to be confined to its instrumental functions or related to specific struggles for power (Bourke 2006; Furedi 2005; Glassner 1999). A similar mode of explanation is also evident in political philosophy. Fear is interpreted as if it were a mechanism for sharpening loyalties and galvanizing collective bonds. Hence, Machiavelli and Hobbes are routinely cited as the philosophers who elevated fear into an instrument that the sovereign could wield in order to preserve both the social contract and power (Corey 2004). By contrast, when attention is turned to the more diffuse ways in which fear can shape the political environment, there is a tendency to adopt explanations that intertwine a subjective experience of doom with a collective wish for salvation by an external agent (Carroll 2002). Tocqueville saw anxiety as a formless state of nervousness that gripped the mass psyche, producing a state of paralysis that left people feeling vulnerable, while also stimulating an unspoken desire for salvation from an authoritarian figure. More nuanced conceptions of the relationship between fear and anxiety can be traced throughout the writings of Kant, Kierkegaard and Heidegger. The problem with fear and anxiety, states Heidegger, is not just that it 'radiates harmfulness', but that the person who is immersed in it 'loses his head' (Svendsen 2007, pp. 42–3).

Historians have also argued that fear played a central role in promoting hostility towards outsiders and stimulating integration into the modern nation-state. For instance, Eric Hobsbawm argued that, at a time when empires were struggling to manage competing forms of religious and cultural pluralism, the nation was 'invented' in order to create social cohesion (Hobsbawm 1994; Hobsbawm and Ranger 1983). Benedict Anderson (1983) also stressed that, as an 'imagined community', the nation promised a sense of fraternity and security to its members, by highlighting the barbarity and threat of the external other. It was postcolonial cultural theorists like Edward Said (1993) and Homi Bhabha (1990) who exposed the logic of this communion and noted that the fear of strangers served a double purpose: to externalize undesirable qualities while concentrating the permissible forms of national identity. This critical perspective paid particular attention to the way that nationalist discourses of belonging were dependent upon a definition of the other as an external and dreadful entity. However, to suggest that fear is merely a manifestation of a local form of insecurity arising from the fragmentation of social structures, or an instrument for mystification and exaggeration that is manipulated by political elites, is to limit its sources and scope to a specific psycho-geographic terrain. In this sense, it is reduced to an instrument that should, and can, be controlled. It is rarely seen as a constitutive force in social reality (Rumford 2008, p. 631).

Paolo Virno was among the first of the social theorists to grasp the centrality of fear and the 'ambivalence of disenchantment' in the transformation of contemporary culture and society. Fear, he argues, is not just the negative effect of experiencing threat, but also the motivating force that now drives contemporary politics and shapes the administrative criteria of everyday regulations. The restructuring of home and work is no longer defined simply by a break with the solidity of tradition but by an activation of the already fragmented state of traditions and an engagement with – a process of putting to work – sentiments, inclinations and states of mind that have been severed from any form of traditional foundation (Virno 1996, p. 15). The mobilization of fear is therefore not just a response but part of the precondition or mechanism for the advancement of specific socio-economic practices. The mutability of economic relations and the fragmentation of cultural values combine to create a mood of collective uncertainty, rather than simply a personal sense of insecurity (Nelson 2010). Or, put the other way, when the instances of a person experiencing insecurity are now commonplace, and the sources that stimulate this response are so widespread, then it is no longer sufficient to speak of fear as if it were a single entity that belonged within a person's subjectivity.

The distinction between fear and anxiety can help sharpen our focus. Fears are, as Freud noted, usually linked to specific objects of dread, whereas anxiety is an uncomfortable state in which the origin or the object of threat cannot be specified. Fear usually emanates from an external source. It hovers above, like a tyrant, or approaches as an enemy from the outside. When we speak of our fears, we usually refer to our fear *of* something. The object of our fear has a definable outline. By contrast, anxiety is diffuse, without precise boundaries, and it appears to emerge from a twilight state – neither in full light nor in total darkness. Therefore, when we articulate this kind of mood, we say that we are anxious *about* the possibility of something happening. Anxiety may lack a clear source of threat, but it is related to what Freud (1948) calls an 'expected situation of helplessness'. It lurks in the heart, it exists in rumour, and it spreads from below. Anxiety can provoke insecurity without sensory apprehension. It produces a far less certain sense of where danger lies, what is risky, and who is threatening. In his extensive survey of the role of fear in contemporary life, Zygmunt Bauman asserts that 'fear is at its most fearsome' when it remains an implicit menace that 'can be glimpsed everywhere but is nowhere to be seen' (2006a, p. 2). The inability to identify the origins or predict the consequences of our everyday fears has, according to Ulrich Beck, made people feel that fear is so widespread that it threatens to disrupt the crucial task of calculating risk. In a rather pessimistic response to the tension between difference and certainty, Beck goes so far as to suggest that the collapse of a risk regime – that is, the ability to measure and control threat – signals the end of modernity (1999, p. 5).

More recent uses of the psychoanalytic theories of projection and anxiety can also help unfurl the link between unconscious and public fears (Papastergiadis 2007d, 2006b). For instance, Julia Kristeva's study of the presence of strangers in contemporary society provides a useful example of the adoption of psychoanalytic concepts of the uncanny, splitting and projection for an explanation of the way fear is mobilized in both the encounter with the other as a stranger and the process by which we become 'strangers to ourselves' (Kristeva 1991). John Cash (2004) has also argued that, in the more paranoid modes of neo-nationalist politics, or what he eloquently describes as the 'haunting of security by the spectre of insecurity', there is a struggle to preserve an idealized self by means of either expelling or suspending the other in a state of unplacement.

A critical feature of the psychoanalytic construction of identity is the deployment of mechanisms for resisting the incursion of foreign elements and for promoting boundary formations. Across this boundary, values are projected that define the characteristics of the self and the other; force, then, is mobilized to ensure that the boundary and the differentiated identities remain intact. Projective and defensive mechanisms also operate in contradictory ways: they tend to both exaggerate and trivialize the figure of the other, while also asserting the right to aggressiveness and minimizing the acknowledgement of violence in the self. For Lacan, projection is linked to anxiety. Anxiety emerges when the individual is caught in an ambivalent state: wanting the comfortable feeling of being human and whole, and yet also discovering the paralyzing and dreaded sense of lack (Salecl 2001, p. 92).

Psychoanalytic concepts can help differentiate between aggressive modes of dehumanization and more inclusive ways of living with difference. However, Freud's psychoanalytic model of identity development, based on this familial triangulation of fears and desires, is not easily transposed to explain the collective formation of ambient fears in the global political imaginary (Stengers 1997, p. 106). Deleuze and Guattari's vision of the social imaginary as a vast, shifting network of desire-producing machines, connecting with each other in multi-directional binary chains and in ever-mutating combinations, offers a more prescient framework for considering the turbulent patterns that are shaping contemporary political attitudes and cultural identities (Deleuze and Guattari 1983). From this perspective, the aim is not to isolate fear from hope, or to oppose repulsion and attraction, but to see how the two responses are inextricably tied in a common creative process. Both occur in the imaginary, and they proceed through an associative dynamic. In the experience of fear there is also a perverse feeling of wonder, just as the encounter with sublime beauty always sends a shiver through your body.

Ambient fear is therefore not just a political effect that is manipulated by a powerful elite. It is more like a collective creative process that spreads through the whole range of communicative devices, from the one-way channels of mass media to the multiple networks of the internet. Passing from one medium to the next, it gets implicated in a near infinite range of carriers. This process of connecting disparate entities in the imagination gives rise to a much more intimate sense of threat. Each new formulation of fear proves to be highly unstable and quickly overlaps with the residual sediments of archaic fears, as well as inserting itself into the as yet undefined fears of the future. Hence, this associative dynamic acquires a self-propelling capacity that is fuelled by both the multiplying effect of additional sources and the process of concatenation that occurs in the rebound between the external sites and the expanded field of fearful sensory apprehension. Rather than trying to disentangle this new emotional and social bundle, I propose to examine the tropes that bring together deep historical fears and wide-open anxieties. As these 'vertical' and 'horizontal' emotions mutually reinforce one another, they are internalized as social 'facts' that provide the spatial and psychic markers for the 'ensemble of possibilities' through which we relate to others, affirm our own idealized self-images, and define a sense of place in the world. Hence it is not just a matter of correcting the flawed and false images of fear, but a deeper challenge to understand how the dynamics of fear *create* a specific worldview.

I will now examine the broadening of fear by discussing the blurring of the boundaries for six fundamental tropes: spatial boundaries, recognizable faces, controlled order, stable media, central leadership and unified organization. Ambient fear arises, therefore, not just from the acts of violation but also from the perception that these tropes no longer operate in their normal way.

De-spatialization of fear

The shift in the form of fear since September 11 can be gauged by the perception that the spatial boundaries of conflict have collapsed. In conventional warfare the aim of conflict is to overpower or disarm one's adversaries. This is usually achieved by superior force or cunning, and the battle usually occurs within the respective territories of the combatants. Even in the most paranoid accounts of war there was always an actual location from which the enemy would launch their invasion. For instance, shortly after President Ronald Reagan 'warned' America that the Sandanistas were closer to Texas than the Texans were to Washington, a cartoonist drew an ironic picture of the necessary watchfulness that war inspires. It showed, under moonlit skies, two men sitting on a veranda with shotguns on their laps. The son turns to his father and suggests: 'It's a bit quiet out there.' Pa replies: 'Yeah, a bit too quiet!'[1]

After September 11, the fear of the other could not be contained within a single territorial entity or confined to a given place of origin. The previous attacks on US embassies in Africa, as well as the subsequent bombings in Madrid and London, were seemingly connected as part of wide-open conflict, but they happened across a disjointed terrain and an asynchronous time frame. Hence the war was not waged against an enemy with a conventional army, but against the concept of terror and the euphemistic defence of virtues.[2] The ensuing wars in Afghanistan and Iraq lacked the primary characteristics of conventional warfare because there was no front, no clear borderline to divide adversaries, and therefore no territory that had to be conquered and occupied. The enemy could not be pinned to a fixed place, nor did they gather for a once and for all battle over a particular territory. It suddenly became clear that the enemy could be on all sides of any given line. The de-spatialization of the arena for 'war against terror' not only meant that there was no bounded territory that could be monitored, it also created a boundless temporal horizon. Donald Rumsfeld was brazen enough to announce that the 'war on terror' had no endgame, and therefore part of his job was to 'persuade the American people that real victory will never happen, and that the war itself may continue indefinitely' (quoted in Rampton and Stauber 2003, p. 130). If threat could be anywhere and everywhere, it could only exist in a kind of a non-space.

Nameless, faceless enemy

The struggle in naming the conflict after September 11 was nowhere more palpable than in George W. Bush's speech to the nation. He sought at first to draw a link with the need to recall the previous 'righteous' wars in which America fought against fascism and communism. By comparing the attacks to the one on Pearl Harbor, he sought to awaken a spirit of defiance and sharpen a sense of an enemy that must be conquered (Friedman 2001). But who is the enemy now? In what sense can there be a war if no opponent stands up to fight? In what sense is it a war if the field for battle and the appearance of the enemy cannot be identified in advance?

This was not a war that fitted into any of the available categories of territorial conflict. It was neither a national war nor a class war. The enemies in the 'war on terror' neither wore a uniform nor had a uniform identity. Their place in the public imaginary was not supported by a clear set of ideological or territorial claims. Hugo Young (2001), a seasoned commentator on international affairs, was quick to recognize that, while Blair and Bush were trying to establish a comparison between 'the war against terror' and the earlier invasion of Kuwait, he stressed that this conflict was different because the moral outrage could not be neatly attached to an obvious political entity. In the week after the attack, the Bush government invoked the rhetoric of war against terror, but failed to interpret the events legally within the numerous treaties on territorial invasion or international terrorism (Chomsky 2001). They also projected an image of global unity against terror that included the vast majority of 'good Muslims' (Mamdani 2004).

The difference between the insurgents who fought against the US forces abroad and the terrorists who could strike at 'home' was also

blurred by the invention of the classification of 'enemy combatant'.
This term did not correspond to any of the conventional categories
of military conduct and was also exempted from of the civil codes on
criminal conduct. Such ambiguous terms not only exempted the state
from following legal procedures on detention of enemies, it also stoked
the fear of a faceless enemy who could be categorized only outside of
the sphere of human rights (Olshansky 2005, p. 215). The rhetorical
justifications for war contained an ancient strategy that blurred the
distinction between retaliation and self-defence and also invented an
entirely novel strategy – to delink the identity of the adversary from
any of the conventional racial, ethnic or national categories.

The enemy combatant and the terrorist is not embodied in the features of the visible outsider, but rather assumes a more intimate and
less predictable figure, such as the invisible 'sleeper' – one of those
long-term residents with an ordinary job, valid identity papers, a conventional social life and a secret mission. When these enemies become
visible – as in the 'capture' of a bomber on CCTV footage – their visibility is also transient. No sooner is he spotted, such as the young men
with backpacks entering the London tube stations on 7 July 2005, than
he disappears amongst the crowd of other ordinary commuters. His
camouflage is in the ordinariness of his appearance. If the enemy does
not belong to a single entity, then the enemy is no longer a subject with
whom you negotiate, but a vague monstrous figure who is void of any
human agency. Ultimately, this fear that the enemy does not have a
knowable face is, as Žižek (2002) claims, an elaborate process of denial
of the possibility that the enemy is more similar to us than we could
bear to consider.

Small threats that cascade into chaos

Ambient fear spread not just from the insecurity over the invisibility
and unlocatability of the enemy but also from the cascading effect of
their use of unconventional weapons. Alongside the de-spatialization
of the conflict arena and the indistinguishable features of the adversaries came the threat of invisible weapons, such as backpacks that
could explode at any point on a public transport system and anthrax
deposited on letters that circulated in the postal service. This 'spiking'
of ordinary objects amplified the pre-existing anxieties over the loss of
social control and 'brought home' the realization that the West was not
exempt from the new global disorder.

According to Mike Davis (2001, p. 36), the collective consciousness
of America was already gripped by 'inexplicable anxiety'. He claimed
that the susceptibility to paranoia had been set by TV programmes

like *The X-Files*, diseases like AIDS and unpredictable flare-ups of road rage, and had climaxed with the 'millennium bug'. From the race riots in Los Angeles to the rampages in Rwanda, there was a growing anxiety over the spread of chaos. In the eyes of Western commentators such as Hans Magnus Enzensberger (1994), these outbursts lacked any symbolic or pragmatic logic. Devoid of any ideological underpinning, they were seen as just another example of the loss of control and pointless violence. The fear that small acts of violence could cascade into uncontrollable conflicts also informed the commentaries on international security frameworks. The threat to international stability was no longer imagined as a collision between rival superpowers or the deliberate guile of a known adversary. On the contrary, the sources of global unrest were perceived as coming from the reckless chaos of collapsed national sentiment, the spillover from states that could no longer control their own territories, and the upsurge of collective rage that stems from cultural humiliation (Stephens 2001).

The spread of these new forms of threat expanded the frontiers of fear. With the end of the Cold War there was a growing perception that threat is no longer identifiable as a single entity but is a complex amalgam of unpredictable forces that strike on multiple fronts. In one of the most perceptive essays on the complex characteristics of the 'neo-wars', Umberto Eco claimed that the versatility and the multitude of small players, while not cancelling the power of the dominant force, meant that no military leader could ever single-handedly deliver victory (2007, p. 13). This fear that certain parts of the world were spiralling out of control resulted in the production of new geopolitical maps that distinguished between the 'functioning core areas' and the 'non-integrating gap' (Barnett 2004). The binary division between the 'core' and the 'gap' – which includes much of Andean South America, the Caribbean, sub-Saharan Africa, the Middle East, and Central and Southwest Asia – reflects a new political sentiment that the globalized core is now vulnerable to the outbursts from the agents it has bypassed and marginalized. In this new discourse the world order has lost its simple logic of containment and is now precariously poised over unstable frontiers and populated by people in the 'gap' who will lash out against the 'core'.

Mediatized reverberations

While many Americans may have previously taken comfort from the fact the real wars always take place somewhere else, the violent outburst on September 11 not only punctured that illusion but also disrupted the boundary between real and imaginary violence. Physical damage was not an end in and of itself, but a means to a more 'spectacular' kind of destruction. These strikes did not attempt to cripple the military power of the enemy or hamper its civil infrastructure; rather, they were intended to produce a visual trauma that would find symbolic reverberation within the mass media. Psychological warfare has always been one of the weapons of the weak in modern battles. However, given the now near infinite channels of communication, which include direct feeds from the enemy on Al Jazeera, eyewitness accounts from indymedia networks, and Google searches that link George Bush to 'miserable failure', it is rather obvious that these new networks of information have exceeded the regulative powers of any state.

Following 9/11, viewers were not only exposed to the implacable hatred of the insurgents, but also had the opportunity to witness details of the victims' suffering in all their unbearable specificity. The images and stories filed by embedded correspondents were now in competition with the images released by the military. For the first time viewers could not only see the pilot's bird's-eye view of the event but also follow a missile as it approached its target. Between 2003 and 2004, readers of the magazine *USA Today* were given the option of viewing an interactive map of 'Downtown Bagdad'. With a few clicks they could check, via satellite, these urban sites before and after destruction. The consistent use of aerial imagery and representations of Arab cities as 'terrorist nests' was, according to Graham (2006, p. 265), a deliberate attempt to reduce these environments to the flat battlescapes of video-games. These authorized vertical views of destruction were in stark contrast to the horizontal street-level images of dead civilians that Al Jazeera transmitted. Stephen Graham has gone so far as to claim that the USA bombed the Al Jazeera station in Baghdad because it wanted to cut the transmission of the face-to-face effects of destruction (ibid., p. 263).

This did not cease the flow of images from the victims and the enemy. Blogs and websites continued to cover the scenes. Anyone with a mobile phone and a computer could send out a story that could reverberate around the world and appear on the screens in everyone else's home. The resonance between the virtual and the real not only inflamed the sense of insecurity over America's place in the world by highlighting the growing sense of global chaos, it also generated an unprecedented sympathy for the victims of war. During 'the Troubles' in Northern Ireland the British government effectively prohibited the screening of any 'live' voice of a representative from the IRA. By contrast, the Bush government lost control of the voices and images that reached the American public. According to Umberto Eco (2007, p. 15), these new interruptions in the media have compelled the USA to invent a new neutral rhetoric of war that dampens the cult of the war hero and does not glory in the slaughter of the enemy. These are the most documented wars of history, and the sheer volume of 'noise' in the media has meant that it is impossible to produce a stable and coherent message.

Remote leadership

Even when Osama bin Laden was alive he was an ambient figurehead. Killing bin Laden did not eliminate the threats that he represented. The 'war on terror' commenced without a defined sovereign state as the enemy. It was a war against the category of terror, and the terrorists that fought with an allegiance to bin Laden not only operated across borders, they had no specific territorial or political allegiance to any state. Hence, in the absence of sovereign figurehead, bin Laden was, and continues to be even after his execution, an imaginary leader.

Osama bin Laden was referred to as the 'author of terror', but he was an author without a stable text, a symbol without a clear referent. World leaders were quick to deny him any representative status of a specific national or ethnic community. Even Western leaders acknowledged that he was no heir to the civilizational claims of Islam. Media reports did little to distinguish his identity (Girard 2001). Robert Fisk (2005), one of the few Western journalists to interview bin Laden, described him as a simple man driven by a deep sense of injustice, whereas, Thomas Friedman (2002), commenting from New York, described bin Laden as 'a combination of Charles Manson and Jack Welsh – a truly evil, twisted personality'.

While there can be little doubt that Osama bin Laden's identity had been shaped within the specific milieu of the disaffected Saudi middle class and his own experience of the Cold War machinations between the US and USSR power plays in Afghanistan, the US authorities repeatedly framed his vision in terms of innuendo and presumption. Colin Powell promised to present a case proving that bin Laden was the mastermind of global terrorism. The only statement of fact that Powell issued was merely an assurance that the case against him was 'not circumstantial' (quoted in Boyle 2001). When the Taliban offered to hand over bin Laden to a third country on the condition that evidence of his involvement in September 11 was made public, Bush replied: 'There's no need to discuss innocence or guilt. We know he is guilty' (Buncombe 2001). Bush reasserted an ancient demand based on superior power: 'Lay down your leader, or else we will destroy all in our path!' Refusing submission, the Taliban were left with only one other option – uphold the law of hospitality and issue the reply 'Come and get him!' In the absence of the public display of evidence, rational arguments and legitimate procedures, both sides adopted the ruthless logic of unilateralism. As Immanual Wallerstein (2003, p. 223) argued, both bin Laden and Bush seemed to share one disturbing feature – a disdain for world public opinion and a comfort in their own flimsy propaganda.

Acentric movement

An enemy without a national base, that has no ethnic face, uses cheap, easily available and at times invisible weapons, operates without a central leader and possesses an acentric movement: clearly this presents a dreadful enemy that eludes easy categorization. The complexity of this situation exceeded the conventional terms that were used to describe the conflict. For instance, the phrase 'axis of evil' was repeatedly used despite the fact that it was commonly known that the organizational principles of the terrorist networks lacked a centralized command system. Similarly, the appearance of radical and militant Islamic networks was not some simple regression into an atavistic past. These were sophisticated modes of operation that mimicked the new 'parallel systems' in communication technologies. These networks demonstrated the capacity to camouflage their own activities by adopting a non-linear, capillary system of flow, within which agents are highly mobile and able to articulate improvisational response towards external changes. Their structure is not integrated into a centralized body but dispersed along multiple nodes. Units are, at best, loosely connected, and linked into sections where they may remain unaware of their own partners. According to his biographer Roland Jacquard, it was in the nature of bin Laden's organization to plan attacks in advance, choose the commandos who would carry them out, and give them the ability, technology and financing that would enable them to act without needing orders or having to return to their bases (Jacquard 2002).

According to the leading US and UK counter-terrorism and military experts, Al Qaeda is now said to resemble an 'ad hoc', 'fluid', 'self-reproducing' entity that spreads like a 'virus', with each unit or affiliate developing its own capacity to determine its own trajectories and independently disseminate its own vision on the world wide web. Thus it could be concluded that Al Qaeda is not a unified organization – with a clearly defined hierarchy and structure – but an acentric movement that Zygmunt Bauman (2006a, pp. 96–128) calls 'Al Qaedism'.

The Affects of War

I began this chapter by describing 'war on terror' as a catachrestic phrase. While there is no doubt that Al Qaeda violates the conventions of war – its operatives target civilians, don't wear uniforms, function outside the norms of international law, and seem to have no regard for their own lives – the USA and its allies have informed us that a response to this kind of threat also involves an indefinite suspension of the normal rule of law. Hence, Al Qaeda provides a double function: it is the entity that produces terror and an emblem for the affect of terror. The 'war on terror' is therefore executed against both a political entity and a psychological state. It is, of course, absurd to think that you can wage war against an emotional state, but the evocation of this psychological identity is central to the figurative construction of the enemy. Demonization of the other is a common feature of war. By constructing the terrorist as 'something' that is numb to the dreaded cycle of fear, he or she is transformed into a kind of zombie and therefore can be attacked with impunity. For instance, when Tony Blair expressed regret for the taking of innocent lives by US and British forces, he was repeating an ancient typology that distinguished between the civilized armed forces, which showed their humanity in their feeling sorrow, and the terrorists, who are presented as zombies that are immune to their own vicious cycle of violence.

It does not take great imagination to repeat such binaries of good and evil. However, the crucial point is that fear spreads when conflict is perceived as boundless, enemies are imagined as sub-human, world order appears to have collapsed, media reports represent contradictory viewpoints, and the enemy's leadership is as monstrous as its organizational systems are formless. My concern is not to evaluate the current tactics and strategies of the war on terror. How could I, or anyone I know, really judge? We are relative outsiders in this game plan. As I have already noted, critics of the 'war on terror' were quick to protest against the restrictions on civil liberties and to denounce the hypocritical justification that it was *necessary* to suspend democratic practices in order to defend democracy (Wallerstein 2003, p. 7). The anti-democratic effects of war are now well known. However, as observers of these mediatized wars, and in our speculations over the possibility of becoming entangled in terrorist acts, we also express ambiguous feelings about the 'war on terror'. At this level our experience of the affects of war is both more intimate and less comprehensible than the knowledge of the overt effects of war. Ambient fear is the dual insecurity that comes from the perception that we are surrounded by multiple risks and the uncertainty of the actual origins and causes of threat. This broadening and blurring of fear is part of the general aestheticization of social and political life.

With the mass production of digital communication devices and the popularization of practices such as sampling, montage and blogging, the possibility of creating an immersive environment with interactive feedback became a mundane part of everyday reality. Sociologists have now noticed that these immersive environments and new modes of interactive feedback have also affected the forms of attention and apprehension. People who are constantly ping-ponging text messages to each other claim to feel 'ambient intimacy'. Members of online chat groups outsource problems to each other, and by observing the micro-details of their respective daily lives they establish weak ties and form 'parasocial' relationships. However, underpinning these looser and pragmatic forms of sociality, there is also a new mode of compre-hension. Without being physically side by side, people become adept at picking up a mood. They may not know the source, recognize the total configuration, or even pick the precise turning point in a specific sequence of events, but by stitching together numerous micro-details they form an overall impression. Each piece of information may be insignificant on its own, but collectively they coalesce into a complex but fluid portrait of a situation. This form of social knowledge is referred to as ambient awareness (Thompson 2008). Promoters of websites celebrate it as a positive tool for keeping abreast of the fast-moving changes in the world. However, critics such as Peter Sloterdijk (2009) see a more insidious trajectory. Alongside the shift in warfare from an assault on the adversary's primary organ to the infiltration of the imaginary, he claims that we have also witnessed parallel forms of 'atmo-terrorism' that have sought to capture and reconfigure the total-ity of everyday consciousness. Everything from aesthetic experience to interpersonal communication is now seen as a battleground that is under assault.

It is the shifting terrain of affect – the ambient awareness of both intimacy and fear – that Lacan argued operated 'between perception and consciousness', and which Massumi claims was stimulated by security practices such as the colour-coded alert system that was 'used to activate direct bodily responsiveness rather than reproduce a form or transmit definite content' (2006, p. 287), as well as the introduction of new policies and laws that could capture 'aspirational' terrorists by blurring the legal distinction between violation and intent. Being alert to stranger danger was elevated into a crucial civic duty. New border control regulations extended the stigmatic association to migrants and terrorists. Patriotism was unfurled as the answer to the failed experiments of multiculturalism and ridiculous cosmopolitan fantasies. New stealth surveillance technologies were introduced to track suspect movements and the movement of suspects. This discourse and the security practices not only drew upon visual images to depict the state of fear but also relied on a highly reflexive communication system. People were assured that their safety was now dependent on the almost imperceptible information processing strategies. However, this also spread the sources of fear into every atom of everyday life. Fear became invisible and unpredictable. As the experience of fear was projected into the realm of anticipation of the unimaginable, it also left the boundaries of ordinary reason and comprehension.

In one of the most thoughtful meditations on the tropes for explaining the 'war on terror' and suicide bombers, Talal Asad (2007, p. 45) exposed the traps that leading philosophers, anthropologists, theologians and political scientists fell into as they tried to 'endow the dead terrorist with the motives of the living'. Throughout his analysis of these different accounts, which stress notions of religious sacrifice, escape from political oppression, a death wish, or even the pursuit of personal morality, Asad finds the scholarly approaches to be at fault, either for being too partisan to acknowledge that violence is inherent in all forms of political subjectivity or for failing to see that such intense motivations are rarely lucid and one-dimensional, but more likely to reside in a myriad of contingent circumstances. Asad does not correct these shortcomings by taking us closer into the murky ideological and emotional accounts left by suicide bombers. However, having exposed the flaws in the mainstream political debates, he points to the need for an alternative understanding of the fears that haunt our fundamental notions of being and security. In the following chapter I will argue that the fear of terrorism, like the fear of the 'flood' of refugees, is part of deeper social transformations that I have termed kinetophobia.

2

Kinetophobia, Motion Fearfulness

If fear has become a dominant mode by which we relate to others and assume our place in a globalizing world, then what sort of image do we have of the way the local and global are entangled together?

> An Aboriginal girl in Alice Springs cradles her Pocahontas Barbie while she watches the Winter Olympics on satellite TV. Another factory closes in Newcastle because it can no longer compete with Chinese wages. Another Latrobe Valley power station is sold off to a United States energy corporation. Moody's credit-rating agency warns that Australian governments must keep cutting taxes and services – or else. Australian environmentalists and Aboriginal groups mobilise support from the European parliament in their opposition to the opening of Jabiluka uranium mine in the Northern Territory. A public park in Melbourne is taken over for an international car race beamed around the world. A Tasmanian mother frets about her sunburned child and the risk of cancer. (Wiseman 1998, p. 1)

As this survey plots the interpenetration of global influences with local structures, it simultaneously builds a mosaic that shimmers with ambivalence. Almost all the interactions between the local and the global are seen as threatening. The objects of desire and sources of hope, as well as the risks of disease and the exposure to displacing forces, are linked to processes that have remote and multiple origins. In this act of compilation it is the distance *between* these polarities and the complexity *of* their interaction that heighten the sense of precariousness. Uncertainty is magnified by the assumption that a multitude of forces either are operating from so far beyond the horizon or are so intricate that they defy graspable identification.

This commentary on the impact of globalization concurs with Zygmunt Bauman's observation that fear saturates all aspects of life and work, as it trails and frames the reception of all movements. For Bauman, globalization spreads fear because it has unleashed processes that are beyond control. It is not just that there is a vast range of forces interacting together, but the contingencies generate so many variables that the system can no longer monitor, let alone predict, its own outcomes. 'Even the tiniest modification of the initial conditions, or a minuscule departure from the early developments anticipated, may result in a complete reversal of the end-states expected or hoped for' (Bauman 2006a, p. 101). Hence Bauman concludes that the fear of becoming homeless is the most pervasive emotion of the new global condition (Bauman 2002, pp. 112–14; see also Lawrence 2006).

There is indeed much to be nervous about. Manuel Castells (1989, p. 228) has argued that globalization has produced vast chasms within social spaces, with the upper tier connected to global networks, while at the other end of the spectrum communities are segmented into ethnically based groups that rely on their own identity 'as the most valuable resource to defend their interests and ultimately their being'. These ever widening differences have now been thoroughly documented by many political economists, such as Jacques Attali, who have found numerous ways of repeating the chilling fact that 90 per cent of global wealth is now concentrated in the hands of 1 per cent of the world's inhabitants (Attali, cited in Bauman 2007, p. 6). Nevertheless, I am wary of the way that the negative outcomes of globalization have been used as a generalized message of the doom that comes with mobility. Much of the commentary on globalization seems to perpetuate a deep fear of change, and in particular the fear of mobility, or what I call kinetophobia. Drawing on Paul Virilio's extensive critique of modernity through the concept of dromology, and taking a more direct cue from John Urry, I will argue that, in order to grasp the 'systemic features of globalization', we will need to develop a new perspective on mobility (Urry 2003, p. 7).

What is mobility – a state, a force, a set of shifting co-ordinates? How does the definition of mobility shape social attitudes and personal experiences? This chapter examines the use of organic and mechanistic metaphors that have underpinned the classical paradigm for the understanding of mobility in the social sciences. It argues that the global patterns of mobility do not fit well within this paradigm. The limits and kinetophobic associations generated by the classical paradigm are examined through Harald Kleinschmidt's theory of residentialism.

The final part of the chapter outlines an alternative conceptual frame that is based on key terms from complexity theory.

Mobility and the Integrity of Bodies and Machines

Since the late nineteenth century, most of the social and political discourses on migration have followed the core assumptions of nationalist ideologies that defined sovereign states as comprising a population that was both settled within a defined territory and in possession of a unique cultural identity. This viewpoint was also premised on a metaphysical claim that the abandonment of a nomadic lifestyle for fixed settlement was a developmental stage in human evolution. In addition, it was framed by a mechanistic understanding of the negative relationship between movement and equilibrium: human movement was thereby seen as a depletion of energy as well as a threat to the integrity of borders and the stability of social entities. Hence, migration was considered as a deviation from the normal conventions of settled life, and the migrants (or, as Oscar Handlin termed them, the 'uprooted ones') were at best seen as the victims of external forces, and at worst perceived as suspect characters who sought unfair advantage over the residents and posed a threat to the prevailing social order (Handlin 1951; Geddes 2000). This tendency is also evident in sociological accounts on migration that express overt sympathy for the needs of migrants, but then describe them as 'people with problems' (Martin 1978, p. 209). Even when migration has been acknowledged as a crucial feature of modernization, it has usually been framed as if this process was finite and adjustment was a mere transitional phase (Williams 1973). Hence the recent efforts to raise the height of the US–Mexican wall and to defend 'fortress Europe', while perpetuating the fantasy of self-preservation by fortifying the border, has at best temporarily restricted the flows, and at worst encouraged migrants to use higher ladders and develop more sophisticated tunnelling techniques (Huspeck 2001; Harding 2001).[1] Such strategies never fix the 'problem with migrants'. They neither keep them out nor help in the subsequent plans to convert migrants into citizens. Given these negative assumptions on the effects of migration and the status of migrants, it comes as no surprise that the public debates have tended to focus on the degree, rather than the legitimacy, of the imposition of limitations on immigration, restrictions on political entitlement, and the subjection of migrants to additional tests in relation to their biological and cultural fitness.

This negative view on migration is related to a deeper ambivalence towards mobility. Kinetophobia, the fear of mobility, takes many forms. It is most apparent in racist scapegoating, where the cause of social upheaval is projected onto the most vulnerable agents of movement. However, it also appears in the more pervasive and almost invisible oxymorons – 'political body' and 'social engine' – that shape everyday life. In this chapter I will argue that the mechanical and organic metaphors that are used to represent social forms are embedded within a kinetophobic worldview. For instance, in political philosophy there is the common metaphor of the three key parts of the political body – a head that commands, arms that fight battles, and organs that fulfil specific functions (Cheah 2003). The Roman Senate was popularly referred to as the head, while the subordinate plebeians were the limbs. This division between command and obedience, intellectual and manual labour, persisted throughout the medieval and modern structures of religious, military and economic organization. Even the struggle between papal and regal authority was fought in bodily metaphors. If Christ's representative was the spiritual head, then the king was to be relocated into the midst of the chest, as the heart. In the modern period, the rise of new economic models tried to reconcile the tension between a seemingly endless chain of mechanical production and the need to replenish what Adam Smith called the 'toiling body'. Mark Seltzer (1992) has argued that, in a number of disciplines, ranging from political economy to literature, a new body–machine complex was constructed to represent the modern flows of power.

Most of the dispute within political theory has not revolved around the validity of this metaphor, but has focused on the hierarchal position of either the head or the heart in relation to the rest of the body. The absolutist traditions equated the sovereign with the will of God, elevating the head slightly above the rest of the body, whereas the republicans defined the sovereign through a negotiated social contract, and so the head was submerged in the body (Le Goff 1989; Gallagher 1989). The discovery of the body's circulation system also encouraged people to think that clean blood cells and a well-regulated circulatory system were not just a sign of somatic health and purity, but also provided a set of normative values on the necessary conditions for social order and security. Coterminously, heightened bodily rhythms and foreign fluids provided the imagery for invasive threats to the nation (Turner 1992). These metaphors, which recount the combat between good and evil in terms of pure cells and dirty parasites, also articulate a new somatic 'division of labour between executive and judicial and deliberative functions, along with an immune system that defends the body against outsiders, and a nervous system that communicates among its parts or members' (Mitchell 2008, p. 23). As Bryan Turner argued: 'Body metaphors illustrate the fact that we use the body as a convenient way of talking about the moral and political problems of society' (2003, p. 1).

Images of the nation as a body under threat also recur in the populist media coverage and political debates on refugees (Tyler 2006, p. 192) and migration (Renton 2003, p. 75). These negative images of strangers are deeply linked to the images which define the structure of the social system. In the later nineteenth and early twentieth centuries, social scientists turned away from body metaphors and began comparing society to an engine. Inputs and outputs, forces and levers, gears and cogs, fuels and lubricants became the key terms not only for evoking social relations and tendencies but also for setting the parameters for the 'normal' function of society. At the core of the mechanistic model of society is a general theory of equilibrium. In particular, the first law of thermodynamics, which proposed the existence of a singular system of universal energy that was both finite and indestructible, was seized upon with particular zeal by both liberal reformists and utopian socialists. This belief that energy flows could be accelerated and converted to maximize production inspired new visions of progress. The human body, and society as a whole, was constantly compared to an engine. It was, and in many ways still is, popularly accepted that both the body and the social system were composed of parts that could be fuelled to move at different speeds, or modified to have greater flexibility, and that overall stability would be ensured through the greater co-ordination of the structure and tightening of the boundary. The social parts were not just described as being part of a whole, but the idea of a whole both determined the limits and prescribed how the parts fit together. Exorbitant bits and dissipative forces that threatened the internal equilibrium were either shaved off or sealed up. Meanwhile the engine of society was conceived as if it could filter inputs to eliminate impurities, and its borders were imagined as walls that could be fortified against external shocks (Rabinbach 1990).

Metaphors of Mobility in Migration Studies

This mechanistic model of mobility also provides the key conceptual framework that binds together the two dominant perspectives on international migration: macro-structuralism and micro-agency. Macro-social theorists have mapped the flows of migrants according to the fluctuations between supply and demand that establish equilibrium in the economy. According to this perspective, it is argued that, in times of economic expansion in the centre, there is a need for additional sources of labour. Migrants come from the peripheries, but they enter on a differential status. They assume a position that Marx compared to the 'reserve army'. When the economy contracts, then the supply of migrants is either constricted or withdrawn from the labour market. This model relies on the integration of the spatial polarities of centre/periphery into a global system that allows migration to flow as a consequence of structural changes in the economy. Migrants may be drawn from sites that are linked by historical patterns of migration; however, the actual flows are controlled by an interplay between structural needs and institutional regulations for entry and exit. The flows are thereby depicted as if there was a system of pipelines and taps that connect the centre and the periphery. The power of the centre is measured by its capacity to control the flow. This model draws from the mechanistic assumption that contrary forces can balance out and that, while power is concentrated by gathering the surplus energy from the periphery, equilibrium will be maintained by regulating flow. As a model which emphasized the compensatory dynamic between push and pull factors, and stressed the function of chains and pipelines for conducting movement, it was perfectly suited to the industrial age. It classified human energy and trajectory according to the language of mechanization.

Liberal neo-classical economic commentators have always rejected the centrality of structural factors and favoured a micro-model that focuses the energy of migration flows on individual preferences. However, this perspective also draws on a mechanistic theory of flow. While they recoil from Marx's militaristic metaphors of appropriation and exploitation, there is an underlying presumption that movement is a result of an individual decision to pursue economic opportunity, and, in some extreme cases, the collective pattern is represented as if individual movements were driven by the forces that operate within a magnetic field. Migrants from densely populated areas with low incomes are meant to be attracted to sparse areas with high-income opportunities. This voluntarist model focuses on individual choices and is most vividly represented in the metaphor of 'chain migration'. It assumes that individuals have the capacity not only to determine whether conditions are favourable for themselves but also to induce others to follow in their steps. There is further the assumption that in times of economic downturn the migrants will be the first to move on, which would then confirm the optimistic belief that migration maintains equilibrium in the market place (Borjas 1989; Chiswick 2000).

Underpinning both the macro- and micro-model is a set of causal assumptions and linear trajectories. I have argued previously that the Marxist versions of the macro-model exaggerate the determining role of structural forces and that the forms of agency in the liberal micro-model are oversimplified (Papastergiadis 2000, pp. 30–7). In the macro-structural model there is no space for the agent to decide on his or her own migration. By contrast, the micro-agency model stresses that the imperious act of individual choice trumps the all-determining force of structure. Castles and Miller, in their revised version of the influential and best-selling *The Age of Migration* (2003), have also recognized the need for a looser and more dynamic model of global migration. While stressing that most migrants still follow the routes that were first established during the phases of colonialism and industrialization, and accepting that individual motivation is a key force that is amplified by the micro-networks of diasporic communities, their perspective has now expanded to include the role of meso-structural agents. This additional focus on the legal advisers and human traffickers, the twin cogs in the 'migration industry', has helped shift the debate from the deadlocked opposition of structure versus agency. While Castles has argued, in a more recent publication, that the factors at play in the global migration process are so complex, and the effects are so unpredictable, that they defy the bounds of coherent and consistent national policy settings, this has not led him to consider whether there are alternatives to the mechanistic models for explanation (2004, p. 854).

There are many fundamental questions that the conventional macro- and micro-models fail to explain. Why do so many people who could gain an economic benefit from moving actually refuse to leave their home? Why are so many of the world's migrants drawn from such few places? The unevenness in the distribution of the volume in global migration is a genuine puzzle.[2] Thomas Faist's response to these paradoxes is intriguing. He is not satisfied by minor conceptual adjustments, such as the incorporation of mechanistic terms like 'stress threshold' that can address both the tension generated by sudden movement and the need to allow for flexibility within the overall social equilibrium. Migration is, in his eyes, not just a relief mechanism; rather, it is a powerful social force. To address these complexities he postulates a sophisticated version of meso-structural theory. In this stratum there is a network that links both broad structures and individual preferences, thereby facilitating the traffic between specific places. This relational approach is encapsulated in the following crucial and complex sentence, in which he stresses that 'social capital is mainly a local asset; but it can turn into a *transmission belt* when it *crystallizes* in migrant networks' (Faist 2000a, p. 29; emphasis added). I am struck by the disjunctive combination in Faist's explanation of mechanistic and organic metaphors. It is not a mere semantic slippage but a reflection of both the complexity of the migratory process and the necessity to graft different concepts that can track the process by which levers slip into nodes and bases become networks. This mixing of metaphors is not necessarily a sign of confusion, but expressive of the complexity in the linkages and flows of global migration.

Social scientists have conceded that there is no single model, or 'grand theory', that can explain the complexity of global mobility (Portes 1997; Massey et al. 1998), and philosophers now argue that the body politic 'is no longer an enclosed nucleus of identity' (Grosz 1994, p. 103; see also Montag 1999, pp. 62–89, and Balibar 1994, pp. 3–38). However, there is a still a general failure, especially in the social sciences, to reflect on the meaning of mobility and deconstruct the mechanistic frameworks within which migration theories are embedded. The concepts of 'reserve army' and 'chain migration' rely on a boundary in economic production that barely exists today. The micro-, meso- and macro-models have all presupposed that migration patterns are driven by the laws of equilibrium. The explanations of exchange and movement may vary by giving particular stress to either individual choice or economic structures, yet they invariably rely on the transpersonal system of the 'self-regulating' market. The invisible hand of the market always ensures that gains and losses balance out. Such myths defy history and confound politics. No system works so neatly.

Mapping Global Patterns

Migrants move because they are already in the spirit of modernity. They are not passive entities being pushed and pulled along the world's great imaginary pipelines. They may leave home with the intention of returning, but along the way the experience of their journey alters their priorities. They often go back and forth, sometimes checking where to settle and where to work. In this criss-crossing, the causes and consequences of migration enfold. Migration studies, which divide the process into the determinant forces of movement and consequent mechanisms for incorporation, invariably overlook this complex feed-back system. The classical theories of migration simply fail to explain why migrants concentrate in the already overcrowded and guarded metropolises of the North, or, in the words of Hardt and Negri, how they manage to 'roll up-hill' (2000, p. 134). I will now present a brief characterization of the volumes and trajectories of global mobility, as well as examining the subject positions that migrants adopt and the spatial affiliations and institutional forces that shape contemporary migration.

1 Increased numbers of people on the move
Today there are more migrants and refugees than at any other point in history. Between the two world wars, the number of migrants doubled, and by 1965 it had grown to 75 million. In 2002 it was estimated that there were 175 million migrants worldwide, and by 2005 this figure had already risen to 200 million (GCIM 2002). Between 1970 and 1990 the number of countries classified by the International Labour Organization as receiving migrants nearly doubled, and, similarly, the number that supplied substantial numbers of migrants rose from thirty-nine to sixty-seven (Stalker 2000). According to the most recent UNHCR report, there are over 51 million internally displaced and stateless people as well as 16 million refugees. The United States continues to have the highest number of immigrants, but in proportionate terms the heaviest weighting of migrants and refugees is in select parts of Africa, Pakistan, Syria and Iran. In overall terms, most migrants are living in the South. While public debates in the West repeatedly express fear of being 'flooded' by refugees, this sentiment overlooks the fact that most refugees flee to neighbouring countries and that, on average, between 83 and 90 per cent remain within the region of their origin (UNHCR 2008).

2 Multiplicity of directions
'Go West' is not the iconic sign of contemporary migration. The classical perception of migration as a finite journey has also been displaced by a more complex range of patterns, which include seasonal, itinerant, recurrent and incessant movements. Migrants are not heading in any single direction (Zlotnik 1998). Nor is there a structural force that governs the majority of movements. Contemporary flows of migration are multiple and differ from the earlier waves of migration, which were characterized as being generated by the semi-structured push–pull dynamic of the colonization of the New World by Europeans or the recruitment of workers into the industrial centres of the North. Today there is no singular set of co-ordinates that is pulling the major flows. People are on the move in multiple and circular directions. Labour migration is heading towards not only developed but also developing countries. For instance, although Asia has disproportionately low levels of international migration, it is experiencing some of the most complex patterns of movement. While the European Union is now overtaking North America as the primary destination in the West, the points of entry and sites of concentration are occurring in the

less 'developed' parts of Southern Europe (UNHCR 2008). Mapping these turbulent movements defies the conventional polarities of 'cartographic reason' and has resulted in the production of new, continuously updated 'interactive maps (i-Map)' (Mezzadra 2009). These maps no longer seek to plot movements as if they either followed fixed spatial markers, such as roads, or were directed by regulated forms of institutional channels. On the contrary, they are reliant on the latest input of surveillance agents and border patrols that are tracking migrants, who themselves are changing directions as soon as a specific route is closed by border patrols.[3] There are also counter-surveillance maps issued by activist and artist groups that in turn alert migrants to the blockages and movements generated by border patrols (Cubitt 2008).[4] The feedback of these mapping exercises and counter-movements produces an image of chaotic motion that is both labyrinthine in appearance and highly contingent. Aggressive surveillance and interception techniques are thereby not only causing migrants to shift the points of access across jagged borderlines, but also resulting in the adoption of dangerous and circuitous sea journeys or new land routes that take people towards their intended destination via the less regulated 'third' territories. These transit zones become so entangled as servicing centres and way stations that they eventually become 'proxy' destinations.

3 Diversification of migrants

The classical sociological image of the migrant as an uprooted, lonely and impoverished man is not representative of the diverse types of people that are now on the move. While the classical image of the migrant was dominated by the psycho-social type known as the 'marginal man', it also included a more ambivalent figure that Simmel and Schutz sketched out as the 'stranger'. The image of the stranger opened a more positive form of identification, as it suggested that migration was responsible for a broadening of cultural horizons and the introduction of critical perspectives. By contrast, the contemporary figure of the migrant is loaded with stigmatic associations of criminality, exploitation and desperation. In reality, men from all classes and status groups, and growing numbers of educated women, are on the move across the world. The vast majority of Indian migrants leave home with tertiary qualifications (GCIM 2002). In the Philippines, the second largest 'exporter of labour in the world', not only does the number of women migrants vastly exceed that of men, but their remittances have prevented the national economy from total collapse (Go 1998, p. 147). The recent studies on the feminization of migration have shown that women have not simply followed men's footsteps but have pioneered new journeys and patterns of circulation (Anthias and

Lazardis 2000). The UNHCR has noted that, of all the people that they oversee, 47 per cent are women and 44 per cent are under the age of eighteen. These people are not easily classified in discrete categories such as economic migrants and political refugees. People who flee from violent societies also tend to be the victims of collapsed social orders that are the result of the global economy bypassing whole regions (Duffield 2001). As the distinction between political or religious persecution, systematic discrimination and structural disadvantage starts to blur, more and more commentators are calling for a fundamental redrafting of the 1951 UN Convention and Protocol Relating to the Status of Refugees. In this complex world there is now a multitude of factors that force people to be on the move, and there is a range of new terms, such as 'transmigrant'[5] or 'transilience', that were once applied to mobile elites, but are now just as relevant to a wide range of people who have the capacity to move and live in and between different countries (Richmond 2002, 712).

4 Complex forms of agency and spatial affiliation

The motivation for migration can no longer be confined to an economic calculation of wage increases. The recent acknowledgement of social, cultural and political factors as being active in the *whole* of the migration process has a dramatic impact on the way we also understand spatial attachment. By contrast to the earlier practices of assimilation, in which it was assumed that migrants gave up their loyalty to their original homeland and adopted the values of the host society, or segregation, in which the migrants were confined to specific zones before being repatriated, the current understanding of migrant communities is directed more towards the way they create transnational and diasporic cultural networks (Hess 2006; Babcock 2006). Regular commuting and communing across distant places has led to the creation of new forms of cross-border economic, political and cultural exchanges. While some diasporic communities remain relatively fixed in their adopted homeland, they also channel their media services through new satellite networks (Bailey et al. 2007). These triangulated media delivery systems that hop across vast horizontal distances also twist the proximate forms of day-to-day intimacies. The contemporary patterns of cross-cultural interaction include both complex forms of hybridization and jagged segmentations that do not fit easily into the categories of an aggressive assimilationism or even the emergent forms of multiculturalism. Diasporic communities are becoming more self-directive and bifurcate as they engage with dominant structures and utilize new communication technologies. Transformations in the methods of production and the dissemination of global commodities are also undermining traditional forms of spatial attachment. In this context, the North is consistently emitting contradictory signals: encouraging the illusion of freedom and mobility and promoting its own commodities and values, while also restricting human migration and devaluing other traditions. Despite the contradition between the rhetoric of global connectedness and the practice of exclusionary policies on immigration, complex migration networks are constantly emerging. For instance, while most forms of migration occur across relatively small distances, such as the route from Burma to Thailand, the changes in communication networks and the use of the airplane for mass transportation have also transformed the relationships to space and place. As a consequence, members from closely knit rural communities in China can find passageways into receptive enclaves in New York. Information networks between friends and families now create a sense of adjacency between places that are separated by vast distances. Migrants thereby choose their destination according to personal knowledge and available transportation systems rather than by geographic proximities (Massey et al. 1998, p. 12). As many commentators have observed, the capacity of migrants to adapt to the new 'liquid' social structures gives the impression that they are spearheading the broader social transformation from the 'space of places' into 'spaces of flow' (Bauman 2006b; Castells 1996).

5 Governance and transnational flows
The contradictions and tensions between national governance and global migration patterns can also be considered in relation to shifts in policies towards the facilitation of new links with the diasporic communities abroad and the increasingly restrictive policies on immigration. In the past decade, many of the nation-states that have large diasporas spread across the world have started to implement policies that create economic, political and social mechanisms enabling migrants to participate in the national development process from afar (Levitt and de la Dehesa 2003, p 588). These new policies not only facilitate more efficient means for transferring money but also encourage higher levels of political involvement and cultural exchange. This has led some commentators to observe that the rise of these transnational networks reconfigures the sovereignty of the state (Appadurai 1996). Immigration and refugee policies have also undergone dramatic changes since the 1970s. In 1976 the UN had calculated that only a small minority of countries had policies to lower immigration, and this was matched by a slightly larger number of countries that were seeking to raise levels of immigration. By 2001 almost one-quarter of all countries viewed immigration levels as too high, and almost half of all developed

countries were introducing more restrictive policies. Canada and Australia, two of the classic destinations of permanent migration, now offer a wide variety of visas as a response to the fact that the number of temporary residents and demand for business visitors exceeds permanent settlers (DIMA 1995). In this 'managerial approach', which first began to emerge in the early 1990s, the state's migration policies, on the one hand, placed greater onus on normative requirements such as stricter citizenship tests, created new temporary residence visas for refugees with probationary conditions and restricted the rights for asylum seekers, and, on the other hand, in order to be able to attract highly skilled migrants, also granted new business visas on a more contractual basis (Kofman 2005; Flynn 2005, p. 465). In other parts of the world, the dismantling of official migration recruiting agencies, deregulation in the market place and the increased restrictions on asylum policies have collectively spawned new informal and illegal networks for smuggling people across borders. In the absence of proximate and secure institutional spaces for the processing of asylum claims, legitimate refugees are increasingly reliant on traffickers to organize their escape, transition and entry into a safe country. The sanctions on airline carriers and employers, the adoption of the safe country of origin and safe third-country principles, and the introduction of a new range of detention and deportation practices have not stemmed these flows. 'Snakeheads' in China, 'coyotes' in Mexico and the new Russian mafia are creating their own illegal trafficking networks of migrants and developing a trade in sex slaves which is now calculated as being as lucrative as the sale of drugs and arms. As one pimp boasted, drugs and guns can only be sold once (Pope 1997). These traffickers are well informed of legal loopholes and follow the most effective routes. They are highly mobile and operate through transnational networks. The widespread reporting on human trafficking, and in particular some gruesome cases of sex slaves, prompted the UN Commission for the Prevention of Crime and Penal Justice to develop a definition of trafficking. While this was a welcome addition to international law, as one commentator observed, the concept reinscribed a gendered distinction and once again conflated migrant with victim (Agustin 2006, p. 42). The 'data vacuum' on irregular migration, the 'fluid character of irregular migrants', the regulative void that sits between the national and the global, and the tension between citizenship rights and human rights have meant that much of the public debate on this issue has been dominated by unfounded generalizations (Grant 2006, p. 17). Despite the promotion of arguments by the United Nations High Commission for Refugees, the Global Commission on International Migration, and the International Organization for Migration that migration is a global issue, there is still no single regulative authority. Hence, these transnational institutions do not even have the power to enforce states to uphold laws and conventions to which they are already signatories. This tension in the regulative procedure has only heightened the contradictions in the migration process: restrictive national policies have in effect exposed migrants to criminal networks and encouraged a higher rate of asylum, while also fanning populist fears on cross-border movements and avoiding the long-term consequences of migration.

This brief outline of the scale and diversity in trajectory, as well as the forms of agency, modes of communal living and relation to institutional forces, reveals levels of interconnection that are rarely registered in public debates. Two factors continue to dominate public perceptions of migrants: the need for control and the calculation of benefit. In recent times, Jagdish Bhagwati (2003) has wryly noted that the 'ability to control migration has shrunk as the desire to do so has increased'. This fear that migration is now out of control is compounded by the paranoid assumption that migrants will 'steal' our way of life.[6] While there is now considerable historical evidence and economic data that demonstrates the dynamic role played by migrants, these 'facts' never seem to shift the kinetophobic values and attitudes.[7] Even anti-racist activists and migration experts often fail to pick up the implicit linkage between stigmatic claims against migrants and the inherent ambivalence towards mobility in the broader cultural frameworks for representing belonging.

Residentialism and Kinetophobia

The fear of migrants is not unique to modernity. While populist media commentators and politicians commonly blur the identity of the migrant with a figure of external threat and treat migration as the temporary disruption to the timeless feeling of national belonging, these images contradict historical reality. Rather than seeking to reverse this typology, I will now draw on historical accounts that demonstrate how the ambivalence towards migrants and mobility is the outcome of nineteenth-century discourses on nationalism, which inherited a mixture of romantic and positivist ideas on belonging and social unity. The promotion of nationalism in the nineteenth and twentieth centuries was based on the need to extend or realign people's sense of belonging within new spatial and administrative boundaries (Weber 1976). When the question of belonging was posed to peasants throughout the nineteenth century, the common response was not

defined in national terms; they would point to their village and reply:
'I come from here and thereabouts.' To them, foreigners started in
the neighbouring province rather than in 'other' countries (Torpey
2000, p. 9). Community was confined to the people they knew and the
territory within which their lives were concentrated. The nation-state
transformed and extended the relationship between space, community
and knowledge. In the famous phrase of Benedict Anderson (1983),
the nation-state was internalized as an 'imagined community'. In the
building of a single state and a unified nation, local attachments had
to be reconfigured and the diversity of identities had to be repressed.
Nation-building was a project that attempted to construct a homogeneous culture by addressing the 'greater whole' and the integration of
the different parts as if they were all members of a 'family'. Anderson
stressed the role of the new printed media, especially newspapers and
novels, in constructing either a daily image or a deep narrative of the
nation as a single body.

Metaphors of the body helped transform the borderlines of these
administrative units into collective feelings that are more 'homely' and
'familial'. Seeing the nation through the metaphor of the body not only
helped give shape to the otherwise abstract and vast 'imagined community', it also established a specific way for the individual to express his or
her sense of belonging. The bond between the self and the nation is, as
Yael Tamir (1993) noted, exemplified by the use of the magic pronoun
'my'. However, in order to go beyond the kinetophobic assumptions
that frame the classical paradigm on mobility and belonging and, in
particular, to decouple the stigmatic associations of either human lack
or monstrous excess from the migrant's identity, it is worth turning to
the work of Harald Kleinschmidt, in which he challenges the 'residentialist' foundations of the nation-state and demonstrates the structural
bias against migrants and mobility in the dominant methodologies of
the social sciences (Kleinschmidt 2006c, 2003). While nationalist ideologies tended to define belonging in terms of a singular identity that is
contained within a territorial boundary, Kleinschmidt argues that this
mode is not necessarily superior to earlier forms of socio-political allegiance, and he postulates that it is unlikely to survive for much longer.
In the Middle Ages the form of group membership was loosely structured around principles of allegiance and security. Belonging was not
constrained by a generic sense of group identity such as the idea that
everyone in the group was part of singular notion of a people; rather, it
arose from a more pragmatic identification between protection, place
and power. Allegiance to a specific ruler was not predetermined by the
uniformity of cultural identity of the group, but was gained through a
set of pragmatic political decisions over security. Kleinschmidt defined

this pluralistic mode of social organization as 'heterodynamic', as he claims that it was both responsive to the regular patterns of human migration and underpinned by feint rather than hard moral distinctions between members and foreigners. In this context, immigration was generally seen as a positive asset, as rulers tried to lure immigrants in order to redress high death rates and provide military manpower. Population stability and security was therefore equated with immigration and relatively open borders.

In essence, the emergence of the nation-state in the eighteenth century created a new social and political entity. It transformed the rights of citizenship in relation to modulated forms of access to territory and redefined the claims to belonging and cultural value. This social change followed a long history of urban concentration, in which the tension between trade and settlement reshaped attitudes towards mobility and attachment, and a process of democratization, in which the nexus between power and governance was dislodged from a sovereign figure and claimed by collectives of individuals who sought to codify the terms of protection within a bounded place. As new institutions were developed for policing public space and new images were proposed for imagining a common well-being, Kleinschmidt claims that society shifted towards what he calls an 'autodymamic' mode of social organization. Hence the image of society, which was previously conveyed through the quasi-biologistic paradigm of a divine body, was increasingly supplanted by various mechanical metaphors such as the clock. These mechanical metaphors stressed that the function and structure of society was also defined by its regularity and centralization. Such metaphors articulated the prevailing view that the integrity of the social system demanded careful calibration of its constituent parts, while also highlighting the necessary scrutiny to keep its engine clean of impurities or other extraneous elements that would disrupt its precise rhythm. Thus, the social expectation of conformity by its residents, and the right to regulate the movement of foreigners, was not just part of the individual's political and moral rights but was embedded in the existential claim of the nation-state. Migration policies in this period pursued the often mutually contradictory objectives of social cohesion and economic development. So, even in times of industrial growth and in places where migrants provided vital economic functions, mobility was still regarded as a deviation from residentialism, and migrants were perceived as deviants that required careful scrutiny and surveillance.

One of the main obstacles to understanding the complexity of flows that shape contemporary forms of belonging is the prevalence of state-centric paradigms in the social sciences. As Harald Kleinschmidt observed, information ends at the borders of the state. Empirical studies of migration tend to focus on the national impact, such as the cost of accommodating refugees or the assets that are transferred by migrants. This data presupposes that the cost–benefit analysis can be measured at the original point of entry, and it rarely addresses the complex mobilities and historical patterns of transnational forms of spatial cohabitation.[8] Borders are usually 'fuzzy' at their edges, and, as Kleinschmidt reminds us, neither the territorialized social structures associated with nationalism nor the stigmatic attitudes towards migrants are a constant feature in human history.

The now vast literature on globalization consistently touches on the process of mobility as a dynamic force in contemporary society and acknowledges that the forms of subjectivity, structures of spatial attachments, and institutions for regulating cross-border flows have also altered. However, as Papadopoulos, Stephenson and Tsianos (2008) have also argued, this discourse has not necessarily displaced the fantasy of border control. For instance, they draw attention to the way European policies on migration now direct funds towards the militarization of border control; the development of new transnational databanks; the implementation of stealth surveillance techniques; the construction of temporary camps; the use of off-shore processing centres; and the forging of treaties that legalize the 'transfer' of migrants to safe third countries. They characterize these efforts and the more general discourse that promotes the illusion of 'fortress Europe' as a kind of ideological smokescreen that masks the more complex reality of flow and porosity. Their alternative conception of the migration process gives greater stress to the evolving network of trajectories that pass through porous institutions and the multi-directional patterns of global migration.

John Urry (2007, p. 44) also promotes the need for a new mobility paradigm within which scholars can investigate the issues regarding displacement and settlement, networking and conviviality, as well as the effects produced by new communication and practices. This new mobility paradigm will need to overcome the methodological limitations of the state-centric views on belonging, and thereby refute the residentialist claims on social evolution (Malkki 1995a, 1995b). Recent advances in the sociology of migration and multi-sited ethnographies have already shown both a finer appreciation of the complex feedback systems that arise from relationships formed across borders and an affirmative valuation of the impact of mobility on social structures, cultural formations and personal experiences (Marcus 1998; Hannam et al. 2006; Urry 2003). From this perspective, migration is now seen as a dynamic and constitutive feature of social life. Similarly, migrants are no longer typecast as either passive victims that are 'pushed and pulled' by external forces or deviants that threaten social order. It is therefore more appropriate to consider the way migrants plot their journeys and utilize extensive networks of information as part of the normal and conscientious efforts by which people dignify their lives. In Hardt and Negri's (2000) spirited defence of a new form of critical agency, migrants are pioneers of what they call the 'multitude', and, as Kleinschmidt (2006c, p. 65) argues, the new discourse on migration has the potential to extend the notion of citizenship to 'universalistic principles of human rights irrespective of loyalty to a particular institution of statehood'.

The concept of citizenship and the formations of the nation-state are undergoing tremendous strains. At one level, the heightened mobility of various agents and the dislocative forces of globalization are inspiring a neo-nationalist backlash, while at another level nation-states, in the spirit of global competitiveness, are fragmenting the institutional structures that secure the feeling of belonging and security. The status of the migrant is also caught in the crossfire of contradictory trends, at once an exemplar of the subject who has the formal right to rights and the convenient object that is filled with contempt, suspicion and paranoia. As Saskia Sassen (2006) argues, this tension between formal and substantive rights has the potential either to shrink or to expand the terrain upon which social and citizenship issues are articulated. In order to capture the possibilities that arise from this tension, I am proposing that we not only debunk the old passions that objectify the other and correct the cost–benefit evaluations of the migratory process, but also develop a new conceptual understanding of the interplay between mobility and belonging.

Mobility and Complex Systems

As I write, the world's largest scientific experiment has commenced its search for the origins and proof of the existence of dark matter.[9] The experiment involves the collision of particles at the near speed of light. Will the collision reveal the origins of matter after the big bang or open new questions of time, space and movement? What is now clear is that the classical theories of equilibrium and entropy are no longer the 'natural' explanations for what makes things move. For Aristotle, the natural state of things was rest. Movement was the fulfilment of a potential that was already in an object. Galileo reversed the relationship and claimed movement as the norm. Newton subsequently proposed a model of mechanics in which movement was reduced to the interplay between a fixed entity and external forces (Cresswell 2006, p. 14). According to Newton's theory, movement is governed by the deterministic laws of external causes and effects. Hence, as matter expends energy in movement, it also proceeds towards entropy. However, with quantum theory and the discovery of the 'relational patterning' that is formed by motion, Bohm argued that matter gains mass through the interactions that occur in movement. Scientists thus overturned the longstanding assumption that energy is always depleted and matter diminished as a consequence of movement and reopened thinking on the relationship between matter and movement. The most recent theories of complex systems have gone so far as to claim that survival requires mobility. Capra (1996) claims that all matter is constantly involved in a process that includes the drawing up of semi-porous boundaries, interacting with proximate neighbours, developing responses that accelerate exchange or provide resistance, weaving into clustered networks and producing feedback effects that mutually transform matter itself and its environment. In this system, mere equilibrium equals death. Or, to put it more affirmatively, it is through mobility and interaction that we discover novelty and creativity (Prigogine and Stengers 1997).

According to complexity theory, difference is not a problem that is in need of either segregation or integration. This starting point signals a departure from the dualism between matter and motion and the oppositional logic that dominated the mechanistic models of social transformation. Complexity theory gives us a new way of thinking about difference and motion. In this model, difference does not threaten identity and mobility does not exhaust energy. If we were to rethink social and cultural transformation through this interactive model, it would open new possibilities of thinking about the constitutive relationship between difference and identity, as well as allow us to consider the idea that movement is an intrinsic part of belonging, and vice versa.

However, before giving the impression that complexity theory is a new scientific model that, like its predecessors, can provide an explanation of the totality of social relations, it is worth stressing that, so far in the social sciences, it has been used only as a new toolkit – a set of metaphors and concepts (Urry 2003, p. 120). James Rosenau, one of the most enthusiastic and astute users of complex theory, is also cautious as he notes that there is still a sense that the vocabulary and techniques for representing social change are lagging behind the dynamism that has exploded from the major events of our time. While he warns that complexity theory cannot predict the trajectory of change, Rosenau also maintains that it produces a more optimistic view of mobility and difference, as it is more attentive to the creative links between order and disorder (2003, p. 212). The link between the two remains vital, because disorder is defined not as the oppositional term of anti-order but in the more open-ended sense of not-order (Hayles 1991). Bruno Latour (1993) goes so far as to argue that society has no fixed structure and that all social agents lack any fixed essence. Rather than seeing the social system as a bounded unit, he describes it as a hybrid process in which everything is in an endless state of circulation.

From this perspective, complexity can be seen as an operational modality that is neither totally ordered nor tumbling from one random encounter to the next. It refers to a process of relational interactions that exists between and within the 'closed' space of structure and the 'open' spaces of chance. Flows occur and shapes emerge through a network of circulation and modification. The effect of these flows is unpredictable. A singular action can have multiple effects in different parts of the system. At some point it can proceed in an incremental manner; at other points it will link up with other effects and cascade away from its intended path. As has often been stated, a complex system is non-linear. This means that there is no proportionality between cause and effect. 'Outcomes are determined not by single causes but by multiple causes, and these causes may, and usually do, interact in a non-additive fashion. In other words, the combined effect is not necessarily the sum of its parts' (Byrne 1998, p. 20).

This shift in scientific perspective has dramatic consequences for the way we understand the integrity of a social system and the risks or benefits of human movement. For over a century, social scientists and legislators have relied on a discourse that understood social change and human movement in light of a mechanistic worldview. Complex systems theory could offer a third perspective on the turbulent mobilities that shape global migration (Rosenau 1997, pp. 55–78). It goes beyond the mechanistic paradigm of migration studies, because it does not simply search for new causal factors or add more links between macro-structures and micro-networks. By contrast, it proposes the view that mobility creates its own momentum, pathways and boundaries. I would argue that the relationship between motivational factors, social networks and institutional forces that comprise the migration process can be redefined as a complex adaptive system. In this dynamic process of fragmentation and integration there is both an interruption of the old structures and the feedback generated by the journey that transforms both the individual and their surroundings. There are no pre-existing structures, only emergent shapes that are made by the constant process of flow. Within this relational system there are also pockets of consolidation and concentration. However, even in these domains, where power may exert greater levels of influence, there is still a looping network of feedback and destabilization that does not necessarily lead to destruction, but inspires reflexive adjustments and modifications. In such a system, flow does not operate under the laws of magnetic attraction and mechanistic equilibrium. When elements are drawn together there are not necessarily compensatory counter-reactions. Gains and losses are not determined on a zero-sum basis. Rather, the system creates clusters out of interactions that share common trajectories.

Migrants have all too often been blamed for causing all manner of social ills. In the next chapter I examine how the ambient fears of migration have led to new modes of stigmatization and the collapse in the spaces for hospitality. I then consider the attempts by migrants to reverse the stigma attached to their identity and give voice to a new vision of human rights.

3

Hospitality and the Zombification of the Other

While hospitality was represented as a sacred duty in Homer's *Odyssey*, the status of the stranger was also framed by uncertainty. A Greek could never know in advance whether the stranger was an enemy or a god in disguise. The conventions of Greek hospitality were therefore laced with a mixture of self-interest and the desire to please the gods. To share food and offer gifts to a stranger was considered the highest form of civilization. By contrast, a monster such as a Cyclops would rather devour his guests. Hospitality was a regulated mode of reception. The stranger was brought into the house according to various rules and customs that reflected their status. The stranger's posture was critical: upright for the holy and prostrate for the poor. The determination over whether the stranger was a friend or enemy, and the willingness to reach out and touch them, followed from the decision formed in the gaze of the host. The host must look and determine the status of the stranger in silence and then offer his hand. After the invitation to enter the house was made, the place of reception and seating arrangement again followed the protocols of status. It was only after food had been shared that speech commenced.

After 9/11 the cultural theorist Gayatri Spivak gazed at the images of the suicide bombers and observed that they 'looked like ordinary graduate students' (2002, 2004a, 2004b). For Spivak, these banal mugshots are taken not as the first sign of an unfathomable enigma, but as a prompt to ask the question 'How can I imagine the suicide bomber as a person who shares the same human consciousness as me?' Taking her cues from Kant's instruction that the aesthetic enables representation to proceed without objective concepts, she argues that the story of the suicide bomber can only enter the field of intelligibility after 'the imagination is trained' to comprehend the other as an agent who is also a knowledge producer. The method for 'accessing' such an understanding is not confined to contextualizing the agency of the suicide bomber within his or her socio-political history. Spivak stresses that figurative representations can supplement the realm of reasoned debate and scholarly investigation. The most difficult part of this task is to surrender to the other as an equal, and from this imaginative outreach and assumed equality, or what she calls 'the uncoercive rearrangement of desire', one can then learn from both a coercive belief system that already succeeded in persuading the young to want to die and our own compulsion for 'bestial' revenge. Through this method Spivak proffers a warning that echoes Derrida's philosophy of hospitality: suicide bombing is a message inscribed in a body; 'if we cannot hear the message, then we will not be able to alter the hospitality' (Spivak 2002).

It is worth remembering that Derrida's conception of hospitality is not grounded on a strict code which can determine in advance who is worthy of sheltering and who is to be banished. The answer to the stranger's request for entry into the host's house is never determined in advance of the encounter. By keeping open the space of encounter, Derrida stresses that every culture has the capacity to be hospitable to the other (to receive them without question) and also to colonize the other by receiving them as a guest (to confine their admission to ways which confirm the authority of the host). This tension cannot be resolved in an absolute way, and Derrida recognizes that 'unconditional hospitality' is impossible. However, he also insists that to lose sight of the principle of hospitality is to risk losing the marker of justice (Derrida and Dufourmantelle 2000). The gift of hospitality is held together with strings. An unconditional welcome, a concept that Derrida concedes to be practically inaccessible, is also posed against its opposite, the imperative of sovereignty. The right to mobility must be positioned alongside the host's right to authority over their own home (ibid., p. 55). In this chapter I reflect on the tension between hospitality and sovereignty by examining the contemporary images of the stranger. I will argue that the names given and taken by strangers and, in particular, the common appeal of the term 'zombie' is a reflection not only of the tendency to dehumanize the other but also of the withdrawal of the space of hospitality. Against this trend, I will also trace the efforts of migrants, activists and artists to reclaim the dialogue between hospitality and human rights (Hlavajova and Mosquera 2004).

How Can There Be Hospitality for Zombies?

During the Fordist period of industrial expansion the dominant image of the stranger was expressed in terms of their function as a component in the machine. Images of strangers and even critiques of exploitation drew on a common pool of metaphors of mechanical exploitation and alienation. In the 1970s migration was inextricably linked to the process of industrialization in the West. The identification of the migrant as a cog in a machine led many commentators to conclude that the alienation of migrants was also a metaphor for the general form of alienation under capitalism (Castles and Kosack 1973). The theories of alienation referred to the *reduction* of humanity as it was objectified in the form of a mechanical part that generated profit for the master. Hence, the alienation of the worker was always configured within the Marxist interpretation of the master/slave dialectic.

In the most recent statements by migrants and refugees, the terms of self-identification have shifted more decidedly towards the realm of the spectral. For instance, Arnold Zable's account of a hunger strike against the Australian government's policy of indefinite detention by Sri Lankan refugees on Nauru Island ends by drawing attention to the placards that the refugees composed in which they describe themselves as 'living corpses . . . walking zombies' (Zable 2007; Austin 2003, p. v). Mohammed Sagar, an asylum seeker who was held for seven years in an offshore camp, explained his predicament to a journalist in these terms: 'I don't want to be happy, I just want my life back . . . whether it would be happy or sad doesn't matter. I just want it back. I want to be alive, that's all, because now I'm feeling like a dead living thing' (quoted in Gordon 2006). The fantasy of release from detention is therefore bound by the desire to return to the place of the 'living'. However, even this modest hope is presented as a chimera in the account by the refugee Richard Okao (2006) of living in Melbourne, 'which is the city of the dead for me because it is the city where I realised that I was dead; that I wasn't living'. Amal Masry was a survivor of the *SIEV X* – a people-smuggling boat that sank on its way to the Australian territory of Christmas Island, drowning 353 persons. Masry survived by clinging to a floating corpse. After being granted asylum in Australia, she visited her son, who was exiled in Iran, and recalled the horror of looking into the faces of the other refugees and thinking, 'the color of their skin was bad, they were living but they were dead, like zombies'.[1]

It is not just in the migrant's biographical accounts that we witness the use of the term 'zombie'. Albert Memmi, one of the pioneering theorists of the psychological dependencies that were forged under colonialism, has also searched for a new way of explaining the social effects of the 'unstoppable human waves' (2007, p. 74) of migration on the 'besieged fortress' of Europe (ibid., 81). His scornful vision of the dislocative effect of migration gains focus as he zooms in on the identity of the immigrant's son and finds that he is 'a sort of zombie' (ibid., 119).

The rhetorical shift in the image of migrant subjectivity, from the wog/cog-mechanical to the zombie-spectral metaphor, provides a graphic register for seeing the contemporary form of dehumanization. The zombification of the other accentuates the *extraction* of the slave's functionality in the master/slave dialectic as it links the slave to a theory of the subject as a spectral entity. It refers to the other no longer as an object for use and exploitation but as a redundant or purposeless thing. Given the recent transformations in both the structures of economic production and the mechanisms for disseminating cultural values, I contend that the stigmatic image of the migrant has been decoupled from the racial/mechanical image of being wogs/cogs in a vast industrial machine and now draws on a spectral symbolic economy.

The American anthropologists Jean and John Comaroff (2002) have also noted that the zombie tropes have increasingly been used as a way of making sense of the uncertainties associated with contemporary migration. They have argued that migrants have always been considered frightening because they usually look different and sometimes make incomprehensible sounds, and, since they are from elsewhere, there is a suspicion that they will not conform to the dominant moral categories. The dread evoked by the migrant is, according to the Comaroffs, akin to the experience of confronting a zombie because it is linked with the feeling of looking into the eyes of an alien being and not knowing whether your own image, thoughts and hopes will be reflected back. The encounter with migrants is thus framed by the problems of sensorial appreciation and non-communication. From this wide range of sources, I will show that the anxiety over the migrant's body, their silence and moral placelessness, is linked to the broader transformations of post-industrial society and the global culture of ambient fear. The spectral logic that compares migrants and refugees to ghosts and zombies refers to a kind of abstracted identity that is stripped of national or ethnic markers and a hijacking of agency by malicious and other-worldly powers.

Dogs in the Polis

During the 2005 riots in France, a young unidentified boy from a housing estate in the northern suburbs of Paris was asked by an

English journalist if he felt French. He replied: 'We hate France and France hates us. I don't know what I am. Here's not home; my gran's in Algeria. But in any case France is just fucking with us. We're like mad dogs, you know? We bite everything we see' (Henley 2005). The 'mad dog' boy was part of a gang when he was interviewed. The 'we' is this gang, but it is also a more generic claim of defiance against the idea that the nation can create a 'people'. The boy despises that which despises him but also recognizes that this hate leaves him without a place. He does not see himself as being at home in the same place as his parents. He knows that his gran's home is in Algeria, but where does this leave him? His fellow gang members reinforce this opposition against the French nation. It promises freedom, but all it offers is 'les keufs, man, the cops'. It declares that the republic is an open space, but leaves them stranded in what another gang member, Rachid, calls 'shit dump'. It presents equality as a right for all, but then the boy's companion Sylla reminds the journalist that the former minister of the interior and now French president, Nicolas Sarkozy, 'calls us animals, he says he will clean the cities with a power hose . . . Every car that goes up, that's one more message for him.' The pyrrhic language is the marker of the deeper loss of faith in the neutrality and integrative power of the state. Republican ideals are seen as a façade that hides the entrenched values of the French. The gang members suspect that they cannot enter the 'open' space of the state as they are. They are not part of the 'already French', and therefore would feel duped if they entered into such a social contract. Unlike their parents, who saw themselves as cogs in the state machine, these gangs find themselves without any function. They see no potential in a conciliatory dialogue with the state, and, as other commentators have observed, the proposition that the migrant must excise their identity in order to participate only inflames their sense of indignation, frustration and anger (see also Bowen 2006; Touraine 2005).

When the gang is left outside of the social contract, its members are aware that they are stranded in a no-man's-land. They know that, when the cops taunt and provoke them, their defiance is futile. 'We're sinking in shit and France is standing on our heads. One way or another we are heading for prison. It might as well be for actually doing something.' In their rage they can only become what the state tries to remove from humanity – animality. If France 'hates' them, then the gang threatens to become what France fears most: an animal that is not bound by common ideals, values and laws. By becoming animal, the 'mad dog boy' goes beyond comprehension of not only what he is, but where he is heading. Prison is seen not as the destiny for transgressors or as a space that provides deterrence, but as another marker of his own exclusion from social norms. It exists parallel – no better, no worse – to the world in which he already exists.

The violence of becoming an animal is not to be confused with juvenile rage. These bitter words were typical of the comments made by many of the rioting youths, for whom police harassment was an everyday occurrence and who also expressed the sense that they had no place in the inner city (Schneider 2007, p. 530). In the public debates that followed the riots, most commentators concluded that the actions and statements of the youths were evidence of either the state's neglect or the rioters' savage vandalism (Mishani and Smotricz 2005). However, this debate missed the most obvious question: How can the failure of the state, or the outburst of anger, strip people of their humanity to the extent that they either describe themselves as 'mad dogs' or are perceived as 'zombies'? The horror of a subject becoming animal can be traced throughout many philosophical attempts to distinguish between nature and culture, anarchy and civilization. Aristotle had no compunction in equating the natural slave with a domestic animal, while Giorgio Agamben (2000, p. 9) reminds us of Kojeve's lectures on the limits of civilization, in which he concluded that no animal can be a snob. Or, put the other way around, the art of *not* 'biting everything we see' is the achievement of the civilizing process.

Slavoj Žižek was among the few commentators who noted that the 'mad dog boy', while lacking a clear ideological agenda, was nevertheless articulating his fundamental human 'insistence on RECOGNITION' (2007a, p. 13). This observation echoes precisely the claim made by the 'mad dog boy': 'We burn because it's the only way to make ourselves heard. . . . Our parents should understand. They did nothing, they suffered in silence. We don't have a choice' (Henley 2005). It is significant that the 'mad dog boy' feels both pity for the suffering and contempt towards the silence of his own parents. He simultaneously elevates himself above, and also moves himself away from, his father's position. Detached, he is alone and confronted by the fear that he has no support. In his eyes the symbolic force of the father has been killed by the nation. He can identify neither with the symbolically dead father nor with the deadly state. He knows that the return to 'my gran's in Algeria' is pointless, just as becoming French is impossible. His own identity is thereby left without a place. It has nowhere to come from and nowhere to head towards. It withdraws into a position from which he can only recoil as an object: 'I don't know what I am.' Or, again, as Žižek observed, the identity of the 'mad dog boy' is deadlocked because he is unable to locate the experience of his predicament into a meaningful Whole (2007a, p. 24).

The experience of being trapped in what the gang called a 'shit dump' does not end with a rigid form of paralysis. On the contrary, the negative space is riven with a thrusting tension. While there is no grounding and binding for a social contract in which individual responsibility can take form, there is a paradoxical series of gestures through which the gang grinds out a defence of their hooded identity. The spiralling flames of the burning cars are evidence of both the 'self-fulfilling sense of exclusion' (Olivier Roy, quoted in Schneider 2007, p. 529) and 'the monstrous symptom of social and psychological devastation' that is hostile to society and yet expects 'more subsidies' (Binswanger 2005). Yet these retaliatory and self-destructive gestures are also expressive of the 'worldless' vortex in which a boy becomes a mad dog. He does not seek to redeem himself by extracting some latent image in the national culture or appealing to an image of a distant self that exists in a different place, but he does defend the space in which his own self is embattled. It is a defensive-aggressive strategy that approximates that of a slave, as envisioned by Lu Hsun: 'He rejects what he is, and at the same time he rejects any wish to be someone other than what he is' (quoted in Bharucha 2006, p. 65). The interview ends with the journalist, looking for a sign of hope, asking: Is there anyone the gang admires? The 'mad dog boy' points to Thierry Henry, a black French football star who was the greatest goal scorer for Arsenal, and then lets fall this acid comment: 'Henry never scores for France.'

The haunting references to becoming an animal are also central to Agamben's influential essays on the human condition in modernity. Agamben begins his project by revisiting the classical philosophical claim that a human life is worth living only if it can transcend its original animal status. He draws out the Aristotelian categories that distinguish between a bare life, *zoe*, which is confined to the animal function of nutrition and reproduction, and human life, *bios*, which proceeds with language and its capacity to develop aesthetic pleasure, moral principles, economic planning and political order. Agamben observes that, throughout the history of philosophy, there is a consistent argument that humans realize their potential through the process of gaining representation within the law. In modern times, he argues, the sovereign has greater power to decide the conditions upon which the law can be suspended, and thereby to exclude people from the right of being a subject under law. As an outlaw, one's mode of being is reduced to that of a bare life: he or she is excluded from the circuit of language and civilization (Agamben 1998, p. 181). The extreme example of this argument is the figure of the *homo sacer* – a subject under Roman law who could be killed with impunity, and whose existence can be defined only in biological terms. His life, and more importantly the status of his life, is stripped of any cultural, moral or

political value. Agamben provides numerous other examples of historical figures who represent this animal state. Perhaps the most chilling
is his recall of Primo Levi's description of the camp inhabitant who
was ironically called 'the Muslim'. This zombie-like figure 'no longer
belongs to the world of men in any way . . . Mute and absolutely alone,
he has passed into another world without memory and without grief'
(ibid., p. 185). He is a being so stunted by fear that neither the threat
of pain nor the promise of pleasure can register within him. Language
no longer impacts upon consciousness. In this apathetic state the camp
inhabitant is almost invisible; the guards cannot exert any more power
over him, nor can the other inmates reach him. Agamben's evaluation
of human life in the current political context is driven by a logic that
identifies the negation of will power, the collapse of a moral order,
and the stripping away of all rituals that sustain cultural belonging
with an inexorable state of bestialization. He argues that this slide into
animality is accelerated and intensified by the monopoly powers of the
sovereign. This leaves the subject with no space in which to forge any
form of residual or resistant agency.

How far apart is the life of a camp inmate and that of the 'mad dog
boy' in the Parisian suburbs? Agamben would claim that they are closer
than one might imagine: they both inhabit the non-space of bare life.
From Agamben's perspective, it is not the 'mad dog boy's' transgressive acts of violence that have cast him beyond the law, but the prior
fact of being in a state of abandonment. He does not simply disagree
with French values; he sees himself as being outside of the space of
French culture. By being excluded from the functions that constitute a
human life, he has passed over to the indistinguishable zone of animality (Bull 2007, p. 10). Similarly, Agamben stresses that the *homo sacer*
is not the extreme figure that exists only at the margins, but rather
the exemplification of a generalized state of abandonment to which
everyone is subjected in contemporary politics. Politics, he claims,
begins with the threat of being held in this state of limbo, and he argues
that, in 'the most profane and banal ways', we are all virtually *homines
sacri* (Agamben 2000, pp. 114–15). The spectacle of detention – which,
Agamben reminds us, occurs not only in remote zones but also in
suburban sporting stadia and within the transit zones of metropolitan
airports – is an expression of the power over the other that actually
undermines the foundations of security and integration in society. For
Agamben, the space in which the detainee is suspended is similar to the
complex topology that the 'mad dog boy' claims for himself: it is both
inside and outside society, the place where sovereign power is exerted
to the maximum but also where the rule of law is reduced to a bare
minimum. This doubled location also exposes a threshold point from

which, Agamben concludes, the citizen's worst fears emerge: the camp has subsumed the home and the city. The detainee is suspended in the camp not just to protect the citizen but also to display the possibility that everyone can be abandoned. As the logic of the camp stretches over the whole of society, Agamben concludes that the integrity of the boundary between human and animal is 'taken away forever' (ibid., p. 188).

Is the 'mad dog boy' an example of Agamben's definition of the *homo sacer*? He says he is in limbo and will 'bite at anything', and for Agamben this declaration is evidence of his lost humanity. The 'mad dog boy' declares himself to be in opposition to the dominant definition of humanity, but, unlike Agamben, I do not see his words and gestures as markers of his expulsion. The position of the mad dog is more complex. It rejects the authority of the state but also inverts the claim that his 'savagery' renders him inhuman. To return him to the status of speaking subject is neither to redeem nor to excuse his actions. My concern is not with justifications but rather with an examination of the available categories for representing humanity. While the state now revels in the use of spectral terms for representing refugees and terrorists, it is my aim to consider how this discourse also intimates towards a more fundamental claim for identity amidst the loss in subjectivity (Grey 2006; see also Rice 2007 and Meeropol 2005).

Spectral Others

Mad dogs, ghost prisoners and zombie refugees – such stigmatic appellations have been an ancient form of addressing the enemy, the foreigner, and even the deviant that lives within society (White 1978). However, it is now difficult to place the mad dogs, ghost prisoners and zombies on the same continuum as the wogs that turned the cogs. These new names shift the position and the integrity of the boundary between humans and non-humans. Even when the wog migrant was reduced to a cog there was a begrudging admission of utility, and every migrant hung onto the hope that one day he would either return home to become a whole man again or his own child's entry into society would redeem his sacrifice. At some point, the migrant wog imagined completeness. While the wog-cog featured as a stigmatic figure in the nation-building narrative, the wog zombie languishes and then erupts as the ultimate threat to the nation. In fact, the wog zombies are now being blamed for the destruction of the will to build a nation.

It is worth recalling that the emergence of ghost stories in the modern era is linked to the Enlightenment and the French Revolution. The Age of Reason sought to banish capricious myths, malevolent superstitions and irrational belief systems and to construct a transparent system of governance that was based on rational modes of explanation. It is now well accepted by cultural historians that the emergence of the ghost genre is a vehicle for expressing both the mysteries that exist at the edges of the illuminated spaces of reason and the passions that elude the powers of rationality (Roberts 2006; Malik 2002). Malcolm Bull goes so far as to argue that the account of human consciousness in Hegel's master/slave dialectic ultimately relies on magnetic theory and the figure of the somnambulist. Hegel's account of the transition to full human consciousness begins with the slave's primal sense of deficiency, and, despite his unequal struggle with the master, he gains a double recognition of himself and of his master's needs. It is through the act of labour that the slave produces both a sense of self and a sense of the self that exists in the other. In order to complete this theory of double consciousness, Hegel drew on popular scientific claims of the capacity of the magnetizer to influence a somnambulist to the extent that two separate individuals may come to function as one. Hegel also stressed that the flow of influence can be reversible, and it is by this process of open-ended mediation that the slave can rise to slay the master. Bull makes the further claim that W. E. B. Du Bois's rearticulation of Hegel's magnetic theory in his account of the African American's 'veiled identity' and 'gift of second sight' has also served as a foundational point for subsequent generations of postcolonial and feminist perspectives on hybrid subjectivity (Bull 2000, p. 240). The spectral thus lingers throughout the theories of emancipation and revolution, and now it resurfaces in the imagery of blowback (Burbach and Tarbell 2004).

In the literary and horror film genre, the status of zombies is not confined to aliens that haunt the borderlands but also encompasses figures that enact the suppression of the other under capitalism (Wood 1986, p. 213). In anthropological accounts, there is the similar observation that the depiction of migrants as zombies not only provides convenient scapegoats but also heightens the vulnerability of social laws, norms and values (Comaroff and Comaroff 2002, p. 796). Their mobility is presented as if it were a liberation from the rules that bind people to the laws of a place. Hence the anxiety over the migrant's arrival is not confined to the initial transgression at the border, but extends to an unbounded fear that migrants, like zombies, possess an insatiable appetite and that predatory behaviour will destroy all forms of social control. It is therefore worth pausing to consider the link between the dehumanizing image of wog zombies and what the American anthropologists Jean and John Comaroff call the 'experiential anomalies and aporias' (ibid.) in the dominant sources of power.

The zombie is a figure that appears to be alive but is also dead. In folkloric and anthropological literature it has been noted that the dead coming back to seek revenge against the living has recurred in almost all cultures. Archetypically, the zombie can move but has neither memory nor will. Either its primary senses have been mutilated – the tongue is cut and the voice seems to come from the nose – or it has been stunned – its eyes are open but the stare is remote. Deprived of these senses, it lacks the means for communication. The image of the zombie often oscillates between the dead person that has returned to life and a body whose soul has been stolen and forced to work for an evil master. Even the meaning of the word is uncertain. It is akin to the Kongo word *nzambi*, meaning 'god'. However, it could be derived from either the French word for the shadows, *les ombres*, or traced back to the West Indian term for ghost, *jumbie* (Ackerman and Gauthier 1999).

In postcolonial literature the appearance of zombies has been linked to the sudden upheaval of social structures, the collapse of traditional forms of moral authority, and the rapid collisions between different worldviews such as colonialism, industrialization and the world wars. Most recently, Jean Comaroff and John Comaroff (1999) have noted an unprecedented increase in the reports of the existence of zombies in the turbulent post-Apartheid period in South Africa. The reports ranged from tales and rumours that circulate in small communities to journalistic claims and state commissions that investigated the motivations for the outburst of violence against migrant labourers. In line with earlier associations between zombies and violent social rupture, the Comaroffs posited a link between the proliferation of these reports and the social and moral implosion caused by neo-liberal capitalism. They argue that both the imagery of zombies and the flows of capitalism are governed by a spectral logic. The increasingly 'opaque, even occult' conditions for the production of wealth in contemporary society have, according to the Comaroffs, left people unable to find a rational understanding of the social change and led them to draw on supernatural imagery as a form of social explanation.

The Comaroffs argue that the experiential conditions of neo-liberal capitalism are framed by a spectral logic because the 'hand' of capital is not only invisible, it is also the omnipotent force for social change – no one can point to 'it', but 'it' is the only thing that makes things happen. The mysterious presence and force of this 'it' has beggared description of any model of explanation that relies on a direct connection between cause and consequence. The Comaroffs claim that radical shifts in the process of economic production, and the new forms of conspicuous wealth, have disrupted traditional modes for explaining the exchange value between human labour and human life. Hence the proliferation of 'the disquieting figure of the zombie' (Comaroff and Comaroff 2002, p. 782) is an attempt to explain the otherwise inexplicable contradictions in social value. In short, when the traditional and rational systems for defining exchange value have been rendered defunct, the allure of zombie narratives gains greater currency. These writers also make the more general claim that the zombie is not just an instance of eccentric and local fears, but also an index of a broader cultural anxiety.

By focusing on the reportage of zombies, the Comaroffs are seeking to address the broader cultural upheavals that arise from the transition of an industrial to a post-industrial society. During the period of heavy industrialization, the place and function of the workplace was, in large measure, defined by reference to the heavy tools and solid structures of the machine age. It was no coincidence that the graffito 'wogs turn cogs' also protested against the alienation of the migrant in the language of the machine. In the post-industrial phase, the imagery of the workplace has switched towards light practices, or what Bauman (2000) calls the 'liquid' flows of capital. The goals of capital have thereby shifted, from the concentration of energy into a unified system to the generation of multiple platforms for the dissemination of energy flows. The place of production and the determination of a company culture are no longer fixed to the territory or norms of a specific place, but have been unleashed into a global field of perpetual reinvention. In this field no one has the promise of being a lifelong cog in the machine. For, when global capital pursues its objective of maximizing surplus and minimizing cost, it should come as no surprise that it is also responsible for provoking a violent competition between the mobile and immobile agents.

The process of zombification that the Comaroffs observed in post-Apartheid South Africa is used as a metaphor for the pattern of dehumanization that characterizes the neo-liberal world order. As mobility and uncertainty become the dominant features of everyday life, the Comaroffs argue that society tends towards an apocalyptic scene in which there is a total rupture of the symbolic bonds and the reduction of humans to senseless zombies. This process of dislocation is represented as if it were of a different order to migrants' experience of alienation in the era of industrial labour. As a consequence, the counter-reactions are represented as wilder. Unlike the wogs that turned the cogs – who, as 'mad dog boy' pointed out, 'suffered in silence' – the zombie has the potential for demonic and unpredictable reaction against the machine. The fear of the zombie lies in the fact that it is perceived to be beyond animal, for it not only 'bites', it also needs to 'eat human flesh'. Zombification becomes a metaphor for the neo-liberal order because in this era the migrant has no hope of being permanently resettled, and the global economic forces have severed any link between productive energy and cultural meaning. In this context the Comaroffs present the melancholic conclusion that migrants are irreversibly dehumanized. However, they also imply that, by 'becoming' a zombie, the migrant may wreck neo-liberal capitalism and thereby rescue everyone from its nightmare.

While Agamben defined the essence of humanity in relation to the articulation of will, the Comaroffs stress that human value is forged in the integration of productive energy within an embedded cultural context. Both perspectives assume a territorialized vision of human life and thereby identify the value of a migrant life in a negative binary. From this perspective, there is not only a dehumanizing logic but also a fatalistic account of the consequences of mobility. All the examples of wogs as cogs or zombies have a negative presumption against the forces that have catapulted people out of their previous state of security and certainty. For, while each of these images captures the extent to which the migrant sees his or her body as an entity whose motion is controlled by an external force, they also conceal the possibility that energy is emitted from the 'bodies' of the automaton, beast and living dead. Central to the argument posed by Agamben and the Comaroffs is the claim that neo-liberal capitalism is an incomprehensible process of change because its operating forces are remote, obscure and volatile, and as a result no form of coherent agency can survive in its wake. The spectral figure of the monstrous enters when rational principles and civilizational institutions everywhere are in ruins. Against this plaintive conclusion I want to turn to a different view on the relation between mobility and identity, and then suggest an alternative reading of the metaphor that couples migrants and zombies.

Cyborg Wog

After the 2005 riots in Paris, the immigrant activist Nico Squiglia (2005) declared: 'I am a migrant. I do not want to integrate. I want to be who I am.' It is precisely the kind of comment that makes cultural conservatives and progressive multiculturalists panic (Phillips 2005). The rejection of integration is immediately seen as either a failure of the state to offer a stronger basis for national affiliation or the inability of multiculturalism to generate more inclusive modes of cultural belonging. When Nico Squiglia declares 'I want to be who I am', he could be seen as threatening to oppose the national demand for solidarity and dismissing the civic promise of equality (Roy 2004). Squiglia's comment at first glance seems to justify the fear that there is now a generation of youth that has turned its back on the state. They seek neither to gain access to more of its resources nor to reform its operational logic. On the contrary, they are creating new imagined communities that have no relation to the territorial and bounded form of a national society. Squiglia's declaration is both a rejection of the state and a proclamation that there is an alternative space for the realization of the self. He already claims possession of the fullness of the 'who I am' while also protesting against the forces that block the wish of the 'who I want to be'. His identity proceeds by rejecting the city and nation as places in which identity is formed by coming together – 'I do not want to integrate' – and proclaims an identity that is perpetually in motion: 'I am a migrant.' These paradoxical declarations also occur in the context of both a fightback against the populist backlash that minorities now experience and an assertion of their awareness of the state's dependency on foreign labour and investment (Phones 2005). However, this claim of rejecting integration and demanding the autonomy of identity is also expressive of an agency that occupies a complex topology.

Nico Squiglia was born in Argentina and now lives in Spain. He is a member of the project Indymedia Straits of Gibraltar, a group composed of activists, artists and cross-disciplinary thinkers. The codename for the project is Fadaiat,[2] which means in Arabic 'through space', 'satellite dish' and 'space ship'. Located in a medieval castle on the edge of the militarized southeastern border of the European Union, this project sees itself as a 'mirror-territory of the transformations taking place in the world'. The idea of Fadaiat is both utopian and instrumental. Through its coalition of artists and activists it has created a no-border media laboratory that is engaged in mapping border flows, critiquing the new militarized border economies and developing links with both local protests on migration issues and international human rights organizations.

Throughout the diverse actions of Fadaiat, the free flow of information is seen as the 'connector' between people from different places and for people on the move. Given linguistic differences between the various members, the project has also embarked on an ambitious effort to devise a communication system based on universal spatial-visual symbols. It has set out to learn from and hijack the symbolic codes that have been developed to promote global capital and to redirect them towards the interests of migrants. While this collective is opposed to the existing modes of regulating migration, their method of opposition is not an outright confrontation with global capitalism, but a form of resistance that reassigns value back to the activities that migrants execute in their everyday lives. This method of resistance draws from a system that is generated by diasporic networks, and in this new social space the collective claims to forge a 'new territory for global democracy'. This rejection of the state is thus creating a space that is very different from the void in which only zombies can roam. The ambivalence of place that Squiglia articulates within his identity is in fact a consequence of what Ulrich Beck (2002, p. 24) calls the zombification of the state. As Squiglia claims to be *in* but not *of* the place, he simultaneously affirms the identity that comes in the context of mobility and asserts a right to define his human value in terms that exceed state-centric parameters. Squiglia decrees his right to preserve identity as a universal right. This proclamation takes a double twist: he claims to have access to the rights that are defined by the state, but he also insists that his identity rests on rights that are above and beyond the state. By rejecting integration into the mechanisms of the state, Squiglia does not disavow the hope of realizing his identity in the context of others; he simply rejects the claim that the context of his community is confined to the co-ordinates of the nation-state.

Squiglia's affirmation of his identity as a migrant, and his desire to define his being in the ongoing process of becoming mobile, is not just an expression of narcissistic individualism but corresponds to a new discourse of migrant subjectivity.[3] The Fadaiat collective describes the process of migration as a result of a complex interplay of forces, rather than the product of linear or mechanistic structures. The group argues that migrants are not simply pushed or pulled by one command or driven out of their homes by the structural imbalances in the world system. On the contrary, they see migrants as autonomous political agents who are also self-organizing in relation to specific pressures. There is no singular or overwhelming force that regulates – 'decides for' – the direction or destiny of the migrant. They are all engaged in complex decision-making processes. Rather than being 'cogs' in the machine, they move in order to 'dignify their life conditions'. This experience of mobility, informality and volatility that is accentuated in the migrant condition is, they argue, also a feature that is becoming common in working life. It is from this perspective that they claim everyone is 'becoming migrant' and conclude that the paranoid metaphors of 'fortress, USA, Europe, Australia' are misleading because they are dependent on the illusion of splendid isolationism.

The Fadaiat collective rejects the conventional definition of the border as simply a demarcation point that separates different entities. It is not just an imaginary line that becomes a geopolitical division, but rather a 'crossed-place', where mixtures intensify and new 'social practices put pressure on established limits'. Hence the border is not a fixed location where one form ends and another begins, but a 'threshold' in which transformation occurs in multiple and unpredictable ways. This vision of the border identity is linked to the ambition of hijacking the info-capital networks in order to create a new ecology between bodies and communication systems. In this utopian model, the Fadaiat collective claims that agency is shaped by the freedom of the cyborg: 'Our modernity has its own mobile borders, which, as always, are in search of the other: the external other that we call nature, and the internal other – subjectivity, ourselves in plural.'

Much of the discussion on the cyborgian transformation of subjectivity has revolved around the unhelpful category of 'post-human'. The incorporation of technology to extend communication is often interpreted through a sci-fi vision of the machine becoming one with the flesh. It resurrects the fantasy that Elizabeth Wilson explored so exquisitely in relation to the childish wish that dolls can become alive, and the fear that humans can slip into mechanical states (1988, 38). I would argue that the use of new communicative technologies does not announce a break, but extends the struggle for the realization of humanity. If the central feature of humanity is the capacity for language, then the search for a common language and the means to communicate with everyone marks the most profound humanist ambition. A universal language and the free flow of information is the necessary but never realized dream of humanism. It is a dream that is forever born in multiple and incommensurable translations. Barbara Creed (2003) has also argued that the banal reality of globalization has presented a new ground for thinking about the political and ethical relations in global communication networks. The perception of the world as an interconnected place and the use of new media, have, she claims, not only caused the flow of information to proliferate and heightened the awareness of global forces; they have also transformed the individual's perception of the self. In Creed's view, this transformation has led to a politicization of a new 'global self'.

Creed's claim that the internet and the new 'global self' will lead to a genuine cosmopolitanism is one of the most optimistic voices in the new discourse on identity and belonging. This reclamation of cosmopolitan values and humanist desires is also central to Paul Gilroy's argument that a new 'planetary humanism' is evident in the contingent and multicultural interactions that have transformed both the conditions of everyday urban conviviality and the rise of translocal human rights movements (2004, p. 28). The Fadaiat project is one of many collective art projects that have emerged in the context of neo-liberal society. A common characteristic in many collectives from this period has been the identification of the transversal relationship between subjectivity and location. The fullness of subjectivity is no longer presented as an achievement that can be gained only after the overcoming of alienation, or even in the process of being connected between different places, but rather is posed as occurring in the midst of the subject's movement across and through space. Hence, the forms of solidarity that emerge in these encounters follow from a prior commitment that cross-cultural communication can produce a recognition of mutual human worth, rather than proceeding from the quasi-mystical assumption that being born in a specific place and having acquired specific cultural traits form the basis of one's exclusive identification with 'a people'. It is no longer where you are *from*, or even where you are *at*, which matters; it is more about the way we communicate with others.

The Diaspora: At Home Outside its Home

Speaking at the opening of Refugee Week in Melbourne, John Pandazopoulos, a former state minister responsible for multiculturalism, connected the plight of the refugees held in detention with the experiences of earlier migrants who had arrived in Australia.[4] He spoke with moral indignation against the then federal policies on border protection and with genuine empathy for the plight of people, like his own parents, who were forced to leave their homes. He observed a deeper moral connection with refugees and believed that this would lead to more than a plea for tolerance towards outsiders. He claimed that 'the wheel has turned on these issues', and concluded that, as a consequence, most people now see the refugee's story as being part of the nation's historical narrative.

Pandazopoulos was able to acknowledge the refugee story by first establishing a commonality with the founding myths of the nation. This connection both allays the guilt over the harm done to the refugee and reinstates hospitality as a central feature of the national narrative. By contrast, John Howard, the former prime minister of Australia, consistently denied that guilt was a necessary emotion either for reviewing the legacies of the past or for establishing a connection with refugees. His stance on immigration focused on defending the absolute priority of national security over humanitarian concerns. He also pushed an agenda that reduced the social services and dismantled the cultural policies that were previously directed towards promoting a multicultural society. In general, he insisted that migrants should integrate into mainstream society and rejected multiculturalism as a dangerous and divisive experiment. This position encouraged his ministers to make pejorative remarks about the so-called mushy principles of multiculturalism (Garnaut 2006), as well as singling out for ridicule the grandmothers that dressed in black and refused to learn English (Robb 2006).

The response to these perjorative remarks on the ethnic community radio programmes was described by one of the hosts as a form of 'wailing' anger. One respondent, an old and frail woman who emigrated from Mexico, said: 'We came here with nothing. My English is still bad. However, I did what I could, and with my now dead husband worked very hard to bring up a good family.' Even at the age of seventy-five, presumably alongside her 'now dead husband', she expressed great pride in her children, who are both doctors: 'They cure people now', she said. In response to the suggestion that her failure to learn English was a sign of unwillingness to join into mainstream society and expressive of disdain of common values, she turned the challenge back to the prime minister: 'Just ask him to come to my place to teach me about values. I'll teach him where he should go' (Trumper 2006).

Even with her 'bad' English, from whence is she offering to teach the prime minister a lesson on values? It is not from outside or elsewhere, but from within 'my place'. This place is her home. By placing the values lesson in her home, this woman also claims both her equal place inside the nation and her equal right as a person who can speak the language of human values. The language and place from which she enters this debate may seem uncanny to the sovereign who assumes a monopoly over defining national values; and, yet, it is this assertion of relative autonomy that is the seat of its anxiety, and a glimpse of a value system that privileges the human above any other category. The government's complaint over the failure of immigrants to integrate is contradicted by the response from this old woman, who believes she has succeeded in retaining her human dignity. In her opposition there is both a rejection of the sovereign authority and an assertion of her own cultural value as an absolute human right. She reinstates that she is the master of her own house. The prime minister is warned that she remains unmoved by his authority. 'Now Australia is my country, I can't go back where I came from. I don't like this but I am not going anywhere.' For this 'poor Mexican migrant' who admits that she 'speaks with an awful accent', there is the realization that there is no home to return to and that life is to be drawn from the very landscape that is foreign to her, even if in this landscape there are voices that condemn her as being among the dead ones. In a letter to the photographer Frederic Brenner, Jacques Derrida noted that 'the diaspora is at home outside its home, it remains outside its home at home, at home at the other's'. The 'mad dog boy' in Paris, the artists in the new collectives and the old woman from Mexico may respond to the challenge in different ways, but they all proceed from the same insistence: I am who I am, and the national values are not the absolute containers of my humanity. Let me repeat the warning issued by the old woman to the prime minister: 'Just ask him to come to my place to teach me about values. I'll teach him where to go.' Like the 'mad dog boy' she is angry at the lack of respect. She also proclaims that she has the moral authority to 'teach him where to go'.

Translation and Universality

The power of the sovereign has in the modern period increasingly been defined by its ability to encroach into the private lifeworld of subjects. Inside the government's complaint about the old migrants stuck in their ghetto is another fear –the failure to gain influence over these communities as they are gaining new connections with other worlds. With satellite dishes pointing elsewhere, there is a new fear of the death of national culture as it is bypassed and even vilified in the pursuit of an imaginary life in diasporic cultures. This fear that the nation will fragment into antagonistic ghettoes, alongside the supposed inter-generational gulf that is evident in the nihilistic rage of the 'mad dog boy', is indicative of what Albert Memmi (2007, p. 111) calls a new social divide. Sociologists have always recognized that the corollary of modernization is detraditionalization (Helas et al. 1996). However, as James Rosenau (2003) argues, the fragmentation of traditional forms of authority is also a stimulus for the reintegration into new social collectives and a redistribution of individual rights.

Rosenau's 'optimistic' approach towards the crisis in authority is consistent with the new paradigm of migration that adopts a transnational and complex feedback perspective. This perspective is not a utopian promise to overcome alienation, but it does offer an alternative to the melancholic disposition towards the decline of the nation-state, and it avoids the denigration of migrant subjects as figures of death and destruction. Butler, Laclau and Žižek also argue that there is a need for an alternative approach towards the understanding of the universal rights of the human subject in the context of cross-cultural communication and global mobilities. Butler gives focus to this argument by contending that, if translation can now be thought of as an unending exercise that is unleashed from the binary of original and copy, then it also provides a new framework for grasping the dynamic interplay between particularity and universality that would accompany the move from spectral humanity into the political. This implies that, within each invocation of becoming animal or turning into a zombie, there must be also be a rearticulation of what it means to be human.

However, as Butler (2000a, pp. 178–9) observes, this simultaneous entry into language and assertion of the humanity of the 'spectrally human' also requires a movement between languages, and an 'opening towards alternative visions of universality that are wrought from the work of translation itself'.

Rethinking universality through the prism of cultural translation opens up the vexed relationship between human rights and cultural difference. Hospitality is now poised over a more complex terrain. What are the visual signs that represent the status of the stranger? When do we touch each other? What is the point at which dialogue commences? It is clear that declaring that multiculturalism is a failure provides no answers to these questions. In Australia this dead-end was predicated on constructing the 'wog grandmother' as the image of death. The 'wog grandmother' was singled out as this deathly force that must be eliminated in order to preserve the integrity of the nation. And, yet, she turns the image of death and life in and around each other. It may have been a translation error when she boasted that, alongside 'my now dead husband I worked very hard to bring up a good family', but it is this linguistic error that reveals the interplay between death and life in the diasporic imaginary.

Here lies the paradox that was first touched upon in Marx's understanding of alienation, and also suggested by Derrida in his revision of the border between human and animals: it is those who were regarded as mad dogs, mutes and zombies that now make a stand for all humanity. They are not asking for their dignity to be returned or for greater access into the national imaginary. They recognize the futility of both requests, and are making a more perplexing summons for the recognition of a humanity that is already embodied in their presence but not yet represented. They are not justifying their equal rights because they believe that they are already like, or want to become like, those who possess national citizenship; rather, they issue this plea from a bodily claim of equal human existence. Their body is already here. Each individual has a singular existence that needs to be acknowledged as being part of a whole. If the body is the only possession, the only means by which the excluded can make themselves visible and audible in public space, then it is also the body that must become the site upon which the protest occurs. By being in a place, each person exists in relation to others. As bodies, with inherent biological functions and human values, the real and fictional figures that I have explored in this essay do not simply represent the depths of dehumanization but also express a process of rehumanization. In the struggle to makes themselves heard they are articulating a form of political resistance that Žižek (2007b, p. 70) calls the 'embodiment of society as Such, as the stand-in for the Whole of Society in its universality, against the particular power interests'.

Even in this reaching phrase by Žižek we can see the struggle that theorists encounter when they seek to give form to the complex interplay between dehumanization and rehumanization. The effort to dehumanize the other always reveals much about the fears that lurk in the self. From the examples I have surveyed here we can witness the way the migrants are perceived as automata, animals and zombies. As Hayden White (1978, p. 152) has argued, this 'ostensive self-definition by negation' is an ancient strategy. It is a paltry attempt to achieve superior dignity by impugning the identity of the other. However, it is also worth recalling that this strategy is pushed to its most extreme limits during times of heightened vulnerability. The suspicion, contempt and hostility now projected towards migrants are testament to a deeper ambivalence towards mobility. The fear of the migrant is always expressed through the suspicion that they cause harm and then move on. However, underlying this fear is a presumption that the migrant has rejected the settled life, and the citizen then is forced to consider: What sort of a human wants to be on the move, and to what extent is society dependent on mobility? The challenge of living together is averted by answering that only cogs, animals and zombies live on the move. A human on the move is threatening to the citizen not only because of the initial transgression at the border, but because the possibility of ongoing mobility renders the totality of the experience and every future encounter uncertain. This uncertainty cannot be resolved by pinning their identity back to the place of origin. The dread of the migrant is not confined to the fact that he or she is someone who is from somewhere else, but is increasingly linked to the anxiety that they and everyone else must exist in an unbounded state of global roaming. So who are they, and what will happen to us if they enter? What would it mean to accept that they too are humans with bodies and dreams?

These questions haunt the national imaginary because they reveal a subject that claims to possess an identity that is both fully formed and unsettled. This cosmopolitan subject appears both full in its proclamation of humanity and spectral because it does not seek to be regrounded in the form of the national citizen. I began this essay with the graffito of 'wogs turn/run cogs'. Under the conditions of national capitalism, the migrants' alienation was expressed as their labour was appropriated from their bodies and rendered as cogs in the machine. Marx argued that the alienated man is torn from his own body, nature, productive capacities and human essence. The emancipation of man is also a successive 'return' to a state of 'species being', where the individual man has absorbed in himself a state of being in a politically equal society and possessing an equal humanity. According to Marx, it was this negation of identity that also created the class of proletariat that he saw as the agent of change. Under global capitalism the migrant's alienation appears like a ghost in search of the machine. Hardt and Negri have extrapolated the Marxian axiom to argue that the new deterritorialized proletariat will become the agent of freedom in the name of a global humanity. This is a big call, and I do not reject it as mere idealism, because at the centre of the stories on automata, animals and zombies that I have surveyed in this chapter is the dialectic between alienation and freedom. In these narratives there are traces of the cosmopolitan yearning and the demand for the migrant's right to be here that relies on nothing more or less than his or her humanity.

Part II

The Politics of Art

4

Aesthetic Cosmopolitanism

The term 'cosmopolitanism' is both the product of an idea of the world and an ideal form of global citizenship. Everyone who is committed to it recalls the phrase first used by Socrates and then adopted as a motif by the Cynics and the Stoics: 'I am a citizen of the world'. Indeed the etymology of the word and its theory appear to be in wondrous symmetry. There are no records that demonstrate the existence of a cosmopolitan society and yet, throughout history, the concept of cosmopolitanism has continually surfaced as a term to express the basic idea of human unity and a harmonious form of universal governance. In 1939 H. G. Wells reflected on the paradoxical persistence of the cosmopolitan ideal: 'All history is against it. But all reality is for it' (quoted in Heater 1996, p. ix). This comment suggests that the survival of cosmopolitanism is itself a paradox. It exists but always in the form of a future-oriented nostalgia. It can be traced back to the mythological fascination with the abyss of the void and the infinite cosmos, as well as recurring in almost all the philosophical debates about the relationship between individual freedom and universal rights.

Diogenes, the maverick founder of the Cynics, adapted the Socratic ideal of the world citizen as a rebuke against the authority of the polis. The idea that one could claim a moral connection to the whole world was passed on to Crates, and he in turn taught Zeno, who developed a school that gathered in the stoa – the arcades that surrounded the agora of ancient Athens. The eponymously named Stoics were the first to develop a cosmopolitan philosophy: they articulated four principles that continue to influence contemporary debates on cosmopolitanism.

First, they rejected the polis as the absolute limit point to political belonging, and defined the idea of community through the incorporation of the whole of humanity. Second, they asserted that human rights were not constrained within geopolitical boundaries. Third, they adopted a non-hierarchical vision of cultural value. Fourth, they encouraged an attitude of self-awareness through genuine curiosity and open exchange with the other. By pricking the narcissistic chauvinism that marvelled at the existing political forms, encouraging an attitude of wonder and curiosity towards foreign cultural forms, and developing a mode of cross-cultural comparison that was based on equal respect, the Stoics proposed a moral, spiritual and aesthetic outlook that extended the principles of rights and obligations to all people rather than confining them to members of a community within a territorial boundary. For the Stoics, this notion of being and belonging was expressed in a complex way – there was a spiritual sense of interconnectedness and an aesthetic interest in difference, as well as a sense of political equality and moral responsibility towards all humanity. It is crucial to note that the Stoics emerged after the collapse of the classical Greek polis and in the wake of Alexander's imperial adventures. Although the Alexandrian vision of a fusion between Greek and non-Greek was short lived, this new imperial context provided the setting for a unique and complex cosmopolitan vision.

Since the Stoics, the spiritual and aesthetic dimensions of cosmopolitanism have been slowly disregarded. Roman Stoics like Tacitus and Seneca were the first to link the moral values of prudence, endurance and steadfastness with imperial governance. In the sixteenth century the Dutch philosopher Justus Lipsius put further stress on the Stoic virtues of moderation, courage and toughness, as he defined the principles of good governance through the ethos of emotional self-restraint. Henceforth, the cosmopolitan vision of conviviality and justice was dependent on the moral fortitude of the leaders and a state system based on reason (Oestreich 1982). By the time Kant adopted cosmopolitanism as a key concept for thinking about global peace, the focus was almost entirely on deprovincializing the political imaginary and extolling the moral benefits of extending a notion of equal worth to all human beings. However, unlike the early Stoics, who saw the cosmopolitan ideal flowing from the animating force of love that is present in every person, Kant argued that the historical development of reason and its embodiment in Western legal-political frameworks enabled the proposal of a more extensive form of civic obligation (Kant [1784] 1963). He imagined a broad political and moral vision of a world order in which the respective nation-states were bound by common principles of freedom, equality and legislation. The progression from local to national and then international affiliation was, in Kant's thinking, a result of the historical developments in political organization. Kant also adopted a view on human nature that privileged the instincts for destruction and placed the collective capacity to share common feelings as a weaker and more fragile human quality that needed protection by political norms and legal regulations. Kant asserted that humans have common sentiments and the capacity to communicate this sentiment of commonality. However, he also noted that the faculty of shared feeling and the principle of *sensus communus* was never used as the primary basis for establishing a political community.

This reflection did not lead Kant to conclude that a cosmopolitan state may remain only as a perpetual aspiration. While also rejecting the view that 'universal civic society' could be developed from pure philosophical reflections on human interaction, he nevertheless argued that it could emerge as a consequence of the logical and historical unfolding of successive political formations. Hence, without the successive passage from primitive, feudal and, finally, nation-states, a new cosmopolitan order would be incomprehensible. Thus, Kant placed the historical process of development in political reasoning and rational deduction, rather than subjective feeling and aesthetic experience, at the core of his philosophical discourse on cosmopolitanism. Cosmopolitanism is thus not a virtue that is to be pursued for its own qualities, but is dependent on the developments within a political process that seeks to control the destructive drives in human nature, as well as to temper the tyrannical abuses of power. Kant also argued that cosmopolitanism is not a moral claim for a borderless world. Cosmopolitanism is, in his schema, differentiated from unlimited hospitality, as it is ultimately subordinate to the rights of sovereignty. Hence, as one commentator observed, 'with a mixture of dignified self-assertion and self-deprecating good humour', Kant proposed that political leaders would require the advice of idealistic philosophical moralists like himself in order to keep the principles of hospitality and cosmopolitanism alive (Wood 1998, p. 61).

Since Kant, the debates on cosmopolitanism have been even more tightly bound to the twin notions of moral obligations and the virtue of an open interest in others. In more prosaic terms, the concept of cosmopolitanism now serves as a catchphrase for expressing the 'duty' to live with all the other people in this world and the moral challenge that humanity should rise up to (Appiah 2006). This approach influenced many of the modern innovations in international law and human rights and has served as the main starting point for almost all the contemporary approaches in the theories of cosmopolitanism. It has become a key theme in debates on the shifts in the order of international relations, the powers of the nation-state, the forms of cultural production, the social processes that are transforming the conditions of everyday life, and even the sense of personal belonging. It has also become a useful scholarly perspective that has been deployed by political theorists exploring the ideological impact of mobility and anthropologists who investigate the global patterns of cross-cultural affiliations, as well as in philosophical reflections on the forms of moral interconnectedness (Delanty 2009). In short, cosmopolitanism has been used both as a term to describe the actual changes in the world and as a normative challenge to feel global responsibility in terms of what Martha Nussbaum (2001, p. 348) calls 'concentricity'.

Contemporary Theories of Cosmopolitanism

Political theorists such as David Held (1995) have proposed the concept of cosmopolitan democracy and global commonwealth to advance new norms and rules for transnational governance. Bhiku Parekh (2000) has sought to challenge the national limitations of liberal multiculturalism by adopting a pluralist cosmopolitan perspective to re-examine the relationship between cultural minorities and hegemonic cultures. Antonio Negri has also adopted a perspective on political struggle that resembles a cosmopolitan optic. In place of the national proletariat, Negri (2009) has argued that the key agent for resistance is a fragmentary and loosely affiliated transnational network that he calls the 'multitude'. The site of struggle has also expanded beyond the control of national industries and is now situated on what he calls the 'commons', which includes the material resources, institutions and utilities that are embedded in a local place and also the immaterial tools for global communication and symbolic identification.

In cultural studies and anthropology, the concept of cosmopolitanism has been at the centre of the critical understanding of how ordinary lives are being shaped by the processes of global mobility and that everyone is now required to engage in some level of reflexive evaluation of how their own experiences are entangled in transnational networks of communication and attachment. Homi Bhabha argues that hybrid cultures are not only constituted in the border zones of cultural difference, but they are also producing a 'cosmopolitan community envisaged in marginality' (Bhabha 1996; see also Gilroy 2004 and Nederveen Pieterse 2007). Mica Nava (2007, p. 8) also refers to this transformation of everyday life through the terms of visceral and ordinary cosmopolitanism: the emotional forms of attraction and identification with otherness. One of the pioneers of this field, Néstor García Canclini (1995), has claimed that, in contemporary society, 'everyone translates'. In other words, everyone is to some extent living in a border zone, negotiating the flows of cultural symbols and meaning of artefacts as they circulate across numerous cultural boundaries. Amidst these complex interactions, García Canclini claims that people from all classes and backgrounds are involved in adjusting the given frameworks and simultaneously creating new interpretations of their experiences. This perspective gives particular emphasis to the popular and hybrid practices of diasporic culture that have shaped metropolitan life. Manray Hsu (2005, p. 76) also observed that the concept of cosmopolitanism has been useful in facilitating 'the move away from the issues of cultural representation to those of globalization, including the emergence of global culture alongside a global civil society'. However, he further claims that the radical implications of living side by side with cultural differences have not been fully appreciated, and that the 'network-nature' of contemporary culture has shifted cosmopolitanism from the abstract domain of ideals to a habitual condition that presents a profound challenge to the way we understand our responsibility of sharing the world we live in. Hence, Hsu proposed a concept of 'decentralized cosmopolitanism' to address the complex network of cross-cultural and self-organized collectives that are formed in specific localities. In cultural studies, cosmopolitanism is not a 'top-down' perspective but a term for referring to 'bottom-up' practices.

The sociological debates on globalization have also adopted cosmopolitanism as a key tool for addressing the impact of global mobility and the new modes of transnational communication (Urry 2007; Cheah and Robbins 1998). Ulrich Beck (2006) has been at the forefront of utilizing the term 'cosmopolitanism' to describe the erosion of nationalist barriers, the development of new forms of transnational governance, and the emergence of co-operative social networks, as well as the perception that many economic and environmental issues can no longer be managed and regulated from within a nation-centred view of the world. Beck argues that the new cosmopolitan realities require not only a greater empathy for the dynamic specificities that are forged by the fluid processes of social transformation but also a kind of spherical consciousness that grasps the new transnational alignments and global flows. This perspective is consistent with the general view that society and culture are undergoing radical transformation through the intensification and diversification of the processes of mobility and mixture. Hence, Beck claims that the concept of cosmopolitanism is best used to refer to the processes that connect global forces to local structures, as well as providing a new conceptual frame for defining the context of social investigation. Beck argues that, unlike the nation-centric approaches that directed social analysis throughout most of the twentieth century, the current predicament requires a new cosmopolitan methodology. The benefit of this approach is that it not only widens the scope for measuring social processes and extends the boundaries for mapping the social context, it also encourages investigators to thematize the relational patterns between the local and the global. In short, Beck claims that this perspective is better suited to the new social movements as well as providing an 'epistemological shift' in the understanding of the interconnectivities between local and global processes.

Beck sees cosmopolitanization as the affirmative side of globalization. At the other end of the spectrum, the Marxist cultural geographer David Harvey takes a more pessimistic view of the relationship between cosmopolitanism and globalization. Harvey (2009) rejects the claim that cosmopolitanism can furnish a critical stance against globalization. For him, globalization is the driving socioeconomic force that has deepened power differentials. He is dismissive of the use of cosmopolitanism as the basis for a universal ethic, as he regards it as mere rhetoric that masks the exploitative logic and divisive social reality of global capitalism. A similar stand-off can be found in the debates over the impact of the discourse on cultural difference in contemporary art institutions. Okwui Enwezor (2003–4, p. 102) not only argues that the visual practices that emerged in the context of the debates on multiculturalism and postcolonialism were instrumental in radically revising the parameters of modernist subjectivity, he also acknowledged that they played a key role in the reconfiguration of the museum as a platform for cross-cultural exchange. By contrast, Boris Groys argues that the emergence of the 'postmodern taste for cultural diversity' was 'formed by the contemporary market, and it is the taste for the market'.[1] For me, this is a bad case of throwing out the baby with the bathwater. Groys has always celebrated the capacity of art to exert 'an autonomous power of resistance', so why would artists that engage with cultural diversity 'emerge' only in order to fulfil the cannibalistic hunger of capital?

The ambivalence towards cosmopolitanism is most pronounced in the philosophical debates that have examined its Eurocentric legacy and the reliance on a theory of universalism that is perceived as exclusivist and ethnically biased. A crucial feature of these debates is that, while the humanist and Enlightenment theories of universalism have been subjected to thorough scrutiny, this has not entailed a wholesale rejection of a cosmopolitan vision of humanity. For instance, Paul Gilroy (2004, p. 28), who has been a staunch critic of the complicity between Western philosophy and slavery, is nevertheless an advocate of the need to develop a global framework for human rights and a platform for what he calls 'planetary humanism'. Alasdair MacIntyre (1998, p. 9), whose entire philosophical project has been a struggle with the pitfalls of both universalist and relativist truth claims, has persisted with the aim of constituting a third culture as an ideal space for negotiating competing moral and cultural claims. Gayatri Spivak (2003), having demonstrated the utility of deconstructive methodology in exposing the semiotic multiplicity and radical difference in the narratives of origin, also asserts that all forms of representation have a necessary commitment to what she calls 'strategic essentialism'. The political philosopher Etienne Balibar (2002, p. 165), who acknowledges that universalism can no longer be defined as if it possessed a singular cultural setting or developed along a linear historical pathway, also reiterates that 'ideal universality' is always formed in the gap between theory and practice. Universalism is therefore not a fixed moral code but a critical perspective that is constituted in the gap between the principle of universalism and the consequential enunciations that invariably fall short of total inclusivity.

While all these perspectives reject the presumption that a universalist viewpoint can be confined either to reflecting the cultural values of a specific point of origin or to operating according to a totalizing schema based on a predetermined evaluative hierarchy, they do not amount to an anti-universalist position. The point shared by these diverse theorists is that universalism is both a necessary ideal and always contingent upon the specific circumstances and diverse needs through which it is articulated. Every attempt to enlarge the form of universalism will always reinscribe a particularistic perspective. The aim of these theorists is thus not just to update or widen the categories for determining universalism, but also to sharpen the focus on the logic of exclusion. Walter Mignolo (1998) coined the phrase 'diversality' to describe the project of rethinking universality through diversity, and he identified this as the key task of a 'critical cosmopolitanism'. This critical approach is in marked contrast to the ideological function that universalism has achieved in the context of globalization. The growing pressure to achieve global standardization in economic exchange mechanisms, communication platforms, political organizations, legal frameworks and even aesthetic forms is now well documented (Jonsson 2010, p. 115). However, as Balibar argued, there is a clear distinction between the ideological versions of universalism, which have invented new scales for measuring equivalence in order to perpetuate competition amongst rival identities, and the critical approach, which seeks to address the terms of equality. By addressing universalism through its essential multiplicity, Balibar also stressed the function of dialogue.

This approach recognizes that, while all claims start from some kind of 'essentialist' position, dialogue can only proceed if the essentialist claim is strategic – serving as a starting point rather than the limit for the field of exchange. From this perspective universalist claims are situated within specific and context-bound positions. It is through their mutual interaction that they forge an evaluative mechanism that enables both reflexive self-critique and a creative alternative. Hence, this universalist approach is not based on fixed foundations, but unfolds through the interminable process of cross-cultural dialogue. This revised version of universalism is a key plank in a critical theory of cosmopolitanism. By moving the vision of universalism from a competition among rival claims to a dialogue between alternate interpretations, it also mobi- lized an iterative process whereby cosmopolitanism is conceived not as a state that is comprised of fixed categories, but as the ongoing activity through which multiple identities communicate with each other within an arena of mutual recognition (Walzer 1989).

From Critical to Aesthetic Cosmopolitanism

While these contemporary approaches towards cosmopolitanism have revised the Eurocentric bias and reconfigured both the scope and the relational process of universalist claims that underpinned the Kantian vision, one crucial aspect has escaped its due scrutiny. Kant's vision of cosmopolitanism inscribes a fundamental hierarchy between reason and imagination. Unlike the Stoics, who believed that cosmopolitan- ism could develop through the aesthetic dimension of imagination, Kant promoted the alternative view that it was forged through a his- torical chain of reasoning. This vision of cosmopolitanism presumes the necessary triumph of reason over the faulty, fleeting and flighty genius of the imagination. It therefore takes as a given that human nature and the prevailing social order is destructive and provincial and that it needs to be modified, cultivated or uplifted in order to become cosmopolitan. Thus the task of patrician leaders and enlight- ened educators is to promote a superior worldview of conviviality and harmony. Although most critical theorists would abjure this characterization, as Etienne Balibar (2007) has observed, much of the theoretical discussion on cosmopolitanism has proceeded within a deliberative paradigm that stressed the role of reasoned argumentation in the delivery of a new transnational public sphere.

Cosmopolitan visions have been most vivid in times of systemic expansion and in the ruins of imperial adventures (Pagden 2000, p. 6). When states break up or new unions are formed, and the intensity of living with difference reaches a critical level, then the ideals of cosmopolitanism provide a perspective for the entanglement of cultural differences. Cosmopolitanism tends to force itself into the public imaginary when the elements in the world interact in unassimilable ways. Therefore it is no coincidence that, amidst the current phases of turbulent globalization, the reaching out for cosmopolitan thinking is at its most intense. My aim is not to question the efficacy of either the patrician visions or the decentralized vernacular perspectives on cosmopolitanism. It is my belief that cosmopolitan ideals do not rest exclusively at either end of the spectrum. It is unlikely that the flow of cosmopolitanism is either top-down or bottom-up, and more likely that the two positions are dependent upon each other. I would suggest that cosmopolitanism is an ideal that is articulated in the moments of critical intervention through a complex interplay of reasoned and aesthetic modes of thinking. It does not emanate solely from above or from below but from the middle of social consciousness (Guattari 1995, p. 129). Felix Guattari also argued that 'collective intellectuality' comes from the midst of cultural flows and social circumstances rather than from the bottom up. He stressed that creativity does not follow a straight line of historical progress or appear as a model that can be imposed from above.[2]

My perspective is informed by the assumption that cosmopolitanism is not only pushed forward by the great transformations of globalization but also occurs in subtle ways during the small moments of transition. If, as Ulrich Beck (1999, pp. 1–18) correctly noted, the new 'earth politics' needs the television to be effective, I will add that the culture of cosmopolitanism also lives within the aesthetic domain of transnational networks and on local streets. The attention that is given to this may require a new perspective that combines a theoretical understanding of global change and a capacity to observe the microconnections that occur in specific places. To grasp the dynamic of cultural cosmopolitanism, we may need not only to consider the big shifts and wide networks of global change but also to ponder over how little commonality is now necessary before people find a connection with others. I will ask whether it is possible to draw any hope from the fragments of idealism and opportunism, absurdity and seriousness, confusion and cooperation that, for good or bad, are creating links between different people. My aim is not to consider cosmopolitanism as an elusive ideal that may one day inform good governance and provide the touchstone of ethical conduct, but rather to consider whether, in the complex process of contemporary culture, there is also an attending cosmopolitan consciousness.

Hence, I will propose an alternative view on the aesthetic dimensions of cosmopolitanism. In particular, I will argue that, through the perpetual function of the imaginative world picture-making, aesthetics is always cosmopolitan. I obviously share the commitment towards securing the moral and political ideals of cosmopolitanism, but the emphasis on ethical duties and deliberative frameworks has both constrained the scope of cosmopolitan ideals and obscured the signs of aesthetic cosmopolitanism. In short, I will argue that the focus on the necessary moral stance of openness has failed to notice the concomitant forms of aesthetic interest. Cornelius Castoriaidis (1997c, p. 3) claimed that the act of the imagination is the principal means for facing both the abyss of the being and the eternity of the cosmos. This act of facing is a big bang aesthetic moment, filled with horror and delight. Traces of this aesthetic encounter with the abyss of being and the infinity of the cosmos can be found in the everyday acts of curiosity, attraction and play. It is from this perspective that I will argue that the cosmopolitan images of conviviality arise not only from a moral imperative but also from an aesthetic interest in others and difference.

The most vivid signs of the aesthetic dimension of the cosmopolitan imaginary can be found in the world-making processes of contemporary art. Imagination – irrespective of the dimensions of the resulting form – is a world picture-making process. Imagination is therefore a crucial starting point for cosmopolitanism. Hence, the appearance of cosmopolitan tendencies in contemporary art is not just a cultural manifestation of globalization. These are the imaginings that combine an old universalism with a new kind of globalism. My interest in aesthetics is therefore an attempt not to announce the triumphant return of the repressed, but to demonstrate the need for rethinking both the general role of the imagination in cosmopolitan visions of the world and the specific visual practices that have emerged in the contemporary art scene.

The concept of aesthetic cosmopolitanism has previously been used to refer to the now normal cultural condition in which locally situated modes of cultural production and consumption are in dialogue with globally hegemonic forms (Regev 2007). My aim is not directed towards outlining the social forces that are defining this emergent cultural field, but rather to reflect on the imaginary constitution of cosmopolitanism through aesthetic practices. I should stress that aesthetic cosmopolitanism does not refer simply to the aesthetic representations of cosmopolitanism, but to a cosmopolitan worldview that is produced through aesthetics. Therefore the attention to contemporary artistic practices is not confined to either the visualization of cross-cultural interactions, or even to the appearance of global processes in artistic practices, but is concerned more with the proposition that the process of world-making is a radical act of the cosmopolitan imaginary. The theoretical underpinnings of the concept of cosmopolitanism can thus be retraced through the recent tendencies in artistic practices.

In the following chapters I will engage with contemporary visual art and how it has embodied a distinctive form of the cosmopolitan imaginary. Artists have proposed a range of social strategies for bringing different people together as part of their aesthetic vision of the world. These aesthetic strategies have raised complex questions about the possibility of mutual understanding and the modes of spatial affiliation. The responses that emerge in these situations, while pointing towards a common ethical and political horizon that is articulated in critical theory, are, however, very different in form and conceptual order. For instance, Paul Ricoeur (2007, p. 5) described the geometry of justice, the fragile equilibrium between taking and giving in civility, and the progression of private ethics to public virtue as 'the search for a just distance in every situation of interaction'. However, unlike the moral philosophers who see this flow in mono-directional terms – that is, what is anterior must 'reveal, expose and unfold itself by passing successively through the filter of moral judgement and the test of practical application in determinate fields of moral action' (ibid., p. 3) – artistic practice suggests a more ambiguous terrain and multi-directional flow. They are drawn to these sites because the topology of 'in-betweenness' resonates with the mode of aesthetic criticality.

It is also worth recalling that, when the Stoics envisaged cosmopolitanism, it was not only as a moral duty towards strangers and a political system for universal governance, but also as an aesthetic engagement with cultural difference. Is it a coincidence that this cosmopolitan imaginary was named after the complex topology of the stoa? The stoa was a shelter from the sun and rain without becoming an enclosed room. It was an in-between and transitional space, neither outside nor inside. Departures and arrivals are signalled in a vague manner within the stoa. One could hover, browse, eavesdrop, rub shoulders and move on. Conversations could commence through casual interruptions. The stoa is a site of gossip, rumour and information.

Why did these cosmopolitan philosophers choose to meet in the stoa? One can only assume it was a deliberate attempt to gain a relative distance from the other available spaces. Between the private space of the *oikos* (home) – where personal needs and interest could be expressed freely – and the public space of the *bouleuterion* (parliament) – which was a deliberative venue in which community defined its collective norms and structures without being beholden to any private interests – there was the *agora* – a relatively open space of presentation, speculation and exchange. The stoa exists alongside the *oikos*, the *agora* and the *bouleuterion*. It is therefore at arm's length from the sites of privacy, commerce and deliberation.

I imagine the stoa as a spatial metaphor for the emergence of critical consciousness within the transnational public sphere. It is a space for criticality without the formal requirement of political deliberation and sociality without the duty of domestication. The stoa is the pivot point at which private and public spheres interact and from which the cosmopolitan vision unfolds. Thinking the place of art within this context is more than jumping from either the local to the global, the private/ *oikos* to the public/*bouletrion*, or even the singular to the universal. It is more like the liminal zone of the stoa.

5

Aesthetics through a
Cosmopolitan Frame

What sort of knowledge of the world does art furnish? The discourse of
aesthetics has, in broad terms, proposed that art is the free play of the
mental faculties. It is capable of giving form to sensation, impression
and intuitions without a conceptual order that is yoked to the logic of
either instrumental function or reasoned benefit. Art represents the
capacity of human imagination to conceive possibilities that have no
necessary objective purpose and, as Kant argued, can appear in an
almost disinterested state of apprehension. However, for all its appreciation of art's creative force, the discourse of aesthetics has generally
viewed the knowledge of art with suspicion. Philosophers acknowledge
that art can constitute its own subjective world, but they tend to argue
that truth does not reside in art. This fundamental distinction between
art's ability to constitute its own image of the world and the role of
reason to deliver the truth of the world has vexed all the debates on
aesthetics and politics.
    My concern with this distinction is not guided by a desire to assert
the priority of aesthetics or to wrestle with the superiority of reason's
access to truth, but rather to highlight the knowledge made in art as
a world-making activity in order to recast the debates on aesthetics
and politics through a cosmopolitan frame. Putting aside the recent
flutter of hope that neuroscience can provide a new psychologism to
explain the mystery of creativity, the dominant trend in the discourse
of aesthetics continues to persist along two broad trajectories. One
stresses the primacy of formalist concerns, and the other emphasizes
the structural significance of social and political forces such as race,

class, gender and power. This division is rarely articulated in absolute terms. For instance, while the artist Liam Gillick openly acknowledges the influence of theory, even his most loyal commentators would nevertheless assert, in a somewhat anxious tone, that he also remains 'judiciously peripheral' to the critical discourses that intersect with his practice (Szewczyk 2009, p. 29). Such hesitancy is symptomatic of the dread of being associated with a form of political art that occupies a position of 'complicit alongsidedness' with the dominant social forces. Of course, there is no shortage of examples in which art has been co-opted either to decorate a corporatist agenda or to promote activist propaganda. This uncertain relationship with politics is understandable because art does not exist in a pure space outside the messy complicities of institutional objectives and economic imperatives.

The ambiguous status of art, its unstable social value and its uncertain political function has been a problem that has never been resolved in art history. Explanations and validations for art have been sought in many different directions. Victor Burgin (1986, pp. 145, 204) argued that there was an 'unbroken thread' in art historical treatises that sought to establish a correlation between the social value of art and non-aesthetic qualities such as spiritual sensitivity or political commitment. T. J. Clark (1982) has promoted the view that art becomes revolutionary through its ideological critique of the everyday. Arthur C. Danto's exploration of the triple transformation of art in its transfiguration of the ordinary is another example of the common argument that art acquires an elevated status as it is embedded within the social or propelled by external political forces (1992, pp. 3–4). These approaches were well suited to the task of explaining the discursive affiliations, unpicking the political premonitions in the medium of art, and demonstrating the formal services of art in social transformation. However, I will depart from these art historical approaches because they place the aesthetic knowledge of the world in a kind of limbo. At best, the artistic imagination is perceived as occupying a space of speculative detachment that is separated from the activity that produces social change, and in the worst cases the function of the artwork is reduced to 'a mute form of political economy' (Lutticken 2009, p. 93).

However, a more fundamental reason for departing from these art historical approaches is driven by the recent tendencies in art that demonstrate a different mode of engagement with the processes of social transformation. In the field of contemporary visual practice, the critical engagement with the medium of art can no longer be confined to contemplation of a fixed object. The use of non-material media and processes of collective participation have demanded a rethinking of the relationship between aesthetics and theory. Although artists are forever denying that they are part of something that is recognized and defined by others, artistic practice is a medium for constituting 'the social' in contemporary society. Given the politicization of contemporary visual practice and the aestheticization of contemporary politics, the discourse of aesthetics is now propelled into the ambient field of image production and circulation. The ubiquity of images and the constant enhancement of the modes for public participation have not only disrupted the conventional division between the agency of the artist and collective authorship but also underscore the necessity to rethink the function of the imagination as a world-making process. Arjun Appadurai stated it most succinctly: 'the imagination is today a staging ground for action, and not only escape' (1996, p. 7). In particular, I will argue that the emergent artistic tendencies require a new cosmopolitan conceptual framework. This framework would depart from the traditional approaches that focus on the capacity of an artwork either formally to embody or pictorially to represent the social changes that society is yet to recognize (Williams 1983; Katsiaficas 2006, p. 215; Gillick 2010).

By drawing together insights from the recent work of Jacques Rancière and Gerald Raunig, I will argue that it is possible to move beyond the dead-ends that appeared whenever the relationship between art and politics was defined as either the pictorial representation *of* political messages or the political inspiration that is drawn *from* art. The concept of aesthetic cosmopolitanism overcomes this impasse as it addresses the transformation that occurs *through* the interplay between the creative imagination and intersubjective relations. Against the grain of art historical approaches that retain a primary focus on the objective forms of art and its placement within a regional cultural context context, I will argue that the current tendencies in art, as well as the role of the image in the ambient spectacle of war, are begging for a different perspective on the significance of place and the flow of ideas. Such a critical methodology would not only go beyond the Eurocentric foundations of art history by acknowledging the diverse contributions to contemporary global culture, but it would also proceed towards developing new theoretical approaches to the relations between different cultural and geographic fields, as well as re-evaluating the function of both individual and collective imagination in contemporary knowledge production (Belting and Buddensieg 2009). Aesthetics is thereby taken to refer to the individual and collective capacity for making an image of the world. This cosmopolitan frame thus serves as my standpoint for reviewing two of the key figures in the recent debates on aesthetics and politics.

Rancière and Raunig

Rancière's work is an unlikely starting point for the reinvigoration of
the debates on art and politics. For decades he operated at the inter-
sections of political philosophy and social history. This culminated
in a path-breaking book called *The Ignorant Schoolmaster* (1991), in
which Rancière ruminated on a pedagogic approach that unsettled
the master/servant dialectic and provided a marvellous illustration of
his key concept 'the equality of intelligences'. Then in the early 1990s
he wrote a number of essays on the significance of the avant-gardist
experiments with everyday life and the invention of new techniques
of visual and literary representation. At one level, this turn towards
aesthetics was consistent with the enduring question that frames the
entirety of his life's work: What is the relationship between knowledge
and emancipation? Or, to put it in his own words: 'How do individuals get some idea in their heads that makes them either satisfied with
their position or indignant about it?' (2004a, p. xxv). Throughout this
investigation on aesthetics, Rancière has deployed a two-pronged
approach, both a clearing away of the fundamental misconceptions on
the status of the image and the outlining of an affirmative conceptual
framework based on what he calls the 'distribution of the sensible'.

Rancière has stated that the aim of his book *The Politics of
Aesthetics* (2004b; see also Rancière 2009) had been to challenge the
long history of aesthetics that repeats a stigmatic hierarchy between
the image and truth, and thereby create some 'breathing space' – an
intermediary zone that enables an affirmative engagement with the way
art can modify the realm of the 'visible, sayable and possible' (2007a,
p. 259). Rancière's approach represents a break with contemporary
theorists and artists such as Guy Debord and Pierre Bourdieu, who
he claims repeat the 'Platonic disparagement of the mimetic image'
(2007b, p. 274), as they repeatedly set up visuality, spectacle and spectatorship as the source of deception, superficiality and alienation. He
utterly rejects the assumption that the image invariably imposes an
ideological distance between reality and interpretation, and that the
subject, by being trapped in the abyss of images, is separated from
the essence of his or her real humanity. Rancière also disputes the
radicality of 'formalist' innovations that seek to empower the viewer to
decode or embody the artwork's intended political message, because he
claims that they reinscribe the presumption that the primary position
of the audience is passivity (ibid.).

This rejection of the negative relationship to the image parallels a
shift in contemporary artistic practice. Since the 1970s it has been commonplace to observe artistic projects that sought to 'awaken the public

imagination' either by inviting public participation or by incorporating critical theory into the framework of the art project. The aim of these projects tended to be defined in terms of revealing or demystifying the machinations of dominant power structures. The aesthetics of resistance in contemporary art assumes a different stance towards public participation, aesthetic form and political theory. A critical stance is defined not simply by claiming to be standing outside or against power, but also by finding ways to rework the meaning and form of power through collaborating with the public. The point of art is not the exposure of the truth but the creation of public situations for reimagining reality.

Rancière's contribution to the debates on aesthetics and politics has, in part, come through his engagement with contemporary artists, but its roots lie in his historical investigation into the emergence of 'the aesthetic regime in the arts'. He claims that this regime commenced in the late nineteenth century, when visual and literary techniques were invented to juxtapose and relate the visible with the invisible (Rancière 2007c, p. 5). From his analysis of the new visual techniques such as fragmentation and montage, Rancière outlined three basic modes of visual representation: naked images that serve as a depiction of the original; ostensive images that transform themselves as they react against the original referent; and metaphoric images that play on the 'ambiguity of resemblances and the instability of dissemblances' (ibid., pp. 24–5). It is the capacity of metaphoric images to go beyond mere reflection and mystification, and their potential to reconfigure the possible, that lead Rancière to assert that the status of the image is not just a mask that hides truth, or even a foil that can displace our grasp on reality, but the 'supplement that divides it' (2004a, pp. 224–7).

Having identified the productive force of the image, Rancière also set out to challenge the conventional theories of aesthetics. For him, aesthetics not only refers to a discipline for either appreciating the formal properties of a given artistic object or articulating the affect that comes from an encounter with art; it is also the discourse through which artistic practices, sensible affects and thought are constituted through mutual interdependence. His aim is not to separate art and politics, but rather to investigate the knot that entangles art with affects and meaning. First, he claims that art only exists insofar as there is a specific mode of appreciation. This training of the gaze is not the problem that is in need of being cleared away but the necessary starting point for the constitution of art. Second, aesthetics is not just the discipline that trains 'the good eye' – identifying the worthiness and novelty of forms but also the means by which art is made intelligible. Third, the complaint that aesthetic theory fails to grasp the ineffable mystery of art is, he argues, a contest for sovereignty over the forms of representation and the faculties of reception (Rancière 2009, p. 14).

At the centre of Rancière's theory of the image and aesthetics is the key concept 'distribution of the sensible'. This refers to the symbolic and social transformation arising from the active involvement of people who are normally excluded from the process of defining the rules of the everyday and their ability to create new terms of perception and inter-action. Hence, Rancière defines the process of transformation through the interplay between the rise of new subjects and the emergence of new forms of knowledge. By giving primacy to the distribution of the sensible, he stresses that aesthetics and politics are discernible not in isolation from each other, but as two forms of an underlying imaginary process (2009, p. 26). Hence he proposes that both are formed within their independent 'regimes of identification'. Aesthetics and politics are different ways, distinctive discourses, unique modes of addressing the task of the distribution of the sensible. While they operate within their own system they do not exist in separate realities. They share a common space, and both have their respective capacity to suspend the normal coordinates of sensory experience and imagine new forms of life. In short, aesthetics is engaged in the distribution of the sensible, as it invents specific forms that link the realm of individual affect to a social way of being. Hence the intervention of aesthetics is always political, because the 'principle behind an art's formal revolution is at the same time the principle behind the political redistribution of shared experience' (Rancière 2004b, p. 17). However, while the principle of the distribution of the sensible underpins both aesthetics and politics, Rancière goes one step further, as he claims that the aesthetic regime precedes the political (ibid., p. 34). By stressing that the 'real must be fictionalised in order to be thought', Rancière lays claim to aesthet-ics as a regime of thought that can challenge the established order of politics. While his work challenges the negative ideology of the image, it has thus far remained as a philosophical reflection *on* aesthetics. It provides an extension of the status of the relationship between a viewer and the fixed work of art. However, to consider the transformation of aesthetics in the context of networked practices, we must turn to the recent work of Gerald Raunig, who claims that philosophical reflec-tion needs to be combined with active engagement and commentary *from* the sites of emergent social transformations (Raunig 2007).

Raunig shares Rancière's view that the politics of art is not found in the mere depiction of political struggles. Like Rancière, he rejects the modernist claim of aesthetic autonomy and argues that, while art is not subordinate to politics, the two are discrete fields that rest on the same terrain. Rancière's work begins from a crucial disagreement with Althusserian circles and gained its distinctive perspective as he distanced himself from what he called the 'extravagant topology' of the politicized French intellectuals (2004a, p. 76). Raunig's engagement with art and politics also emerges from a struggle against the academicist discourses of the old left, and he sees himself as being part of a 'broad assembly of artistic platforms of resistance' (Raunig 2002a). His response to the contemporary condition of precarity and his fascination with the crossover between artistic and activist communication techniques is, in my view, framed by a new kind of cosmopolitan agenda. For instance, he repeatedly celebrates the way that the anti-globalization movement and new artistic collectives have sought to re-route information flows and widen the legal and political frameworks, from a state-centric perspective of citizenship[1] to the articulation of a political agenda that 'explodes the national framework, as it were, from the inside' (Raunig 2002b, p. 63).

Raunig makes two bold interventions in the debates on aesthetics and politics. First, he offers a radical interpretation of the legacy of the avant garde, and in particular the function of the 'break'. His evaluation of the historical claims of the avant garde to 'awaken the citizen' and to 'fuse art with everyday life' is far more sceptical than that of Rancière. While Rancière (2004b, p. 63) took inspiration from avant-gardist experiments, Raunig seeks to distance himself from the practices and theoretical models that he claims endorsed the 'diffusing and confusing of art and life' (2007, p. 17; see also Kanngieser 2009). Raunig goes so far as to claim that the main movements in the 1910s and the 1960s not only 'came to no good end' but, on account of their grandiose or abstracted ambitions, also tended to displace rather than overcome the boundary between aesthetics and politics (2007, p. 203).

Second, Raunig introduces a new approach towards appreciating the aesthetico-political dimensions of collective art practices. His emphasis on the shuttling *between* rather than the blurring *of* the fields of art and politics can be compared to Rancière's claim that art and politics have their own specific regimes of identification. However, the contrasting views over the status and effect of avant-gardist shock techniques mark a fundamental disagreement. For Rancière, the use of a break, or what he calls the 'division', is not just a formal technique but the principal means for the distribution of the sensible. The idea of the 'break' in Rancière's texts is both crucial to the materiality of a collage 'which combines the foreignness of aesthetic experience with the becoming-art of ordinary life' and central to his rejection of art that elevated the pursuit of ethical or political goals above 'the sensible heterogeneity which founds aesthetic promise' (2009, p. 39). According to Rancière, the potency of these aesthetic practices resides not in the resolution of the contradiction between freedom and alienation, art and life but in the articulation of a break with the given political order. By contrast, Raunig argues that the radical function of art is not confined to the articulation of differences in the perceptual sensorium but is also evident in the mobilization of differences in social encounters. Raunig's approach towards representing the intersubjective experience and his analysis of the transversal organization of artistic collectives goes beyond the conventional approaches of art history and philosophy. This perspective shifts the meaning of political context from a fixed background to the notion of the field through which the artist is constantly passing. Hence, his approach is directed not to the question of *whether* an artist draws inspiration from his or her political background, but rather to *how* the artist passes through politics. It is an approach that highlights the dynamics of flow not just as an intervention from aesthetics to politics but as a perpetual oscillation between the two fields.

Raunig's conception of flow draws on two Deleuzian terms: 'concatenation' and 'transversality'. Concatenation refers to sequential practices of fluid movements between each field that occur for limited durations and result in the creation of temporary alliances. The dynamics of concatenation are generated by the tensions within and between constituent parts. These complex, unstable and highly differentiated entities interact in a manner that stimulates new lines of movement and resists consolidation into a fixed hierarchic structure. The flows that constitute a concatenation invariably lead towards a mutual transformation in both fields. As movement is ongoing, the identity of the two fields therefore always remains at a point of difference from each other. It is the perpetuation of this difference that also ensures that the dynamic of concatentation does not tend towards any neat reconciliation or cosy consensus.

Transversality is an acentric geometric concept that refers to the movement that occurs across the time–space continuum. Movement is normally thought of as a linear passage from one point to another. Change is thereby defined by delineating the difference in an entity between the departure from one point and its arrival at another. This perspective tends to stress the negative or positive impact of an external force and overlooks the dynamic agency of the entity in motion. Transversality provides an alternative perspective on the transformation that occurs in the time and space of movement. An apposite definition of transversal activism can be found in the motto of the Viennese Volxtheater Favoriten: 'living revolutionary subjectivity in the here and now instead of saving up wishes for changes in the party funds – for the some fine day of the revolution' (quoted in Raunig 2007,

p. 206). Raunig notes that these collectives, like the autonomous movement in general, sought to invent new networks of social organization. However, he also conceded that transversal activism 'required a great deal of energy, incited many conflicts and could only be maintained by most actors for a certain period of time' (ibid., p. 218). A striking feature of Raunig's approach is the combination of philosophical reflection with participant observation, as well as the adoption of an evaluative standpoint that recognizes ephemerality and intensity as a virtue. Raunig has relinquished the effort to create a model of transversal activism that can serve as a master plan for the future. Through his account of the intense and short moments of critical encounter, he gives an insight into the shuttling exchange between aesthetic and political activities. In short, this reflexive method has the distinctive benefits of attending to the persistent tension between utopian ideals and precarious realities, and thereby offers a new framework through which we can view the cosmopolitan dialogues in contemporary art.

Outline of a Cosmopolitan Imaginary

These recent approaches to the vexed relationship between aesthetics and politics take us some of the way towards understanding the significance of the emergent tendencies in contemporary art. Rancière highlights the role of aesthetics in producing a supplement to existing modes of perception and meaning. Raunig takes us further into the transversal relations between aesthetic representation and political organization. Through these accounts we gain insight into the ways artistic practices are producing knowledge in the world, rather than simply reflecting other forms of knowledge of the world. This crucial distinction prompts further reflection on the need for a cosmopolitan conceptual framework for contemporary artistic practice.

Art historians such as David Summers have conceded that the conventional approaches, based on either a visual analysis of the formal resemblances between the artworks or the historiography of the artist's origin, are inadequate tools for addressing both the cosmopolitan dialogues in art and the capacity of art to be a medium for 'the first impulses in which the world is "formed" and made into a characteristic unity' (2003, p. 33). Mark Cheetham has also turned to the ancient and contemporary discourse of cosmopolitanism in order to renew and extend the disciplinary models of art history. While sceptical of the 'lazy cosmopolitan' appellations that adorn art criticism and artistic self-proclamations, Cheetham (2009) has acknowledged that there is a need to find the 'connective tissues that enable artists to be properly placed and appropriately mobile'. However, he also questions the very foundation of the art historical discipline by concluding that the cosmopolitan visions in contemporary art will not be properly concep- tualized via the 'strictures of Kantian reason'.

A sign of the new directions in art history can also be witnessed in Marsha Meskimmon's attempt to track the ways artists engage 'with the processes and practices of inhabiting a global world' and par- ticipate 'in a critical dialogue between ethical responsibility, locational identity and cosmopolitan imagination' (2011, p. 5). This focus on the engagement with global mobilities and participation in the inven- tion of new forms of 'being at home in the world' not only radically expands the contextual framework, but also shifts the attention away from merely decoding what art represents to testing the creation of new modes of social interaction. Art is thus both a reflection of the process of cosmopolitanization and an active partner in the articulation of cosmopolitan ethical agency and spatial habituation. Hence the cos- mopolitan imaginary is, in Summers's account, materialized through the artistic invention of real forms that are inseparable from habitual activities, whereas for Meskimmon it is found in the embodiment of a multicentred cultural vision and the adoption of ethical modes of global citizenship. Meskimmon's account is of particular interest because, like Rauinig, she is not concerned with the representation of art as a static exemplification of moral virtue; rather, her focus is directed towards active situations in which the artist and the viewer are mutually entangled in a 'transitive economy'. The moral and aesthetic function of art emerges from the journey undertaken by participants. Through this transformative relationship between images, objects and ideas, both the artworks and the viewers are mutually changed as they become participants and constituents in a 'transitive economy' (ibid., p. 63).

The zone within which the creative imagination and social habit- uation occur is the imaginary. Cornelius Castoriadis defined the imaginary as a fluid space that accommodates both the inner images of the world and the social practices for living in the world. Although Castoriadis never spoke directly to the concept of cosmopolitanism, on numerous occasions he linked the act of creation with the capacity to grasp universality. It is through creativity that being is given form, otherwise existence is an 'abyss, chaos, groundless' (Castoriadis 1997c, p. 3). For Castoriadis, all the social institutions of our daily life can only exist insofar as they have been imagined. However, while social institutions furnish a worldview that enables the individual to deal with the flux of life, they also tend to produce a sense of belonging that is experienced through the feeling of enclosure and exclusivity rather than an exposure to the world at large. Hence, while Castoriadis argued that social institutions are viable only insofar as people find them symbolically meaningful and are willing to identify with them, he also noted that institutional closures blocked the individual's freedom to question the limits of existing structures, engage with strangers, and develop a genuine interest in the ideas that are formed in one culture but are also expressive of a 'potential universality in whatever is human for humans' (1997a, p. 270). Paradoxically, it is imagination that makes and breaks the limits of social institutions. However, by placing the grip of universality inside the hand of the creative imagination, Castoriadis goes against the grain of Western metaphysics. Imagination is not just a speculative mechanism for producing opinion and fantasy. For Castoriadis, imagination is the primary means for inventing social ideals (ibid., p. 379), and it is through the 'unceasing and essentially undetermined' function of the imaginary that rationality and reality is created (1997b, p. 3).

Castoriadis's theory of creation and his concept of the imaginary extend the field of inquiry beyond the conventional tropes of artistic imagination. According to Richard Kearney (1988), the theories of the imagination have been dominated by three metaphors that highlight, respectively, the mimetic/reflective function, as if it were a mirror that reflects another reality; the generative/creative process, such as a lamp that produces its own light and heat; and the parodic/refractive state, which can be compared to a labyrinth or looking glass in which the object unfolds in infinite variations. For Castoriadis, creation is neither the reconfiguration of existing elements nor the assemblage that results from external pressures. Creativity is the process through which a paradigm of being is distinguished from the multitude of forces that exert influence on it. Castoriadis stressed that creation emerged in the world *ex nihilo*. Thus his theory of creation is different from other versions that put the emphasis on mimesis – the expression of meaning through resemblances – on discovery – the recognition of something that is already there but not quite noticed – or even on synthesis – the novel reutilization of known entities. For Castoriadis, creation, whether it produced the Parthenon or Auschwitz, was always embedded in a specific historical context. However, the boldness of his theory also hinges on his examination of the radical and mysterious form by which creation produced newness. Creation is therefore not just the product of its time, for it also comes out of a void and asserts itself as the new and necessary form for living.

Drawing on Castoriadis's conception of the imagination, I will now turn to the emergence of a cosmopolitan aesthetic in contemporary art. This cosmopolitan imagination is an emergent concept that can generate an alternative sense of being in the world and intersubjective relations. In the following chapter I will outline a wide range of artistic and curatorial practices that have activated new forms of collaborative practice and, through these multiple levels of public interaction and cross-media engagement, articulated a cosmopolitan imaginary.

6

The Global Orientation of Contemporary Art

Baudrillard's much misunderstood claim that the Gulf War only happened on television was not a ridiculous denial of its reality, but an astute observation that the 'real' terrain that was being contested was the public imaginary (Baudrillard 2004). It is worth recalling that in the weeks after 9/11 most US and many Western TV channels were fixated on the image of the planes crashing into the twin towers. In the absence of a hard explanation of the causes, and amidst endless speculation over the consequences, the media kept replaying the scenes of the terrible collisions. The documentary representation of 9/11 was perhaps the first to underscore what the Retort collective called the contradictory 'struggle for mastery in the realm of the image' (2005, p. 15). These images of war not only dominated the banners of newspapers and television broadcasts but also passed from mobile phones to internet sites. Okwui Enwezor (2008b) has gone so far as to argue that, after 9/11, the relationship between the image as a representation of an event and a signifier of a historical epoch collapsed. He noted that, as the image of planes crashing went 'live' from New York, it was met with a global response that was summed up by a headline in *Le Monde*: 'We are all New Yorkers now'. However, the feedback from these spectacular images soon intensified to such an extent that Enwezor claimed they blurred the function of the image as a signifier of an event. Boris Groys also claimed that, from now on, the warrior must also act like an artist, as 'the act of war coincides with its documentation, with its representation' (2008, p. 122).

The interplay between the event and the image in ambient wars has disrupted the conventional function of the image in the time of war. For instance, writing in the aftermath of the images of the Vietnam War, Susan Sontag insisted that the photographer was often entangled in a moral dilemma, on the one hand wanting to stop the acts of violence that occurred before his eyes, but on the other nevertheless committed, if not actually desirous, that the event should continue so that he might capture the image of the horror (Sontag 1986, p. 12). This hunt for the 'decisive image' is now overwhelmed by the endless flow of digital images. On the internet, war is covered from every angle. With cameras strapped to their helmets, soldiers record and then disseminate both their shameless exploits and their heartfelt messages. Such low-to-the-ground visions of the war are the counterpoint to the army's practice of releasing aerial footage of the moments before the destruction of a target captured by missiles armed with a camera. The veteran anti-war filmmaker Brian de Palma decided that the only way tell the story of the war in Iraq was through a montage of images that were produced by mobile phones and amateur video cameras.[1] In one of her last published essays, Sontag (2004) noted that 'the pictures taken by American soldiers in Abu Ghraib reflect a shift in the use made of pictures – less objects to be saved than messages to be circulated'. Julian Stallabrass also proposed that the proliferation of images in ambient wars has displaced the boundary between representation and political intervention.[2]

There is no doubt that the physical act of destruction and the circulation of the images of 9/11 were intended as a single political action. It is also widely recognized that the repeated screening of the footage enhanced the experience of trauma. For weeks after the event, the images not only incited a sense of stunned disbelief but also destabilized the meaning of habitual images of everyday life. Ordinary signs of Muslims doing their daily duties were, according to Talal Asad (2007, p. 16), suddenly switched onto a stigmatic spectrum. Banal signs were compressed with unspecified anxiety and turned into possible images of terror. Of course, paranoid projection of suspicion and fear is commonplace in times of war. However, if the Retort collective is correct in arguing that power is being reorganized 'under the conditions of the spectacle', then this realignment of the function of the image does not only come to haunt Sontag's empirical distinction between the documentary function of an image and the event that it depicts, it also prompts a review of the critical function of aesthetics when politics operates as a form of spectacle.

Throughout modernity, art asserted its criticality through two diametrically opposed strategies: iconoclasm and redemption. Just as it violently ripped apart the symbolic universe it inherited, it also found aesthetic force in the surplus of ordinary signs. Art simultaneously provided a counterpoint to the already known and discovered new resonances amongst the surrounds. However, these two aesthetic strategies also reflect a dramatic shift in the function of the artist. In modernity, the artist is neither the primary nor the dominant generator of imagery. Mass culture is an aesthetics machine. This process of incorporation and the new techniques for dissemination imply that the artist is now a critical navigator in an atmosphere that is already saturated with images, symbols and narratives. With sparkling optimism, Brian Eno (1996) once claimed that ambient music – the genre that he pioneered – had the capacity to exert a surrounding influence: a critical tint to the all-pervasive influence of commerce in the sonic environment. He thought that, unlike muzak, which stripped away all the atmospheric idiosyncracies and replaced them with a cheerful sound intended to alleviate the tedium of commercial space, ambient music would induce a contemplative atmosphere that accommodated many levels of listening attention without enforcing one in particular. Eno's faith in the interaction that occurs between music and the listener revealed a joyful confidence in the open-endedness of this process. It is neither nullified by the intrinsic doubt over the origins nor hampered by uncertainty in its destination. For Eno, ambience refers to the surplus of possibilities from which both the artist and the audience can produce new points of clarification and unexpected levels of connection.

How do we read the open-endedness of art (Eco 1989, p. 4) and, in more general terms, what is the critical function of art after 9/11? If, as I have already noted, the complex circulation of the 9/11 footage, as it was entangled in a near endless sequence of transmissions in both the mass media and interpersonal networks, had the ghostly effect of making the event appear to happen again and again, then in what sense did this chain of unending co-productions, this new loop of 'ambient fear', become the aesthetic field of the 'war on terror'? It is possible to answer this question by arguing that the ordinary citizen became more and more implicated within the spectacle of war because the colonization of everyday life had already intensified the experience of uncertainty. The experience of fear became more diffuse when society had undergone a radical social transformation through the dissolution of the boundaries and the commodification of the practices that were previously contained within the civic, cultural and domestic spheres (Melucci 1989). In this context, the function of art is no innocent bystander. Two sociologists, Luc Boltanski and Eve Chiapello, have gone so far as to argue that it was the artistic vision of authenticity, independence, flexibility and mobility that motivated the reorganization of the culture of capitalism and provided the 'sources of new forms of exploitation and new existential tensions' (2007, p. 468). Boris Groys (2008, p. 122) has also posed the question as to whether the video tactics of Al Qaeda and the documentation of the scenes at Abu Ghraib would have been possible without the history of perform-ance art. Similarly, if the Taliban are so committed to iconoclasm, why were they so scrupulous in documenting their destruction of the giant Bamiyan Buddha sculptures (Papastergiadis 2007c)?

It is difficult to register the precise impact of the 'war on terror' on the public imaginary, let alone the interlinking between avant-gardist state-gies and neo-liberal tendencies. But it is possible to consider the interplay between recent political events and emergent trajectories in contempo-rary art. I turn to art not because it has a superior moral vantage point, nor for its putative capacity to anticipate future forms. At this critical juncture, when the status of the image is transformed by ambient spec-tacles and networked society, and politics is explicitly shaped by a feedback in aesthetic processes, Jimmie Durham claimed that it was an opportune moment to redefine the orientation of art:

> This is a time when we ask: 'Who are we humans?' It's not the American invasive kind of globalization, but globalization where humans try to talk to each other. I think that humanity is trying to talk to itself now, for the first time in human history, maybe. We don't necessarily like each other, or like what we are trying to say to each other, but to me it looks like we are trying to see ourselves. (Durham 2004, p. 119)

It is a matter of considerable significance that Durham suggests that this process commences with the question 'Who are we humans?', rather than with a declaration such as 'As humans we should . . .!' This shift is expressive of a broader rethinking on the fundamental question of being and community in the context of radical mobility. A decade earlier, Giorgio Agamben (1993, p. 85) posited a communal struc-ture in which 'humans co-belong without a representable condition of belonging'. Cosmopolitanism begins in such propositions. It also transpires in the myriad of mixtures that occur in everyday life. When Durham suggests that art is part of a global dialogue on the definition of 'our' common but distinctive identity, he also suggests that everyone enters into this dialogue as an equal. The events surrounding the 'war on terror' also prompted the artist Liam Gillick to proclaim the need for new aesthetic and political models.

> Much postmodern theory was based on how to understand a globalised environment of relativism, subjectivity and simulation. We are now facing a situation of specificity and desperate rationalisation in Iraq and elsewhere.

Art became more and more diverse throughout the 20th Century. The Iraq war is an example of one of the many clarifications that may appear to render art more and more irrelevant. The US army has reconvened and prays to its God for strength. The factions in Iraq pray to theirs. Everywhere we see the routine obscenity. For artists, the combination of piety and pragmatism from politicians on all sides is not worth showing back to them. Documenting the increasing piles of body parts is pointless pornography. What artists can do is occasionally step outside of their normal practice and stand as citizens against the delusions of their leaders. This is an exceptional moment, where it is necessary for some to suspend their normal work in order to make a direct statement. In this context, the ICA exhibition is not an answer, it is a melancholic and sullen response. The idea of creating a memorial to something that is still taking place is an honest concession. It is no good looking back to some earlier moment of apparent cultural consensus. We have to look instead towards art as a carrier of differences and a perfect form for the revelation of paradox. (Gillick 2007b)

Similar attitudes and responses could be found in a wide range of artistic responses to the 'war on terror'. In the description of his project for the New Museum in New York, *It Is What It Is* (2009), Jeremy Deller stressed that 'it is not an anti-war piece, it is already too late for that, it is about the war'. In one sense this may sound like a clever ruse to escape the dismissive label of mere protest art. However, it also echoes Gillick's comment on the problematic function of the place of the artist during a time of war. How can an artist respond after it has already begun? The war itself is a hideous limit point of human violence that defies explanations and justifications. If you cannot stop it, does this mean that you are forced into either silent submission or reportage of the horror? Deller's project takes a different approach. It was an installation that included a banner with the title in English and Arabic, a map of both the United States and Iraq in which various cities had been twinned with each other,[3] photographs from Iraq, the remnant of a car that was destroyed by an explosion in Baghad, and a comfortable and open space in which visitors to the museum could, at different times of the day, speak to a soldier who had served in the war, an academic, a refugee or a UN representative. After its first showing at the New Museum in New York, the installation toured throughout the United States. This project was not offering an answer to the war; on the contrary, it presented the opportunity to discuss the event with someone who had direct experience or knowledge. The banner makes a strong declaration, the photographs have a disturbing documentary function, and the car has enormous metonymic associations with the bodies of war. However, Deller adds that the purpose of displaying these objects is to use them as 'prompts' for new discussions, and he stresses the 'project is about people meeting each other . . . my role is as a facilitator' (New Museum and Creative Time 2009). Hence, we could surmise that the point of the project was not confined to the symbolic meaning or formal properties of the installation, but developed in the interplay between the objects and the creation of a small public sphere.

The function of art in the mediation of public dialogue, which was made explicit in Deller's project, was not purely the result of a revolt against the 'war on terror'. It also drew on an emergent set of aesthetic practices that utilized the form of social encounters and collaborative processes (Bourriaud 2009b, p. 161; Raunig 2007; see also Fischer-Lichte 2008, p. 18). For instance, artistic collectives such as Stalker were concerned primarily with the construction of events in nomadic settings. Similarly, Rirkrit Tiravanija often turned a gallery into a temporary soup kitchen. He used the experience of preparing and serving food as 'instruments' for 'sculpting' hospitality. Tino Sehgal, an artist who invites performers to improvise from his 'constructed situations', is also insistent that the experience of the 'here and now' should be the pre-eminent effect of his work.[4] Francis Alÿs's project *Bridge* (2006), in which he organized scores of local fishermen in Florida and Cuba to link their boats to two chains that headed towards each other's horizon, furnished a poignant image of the yearning for connection and the perils of the crossing. The members of Superflex, a Danish collective that tackles the unequal power relations between centre and periphery by developing innovative links between local organizations with global technology experts, are also concerned as much with the feedback of social effects as they are with the formal qualities of their aesthetic proposition (Larsen 1997). In Mike Parr's performance *Close the Concentration Camps* (2002), the artist sewed his lips and eyelids together as a gesture of solidarity with the refugees. Before the performance, the art critic David Bromfield dismissed the idea as 'false realism' and questioned the vicarious motivation. Writing to Parr, he remarked: 'We both know that it is no good simply becoming a glorified stand-in for a camp inmate.' Parr replied that doing something 'bad' might have a greater social effect (Geczy 2003, p. 45).

But how do we make sense of such artistic experiments with the experience of the journey, the meal, the dance with strangers, or even the encounter between fellow fishermen? Furthermore, why do artists such as Lida Abdul and Tania Brughera keep returning to ruins and pain (Papastergiadis 2006a)? Artists have been drawn to these abuses of humanity and the violent contact zones. They represent conflict by holding together both good and evil. Artists oppose violence and exclusion, but they do not believe that tensions disappear by dramatizing the triumph of either good over evil or vice versa. They explore the heat of pain by, at first, locating themselves inside the prism of contradictory forces. The paradoxical force of truth cannot be found on higher ground, but, as Cesare Pietroiusti (2004, p. 146) says, by putting 'one's finger in the wound'. It would be all too easy to read a general activist intent into these projects, only then either to dismiss them as aesthetic gestures that fail to produce real social change or to grant them the title 'political art' in order to reject any consideration of aesthetic merit.[5] This of course misses the point of art. When artists such as Hans Haacke, Steve McQueen and even the collective Multiplicity confront political questions, they do not abandon aesthetic forms.[6] Art is not justified by adopting an activist stance. However, if an artist decides it is necessary to serve as a host, organize a chance meeting with strangers, or even redeem the fragments amidst the ruins of war, this should suggest that some other kind of appeal, witnessing and symbolic register is being summoned. The artist is not simply becoming a chef or an archaeologist but adopting these roles and returning to these sites because the act of imagination and inquiry has something in common with hospitality and violence. The imagination approaches the space of the other and passes over the ruins and asks, 'Have I been here before?' These relatively traceless practices are in one sense speaking directly to the condition of precarity – the social experience of living without certainty, the fear of loosing moorings, the dread that a life's labour will suddenly vanish without a trace.

Emergent Themes and Global Tendencies in Art

While noting that utopian claims are easily spoiled, Liam Gillick has claimed that there is a revival of the 'utopian impulse' in contemporary art (Bradley 2007, p. 22; Verhagen 2007). With all seriousness, Gillick has compared the effect of his art to 'the light in the fridge door; it only works when there are people there to open the fridge door. Without people, it's not art – it's something else – stuff in a room' (2000, p. 16). The influential political theorist Chantal Mouffe also endorsed Gillick's view that the radicality of art was found not in the clean break with all institutional relations but in the disarticulation of conventional discourses and practices that uphold existing authority. This artistic process of public participation is, according to Mouffe, analogous to her own effort to define an agonistic framework that facilitates the interaction and exchange of different perspectives. In support of Gillick, she also embraced 'the necessity of recovering something of the utopian impulse' without falling into the traps of authoritarian universalism or pure idealism (Mouffe 2009, p. 94).

This conjunction between aesthetic practices and political theory points towards a growing discursive convergence of horizons between art and politics. In broad terms I will map out five artistic themes and tendencies that are expressive of an aesthetic cosmopolitanism – a cultural phenomenon that is born from a productive tension between a globally oriented approach and locally grounded practices. I will outline the emergence of aesthetic cosmopolitanism by tracing the rise of interest in the issues of denationalization, reflexive hospitality, cultural translation, discursivity and the global public sphere in contemporary art. These tendencies have been manifest in numerous studies and exhibitions that proceed under the general headings of globalism and internationalism.

There is now a clear recognition that contemporary art is increasingly engaged in a critique of globalization and the rearticulation of a universalist vision. However, these global tendencies are difficult to map. The artists can be identified in almost every corner of the world, but they also express a deep resistance to situating their work within regional surveys. The form of the artworks has further exploded into a baffling array of styles, media and motifs. Given this diversity, the recent tendencies in contemporary art are resistant to the conventional modes of formal classification. These tendencies possess a complex dynamic and cannot be deduced as mere symptoms of the socio-economic characteristics of globalization. They are enmeshed in the real-time processes of social change. Artists are now routinely presenting themselves as participants in the collective making of a global worldview. In addition, this departure from the earlier model of the belated critic or the avant garde has presented a new interpretative challenge. In response to these recent shifts I will propose that contemporary art is not just reflecting the contradictions of globalization but is also a constitutive force in the production of what I call a cosmopolitan imaginary.

For Marcel Duchamp, leaving home was a de-nationalizing act of disentangling himself from the feeling of being rooted in one place. He enjoyed being away from Europe because, as he said towards the end of his life, it allowed him to 'swim freely'.[7] From this seminal figure in history of modernism we can witness a cosmopolitan tendency that starts from a process of subtraction. The self-defined cosmopolitans of early modernity, such as the avant-garde artists and revolutionary intellectuals, often spoke of belonging nowhere. They eschewed any fixed or authentic attachment to their origins and adopted a perspective that Amit Chaudhuri (2009, p. 96) calls 'worldview as angularity'.

This persistent exilic tendency is now complemented by a form of artistic practice in which the spaces and protocol for receiving the work of art assumes a kind of reflexive hospitality. According to Daniel Birnbaum, the understanding of alterity and the principle of hospitality amounts to an epistemic revolution. For instance, in Olafur Eliasson's artworks, Birnbaum observes the construction of a scenario in which the viewer is not only aware of the process by which he or she sees the work, he also notes that 'a kind of inversion takes place – you are seen by the work' (2008, p. xii). As the viewer adopts an active role in shaping the whole environment, their subjectivity is in turn shaped by the experience of giving in to it. This shift in perspective towards the object of the artwork, and the heightened attitude towards the consciousness of the viewer in the artwork, also amounts to a redistribution of agency. It stimulates a relationship of co-production. The viewer is no longer a passive and detached observer. Given the vigorous interplay between subject and object and the fundamental role of alterity in defining the intentionality of the viewer and the form of the artwork, this tendency recasts the relationship between self and other as a form of reflexive hospitality. A more explicit articulation of this tendency can be found in the numerous artistic collectives, such as No One Is Illegal and the Fadaiat no-border media laboratory. These collectives aim to create a 'mirror space' that reflects back the transnational movements of people and stimulates the coming into being of community that is based on universal human rights.

The proliferation of non-Western artists within the institutions of contemporary art has also prompted critical attention towards the process of cultural translation. For many critics, when faced with the sheer volume and diversity of art that now appears in biennales, there is the instant reaction of horror – how to judge the merits of so many different works, and what model can address both the cultural specificity of the artwork's context and elucidate the capacity of art to transcend cultural differences? This cross-cultural challenge is neatly outlined by the Iranian born but US based artist Shirin Neshat.

> At one moment I am dealing with Iranians who know the sources of my material, and then I am dealing with an audience who has not a clue. To me they both have their advantages and disadvantages. With Iranians, I can never fulfil their expectations because I am an outsider; with foreigners I can never fulfil their expectations because I am Iranian and they are Westerners. And I can never really break down the cultural context of the work. (Quoted in Tao Wu 2007, p. 724)

This neat separation between Iranians and foreigners obscures one crucial fact: Neshat's work is speaking to a new constituency – composed of Iranians and foreigners who know what it means to be outside of a culture but still attached to it, or what Naoki Sakai calls a 'non-aggregate community' (1997, p. 7). Obviously not everything becomes clear to a foreigner, but this does not mean that the artist – as a virtual cosmopolitan[8] – is not able to communicate something. Furthermore, the possibilities for mutual understanding only expand as the artist embarks on the process of translating between the global and the local without the foreknowledge of a known addressee.

The themes of hospitality and the challenge of cross-cultural communication were also formative processes in the tendency that Bruce Ferguson defined as the 'discursive turn' (Ferguson and Hoegsberg 2010). Ferguson was referring to artistic projects like Gillick's that were organized as modest participatory events. While modest in form, they also confronted some grand thematic issues and pursued overarching objectives such as examining the gaps between the processes of modernization and the cultures of modernism, exposing the shortcomings in modernity, challenging the commodification of culture, and encouraging new forms of communal activity. This discursive turn was also evident in curatorial practice. Curators such as Okwui Enwezor, Hou Hanru, Maria Lind, Charles Esche, Claire Doherty, Nick Tsoutas, Vasif Kortum, Nina Montmann, Gerardo Mosquera and the curatorial team that work under the name Who, What, How redefined the function of institutional art venues as 'spaces of encounter' (Enwezor 2008a) and adopted a method of representation that was sensitive to the spirit that Manray Hsu described as 'decentralizing cosmopolitanism' (2005, pp. 75–6).

The discursive turn in artistic and curatorial practice, with its wild embrace of hybrid identities and its committed efforts to hijack capital, was also aligned with a desire to build a new global public sphere (Stimson and Sholette 2007, pp. 4–11). At present it is impossible to ground this desire within a concrete site. The global public sphere has no territorial location, it lacks any administrative entity, and there is not even a coherent community that would claim ownership of the idea. Within the conventional geopolitical categories the global public sphere does not exist. And yet, within the rustling republic of texts and images that circulate in the net, in the weak gatherings of people from across the world at events such as art biennales and social fora, there is as, Immanuel Wallerstein (2003) claims, the beginnings of a cultural and political imaginary that is moving away from an absolutist and nationalist ideology on cultural identity. The Retort collective also found inspiration from the unanticipated appearance of a worldwide community that was assembled in the 'interstices of the Net' and in part constituted from the collective 'experience of seeing – of hearing, feeling, facing up to – an *image* of refusal' as it moved from the virtual to reality (Retort 2005, p. 4).

The Retort collective is right to stress that the visuality of the conduct of the 'war on terror' – that is, the global witnessing of its mode of representation – was crucial in provoking a global protest. However, just as crucial is the cascading effect of witnessing the formation of a global resistance. It is in the interplay of these two processes that this collective of artists and scholars also claims a 'premonition of a politics to come'. This vague definition of the locations, form, constituency and dynamics of the new politics is echoed further on in their text, when they claim that 'something is shifting in the technics and tactics of resistance' (Retort 2005, p. 12). These new alliances are by nature fragmentary, ephemeral and loose, often operating beyond or on the margins of institutions and in opposition to formal structures. Such flashes of creative resistance do not offer simple or even unified solutions. On the contrary, they often take us deeper into the messy complexity of everyday life. They also remind us of a fundamental principle that these days seems to have been pushed to the side of political discourse – that is, when people whose worldview is formed in different civilizations[9] encounter each other, there is not necessarily a violent clash; they can utilize their respective intelligence to understand each other and create a dialogue about what is possible and necessary.

I am not so naïve as to rest my case on such faint claims about the potentialities that occur within transitory gatherings. Nor am I so cynical as to assert that art and activism are incapable of making any difference. Between these two extreme points is the more demanding task of teasing out emergent forms and probing the shape of reconfigured structures. Art materializes thought in all its contradictions. It does not always make the meaning of things more clear. At times, it just comes out of the way things are being lived, with anachronisms still glowing and anticipations not yet reached. If the 'global public sphere', as Okwui Enwezor suggests, has become both the destination of art and the focal point for shaping the politics of human life, then the challenge is also to develop such a universal platform through the incontrovertible hybridity of human subjectivity (2003a, p. 14). Hence, in the next chapter I turn to consider the status of hybridity.

7

Hybridity and Ambivalence

One of the most contentious aspects of the discussions over cosmopolitanism is the status of hybridity in cultural identity and cultural practice. Although the phenomenon of cross-cultural exchange and ethnic mixture is commonplace, there is still considerable anxiety over the use of the term 'hybridity'. This uncertainty was particularly noticeable in the debates around the visual arts. At the time when artists were carefully and imaginatively working with the complex symbols that circulate in everyday life, developing new ways to combine traditional and contemporary media and teasing out the survival of cultural ideas in alien contexts, there was also a growing backlash against the concept of hybridity. Critics either highlighted its dubious origin in eugenics or made dismissive claims that it was the new exotic theory that could gloss the exploitative cultural logic of globalization. This backlash coincided with a resurgence in neo-nationalistic ideologies and the loss of faith in the nascent forms of multiculturalism in Western states. Such polarized claims have done little to address the complex issues that interlink the articulation of cultural identity with aesthetic cosmopolitanism.

In this chapter I will review the conflicting theoretical perspectives on hybridity and explore the viability of the concept in relation to the aesthetic practices of Jimmie Durham, William Kentridge, Isaac Julien and Brian Jungen. I have focused on these artists because their work explores the complexities of cultural transformation and displays a critical consciousness of the legacies of postcolonialism and diasporic realities. Their excavation of forgotten histories, utilization of popular

symbols, fusing of traditional and contemporary media, and exploration of the survival of cultural ideas in alien contexts provide not only
an opportunity to evaluate the radical extensions in the aesthetic forms
of contemporary art but also a series of test cases for the conceptual
reach of hybridity. My concern is directed towards the aesthetic
process of modification and feedback as ideas are transferred from one
place to another. Or, more precisely, the question can be posed in these
terms: Is every cross-cultural encounter predetermined by power differential and embedded cultural values, or does the aesthetic encounter
with difference generate an alternate worldview?

In order to move the debate beyond either the racist assumptions
of biological essentialism or the corporatist hype on mobile subjects,
I will argue that the concept of hybridity can be used to illuminate
three levels of cultural transformation: effects, processes and critical
consciousness. At the first level, hybridity refers to the visible effects
of difference within identity as a consequence of the incorporation
of foreign elements. This is also where most debates on hybridity
end. They either celebrate the benefit of adding one cultural sign into
another system or reject the contaminating effect of foreign elements.
Recognition of the second level refers to the process by which cultural
differences are either naturalized or neutralized within the body of the
host culture. Most conceptions of cross-cultural interaction and the
dynamics of cultural development make some reference to the concept
of hybridization (Nederveen Pieterse 2001). The third level of hybridity is linked to aesthetic processes and can be thematized through the
early modernist techniques of juxtaposition, collage, montage and bri-
colage. More recently, postcolonial theorists have adopted hybridity
as a perspective for representing the new critical and cultural practices
that have emerged in diasporic life (Ang 2001, p. 194). It is a modality
that includes an openness towards the contemporary forms of cultural
life without the renunciation of previous attachments. This modality, which emerges from a critical consciousness towards biographic
experience, is, I believe, a crucial feature in the rethinking of cultural
belonging and creative practice. Hence, I will argue that hybridity is
not just a sign of individual distinctiveness and cross-cultural contami-
nation, but a starting point for understanding the aesthetic dimensions
of the cosmopolitan imaginary.

Hybridity in Contemporary Artistic Practice

The question of cultural identity and the politics of representation for
non-Western cultural practices, which were thrust onto the stage of the

international art world in the 1980s, have been reconfigured in recent years. The representation of cultural difference, which at first found expression on the margins, has not only occurred at all levels within the institutional structures of contemporary art but has gone beyond the neo-primitivist and managerialist version of multiculturalism. For instance, *ARS 01*, curated by Maaretta Jaukkuri, put the concept of hybridity at the centre of its curatorial framework (Jaukkuri 2001, p. 101). Hybridity was used to redefine the cultural status of diasporic or indigenous artists. They were no longer defined in terms of an exotic alternative or as a belated supplement whose incorporation could serve to both expand and reaffirm the parameters of the mainstream. The story of indigenous survival and migrant diasporas, Jaukkuri argues, has become a crucial perspective in the critique of globalization and the rewriting of the history of modernism. The concept of hybridity was also understood as offering a critical perspective on the cultural practices and symbolic meanings that were generated by artists. In this exhibition, hybridity was used as a counterpoint to the idealist categories that confined creativity to either closed forms of tradition or universal forms of abstraction. Unlike the essentialist theories that claim that cultural identity is either rooted in a particular landscape or locked into atavistic values, the concept of hybridity was used to shift attention towards the acknowledgement of the process of mixture and the effects of mobility on contemporary culture.

Numerous works in the *ARS 01* exhibition exemplify the three levels that operate in hybridity. By focusing on the works of four artists in this exhibition, it will be possible to track the flow between the process of mixture, the effects of mobility and the formation of a critical consciousness that are central to the formation of a cosmopolitan imaginary. These works neither celebrate the cultural differences in their own identity nor valorize border cultures. They are hybrid in the way that they examine the complex psychic responses to political structures and the diverse layers that are enfolded within historical symbols. Through Kentridge's and Durham's work, I will examine how the concept of hybridity can both elucidate the production of knowledge about the other and frame the experiences of everyday life. Jungen's and Julien's work on hybridity will be used to consider the ways in which artists both critique the structures for representing the past and maintain the creative practice of cultural translation.

William Kentridge's animated film *Shadow Procession* (1999) and Jimmie Durham's *Arche de Triomphe for Personal Use* (1996) are explorations of the fantasies of colonial domination. In Kentridge's film, which is an evocation of the spiritual and physical degradation of oppressed people in the apartheid period of South Africa, hybridity operates through the process of transmogrification. The film depicts the phantasmagoric transition of human into both commodity and mythic beast by constructing moving images that have been adapted from the indigenous techniques of 'cut out' shadow theatre. This splicing of traditional and contemporary technologies represents one level of hybridity. It is in their combination that one sees not only the persistence of a specific way of interpreting the world but also a reconfiguration of the medium for representation. The film shows workmen stooping with a hump growing on their shoulders that begins to resemble the outline of a city. Women appear whose identity as domestic labourers is extended until their heads suddenly flip open and reveal crude instrumental functions. Throughout the film a giant cat looms over all the human figures. These hybrid representations recall the classical modalities of the mythical imagination. In the place of centaurs and satyrs, the bestiality of the apartheid system is represented as a titanic battle that results in the abomination of the human form as it is mixed with object and animal. Throughout this battle Kentridge is also demonstrating that the nightmares of apartheid are not only in the mind of the colonizer. The displacement effect is, according to Ari Sitas, deliberately unresolved: 'We do not know where they are coming from or whether they are fleeing or in any case, where they are going, but in their movement we know they are determined to get there' (2001, p. 113). Kentridge demonstrates through these disturbing shifts from human being to mythical monster and crude tools that the political regime had penetrated the imaginary of all its victims. The horror of apartheid is symbolically registered by way of the specific construction of hybrid monsters, but the whole culture is also re-examined via the unique splicing of the technologies for representation. In Kentridge's film, both the figures and the perspective are constructed through a hybrid optic.

In a more ironic way, Durham makes a similar point. In his sculpture Durham has constructed a mini archway. It is made of cheap wood and found objects. The imperial function of the archway is ridiculed by its domestication and diminution in value. In an accompanying text Durham adds this wry instruction: 'It can be folded up and carried on a shoulder, set up as a tent. Whenever the owner feels that a personal victory has been scored he or she can set up the arch and march through it, perhaps whistling an appropriate tune' (2001, p. 68). By reducing the monumental and public display of power into a personal item, Durham is also referencing the countless strategies of inverting and displacing political authority through indigenous acts of cultural incorporation and mimicry. Like Kentridge, Durham is not only showing the interplay of different cultural forms and symbols, but also revealing how the ideals of one social order are reconfigured as they are internalized by different people. However, Durham's ironic gesture has a double-edged association. The happy archway can also take on the more sinister appearance of a metal detector. This innocent monument, designed to celebrate the micro-conquests of everyday life, thus recalls the habituated vigilance that is now employed to defend internal borders. In this ambivalent recognition we are reminded that the innovative effect of hybridity can have an uncertain meaning. Hybridity does not necessarily imply conciliatory and harmonious forms of cultural transformation; it can also sharpen the critique of the violent structures of global culture.

Critics who expect indigenous artists to confine their cultural imagination to the territorial boundaries and ancestral techniques of their homelands will be immediately disappointed and disapproving of hybridity. Jimmie Durham (1993), who is from the Cherokee nation, has openly challenged the view that his own authenticity is confined to traditional boundaries. His critical and artistic imagination has roamed across various media and engaged issues that are pertinent to different locales throughout the world. This nomadic sensibility is not necessarily a rootless existence. For in Durham's case it is also a perpetual questioning of the condition of belonging and the politics of difference. From this perspective, hybridity is not just a metaphor for cultural negotiation, it is also a tool for examining the inequalities and exclusion that are established in the guise of cultural purity.

It is more useful to track the way the 'power of hegemonic forces is felt *within* hybridity which is none the less experienced as having its own independent cultural power' (Tomlinson 1999, pp. 146–7). Hence, in order to engage with the artworks of artists such as Brian Jungen and Isaac Julien, it is necessary to think with different kinds of spatial models and recognize the possibility that hybridity can lead towards a cosmopolitan imaginary. A more useful response to these artworks is not simply to label them as hybrid objects, but to examine the dialectic between cultural fragmentation and critical reaffirmation. If hybridity is to refer to a cultural process rather than a fixed object, it will require a different kind of working through the zones of interaction, exchange and formation (Hall 1996b, p. 251).

Brian Jungen's sculptures *Prototypes for New Understanding* (1999) provoked a sense of bemusement when I first approached them in the context of the *ARS 01* exhibition. From a distance they appeared as conventional Northwest American ceremonial masks. They were displayed in typical ethnographic museum cabinets. The presence of stereotypical anthropological museum pieces in a contemporary gallery context was perplexing in itself. On closer inspection, the sense of seeing something 'out of place' rebounded. The masks were composed entirely of tongues, soles, laces and straps from Nike shoes. Even the 'made in China' labels were visible.

These fragments of outsourced labour were reassembled both to simulate the icons of a 'disappearing culture' and to question the funereal methodologies for representing the authenticity of indigenous cultures. Jungen's 'prototypes' utilized the red, white and black fragments from Nike shoes in a way that echoed the improvisational skills of indigenous peoples and the intrinsic hybridity of their cultural icons. Nike may seek to appeal to our conscience by publicizing their practice of recycling old shoes to retread the surface of basketball courts, but Jungen disassembled the new shoes to construct a replica of the old icons and thereby create a disturbing link between colonial melancholy and global corporatism. This link was also explored in a text that was offered as an introduction to the work. As the critic Jeff Derkson noted, Jungen's cross-weaving between the local and the global was deliberately staged to refute the claim that either polarity has a monopoly on authenticity and novelty and to evoke a 'strong strategy which brings First Nation's culture into globalism on a symbolic level in order to rearticulate the spatial relations within the discourse of globalization' (Derkson 2001, p. 101).

The deconstructing of symbolic references, and the reassembling and recycling of material that is made visible in Jungen's sculpture, is also a metaphor for the linguistic and epistemological processes of hybridity. Isaac Julien's films offer another strong example of the aesthetic and political process of cultural mixture. In *Vagabondia* (2000), a double-screen installation, he explores the complex legacies of colonialism by intertwining historical, architectural and linguistic elements into a complex narrative. The film is shot in the former home in London of Sir John Soane, and the narration is in French Creole. The architectural space is loaded with the symbols of colonial wealth. Although the house is now a national museum, it is not structured according to the classical and linear taxonomies of cultural development. In its collection one witnesses contradictory styles and diverse 'trophies'. There is no conventional order in which they are arranged. According to Julien, it provides a 'space in which we perceive the Empire as a precursor for globalization' (2003, p. 150).

The visual narrative, which is like an 'archaeological expedition' in the culture of empire, is counterpointed by the criss-crossing paths of the black conservator and the vagabond/trickster figure. These two main characters also provide two different kinds of dreaming. There is a man who enters the rooms and dances to the rhythm of swaying ships and drunken nights. On a parallel screen there is a woman who is the conservator: she folds the corners and locks the cabinets of the museum. Throughout the film the woman's gaze gently faces the camera while the dancer's eyes are averted from any exchange. She has a caressing voice and speaks in Creole. The film places these two figures inside the museum, creating a further level of dissonance between the structures of representation and the cultural life of the artefacts. The dancer evokes the memory of a black sailor who formerly busked outside of the house, and the woman's voice affirms the survival of a language that was formed by colonial contact.

The trickster figure is inspired by two sources. Julien claims that he was referencing the trances that Jean Rouch captured in his film *Les Maitres fous* (1955). Rouch's surreal documentary included the bizarre performances of a mixture of immigrant and local labourers on the outskirts of Lagos. These men would gather on weekends and played out a frenzied concatenation of ritual trances that mimicked the colonial induction service of the governor general. Rouch saw these events as an inversion of the colonial order. Julien also found fascination in the 1815 cartoon of 'two black London beggars notorious for their costumes' (2003, p. 151). One is depicted wearing a grand hat that resembles a ship. The trickster figure in *Vagabondia* recalls both the trance-like state of colonial cultural adaptations and the nautical experience of swaying melancholy. Mixture seems to come together in a drunken haze and loose-kneed swagger. Beside the wild and gangling gestures of the trickster we are also witness to the restrained and knowingly deliberate steps of the conservator. The narrator's voice is Rosemary Julien, the mother of Isaac Julien. The steady tonalities in her narration are lifted by a seductive musical score. Paul Gladstone-Reid, the composer of the soundtrack, fused gentle and ghostly sounds from African and Oriental sources. He sought 'to evoke the ghosts of past energies who have graced the portals of the decadently grand house of Sir John Soane, although the presence of the African and Oriental contingent may have served only to subvert the context' (quoted ibid., p. 153).

Between these architectural, gestural and sonic narratives there is a tender evocation of both the violent appropriation and the implied desires that exist in the folds of postcolonial history. The untranslated Creole narration also serves as a reminder of the gaps in the colonial consciousness. While the colonized had to learn the words and ways of the colonizer, this learning process was not always reciprocated. In the language of Creole there are traces, innovations and combinations that testify to the complex contacts between the colonizer and the colonized. The statues in Sir John Soane's collection remain silent. Nobody speaks back in the language of the black conservator.

These small gestures – undoing Nike shoes to make masks, making a film that is destined only for galleries and museums – are in themselves minor acts in relation to the machinations of global culture. However, they do pose powerful questions about the effects of difference within cultural objects, the process of incorporating foreign symbols or utilizing different media, and the articulation of a critique against domination. Much of the debate around these kinds of artistic practices has tended to take an absolute position, with critics either celebrating the mobility of culture or mourning the loss of authenticity. The melancholic 'salvation' paradigm that clouds the classical anthropological imagination confines its engagement to the salvation of damaged or weakened cultures. This has not only confined our appreciation of aesthetic innovation but also obscured the understanding of the different modes of cultural survival in the context of both colonialism and globalization.

These examples of hybrid art do not fit comfortably within the conventional art historical categories. They work within a context that neither corresponds to the boundaries of a national school nor conforms to the strict principles of formalist movements. In mainstream art criticism there is both a lag in the conceptual development of the vocabulary for representing the global context of art and a reluctance to engage with the political forces that shape the flows of exchanges (McEvilley 2002, p. 82). I want to reconsider the function played by the artist's social context and cultural background by asking the question 'What is the place of art in contemporary culture?' Art history has provided a rich body of texts that answered this question within the parameters of national identity and formal art movements. However, in the epoch of globalization, this methodology would limit the sphere of interpretation. The questions on the place and function of art have to be asked in a different way. Yet, these new lines of investigation have been blocked by the persistence of cultural paradigms on authenticity and contemporaneity that either reinstate the governing force of national territorial boundaries or elevate the cultural sphere to an abstracted domain of globalism.

The Limits of Culture as Residentialism

I have argued so far in this chapter that hybridity can be used to expand the aesthetic categories of creativity and context (Gilroy 1993; Mercer 1994; Hall 1996a). However, many critics have also used the concept of hybridity as a negative term that merely highlights the pretensions of the new cultural elites of globalization and the process of cultural commodification (Friedman 1999; Araeen 2000; Aijaz 1992; Žižek 1997). This opposition has restricted our understanding of cultural transformation. It is critical to note that consciousness of hybridity is not confined to artists that operate within the global art circuit. At one level these artists are making visible strategies that already exist in everyday life. For instance, in his work on the border culture of Tijuana and San Diego, Néstor García Canclini (1995) has observed that street vendors and fine artists alike tend to draw from a complex mixture of cultural iconography and utilize a diverse range of visual technologies in order to articulate their own underlying condition of hybridity. This suggests that cross-cultural dialogue does not require that all speakers have equivalent political and economic resources. Rather than expecting that the victims of colonialism must reclaim their 'original' history and glue back together their authentic culture *before* they can be admitted into the present, it might be more valuable to recognize the horizontal forms of exchange that are already occurring. As Gayatri Spivak (2003, p. 33) suggests, an alternative modality of co-existence and mutual understanding may occur if the dominant partner is prepared to cede a degree of openness to learning from the other and dispenses with the vertical presumptions of cultural evolution that would condemn pre-capitalist systems to an unending game of 'catch up'. The challenge is not whether the formerly colonized can make rapid advances, but whether the dominant can address the ethical register of other cultural systems.

The contest over the conceptual and political frame of hybridity is underscored by an unresolved anxiety over authenticity. The contemporary theoretical debates have not resolved whether authenticity is bound to the 'roots' of traditional forms of attachment, intimacy and proximity, or whether the multiple 'routes' of modernity are the only pathways to freedom, criticality and innovation. Does authenticity demand stillness? Does innovation require restlessness? To what degree do the physicality of place and the experience of the journey play a critical role in the achievement of these states? Is it possible to have authentic attachments to a place and develop a form of cultural identity that is influenced by movement? Is a critical and innovative perspective available from the confines of the home? These questions have been at the centre of a wide range of debates in the arts and social sciences. The anthropologist Jonathan Friedman has disputed both the mobility of cultures and the capacity of diasporic agents to create hybrid cultures (1999, p. 232). The literary theorist Ania Loomba has challenged the celebration of hybrid subjectivity in postcolonial theory for being 'curiously universal and homogeneous' (1998, p. 178). The artist and critic Rasheed Araeen has also argued that an artist's critical practice is unrelated to their experience of displacement (2000, p. 5). It is not my purpose to respond to all these criticisms. However, by focusing on Friedman's argument, there is an opportunity not only to unpack the supposed link between hybridity and corporate globalism but also to examine the limits of the residentialist perspective on culture.

Jonathan Friedman is an anthropologist who adopts the residentialist conception of culture. According to the residentialist model, culture was the means by which a society defined criteria for co-ordinating symbolic practices that affirmed a coherent identity and differentiated its way of life from that of others. The ideas and values that were perceived as unique to a specific community were also mapped within territorial boundaries. Symbolic practices were supposedly confined to the physical and territorial boundaries of a given place. The model of culture therefore stressed two interrelated features: that identity was premised on the differentiation from others and the capacity to map out its mindset onto a specific place. This immediately poses the issues of mobility and mixture as a problem. For, if culture can only find sustenance when it is rooted in a specific place, what is the fate of those cultures that must co-exist in a common space and what is the cultural identity of people who are on the move? According to Friedman, when an individual is disconnected from his or her original place of belonging, there are the dire consequences of being severed from the cultural system that holds together the whole set of identifications. Cultures that have been disembedded from a specific sense of place are similarly unmoored. The residentialist view of culture not only poses a negative slant on the impact of mobility, it also makes the gloomy prognostication that moving beyond one's place is to risk cultural exclusion and the attempt to transfer elements of one culture to another place is always doomed.

The application of this residentialist conception of culture has led to a number of negative conclusions on hybridity. Friedman has not only interpreted hybrid cultures and identities as lacking authenticity; he also sees them as the exemplars of the new culture of global corporatism and rootless cosmopolitan subjectivity. Hybridity is therefore represented both as lacking in culture and as part of a force that is attacking traditional and national cultures. In a final sweeping claim, Friedman states that the theoretical representation of hybridity as a form of 'cultural globalization is the correlative to the argument for economic globalization' (1999, p. 234). Before one accepts this linkage, it would still be necessary to establish evidence of how the aesthetic work conducted in the global cultural sphere serves the interests, reproduces the worldview and promotes the same values of economic globalization. Rather than challenging this assertion on an empirical level, I will seek to unpack the conceptual links between hybridity and cultural transformation.

There is a fundamental contradiction in the way scholars such as Friedman have adopted the residentialist model of culture for the purpose of anthropological investigation and in defence of national cultural formations. First of all, there is a reliance on cultural values of distinction and taste that presupposes a hierarchical differentiation between high culture as the embodiment of cultivation and reason and low culture as a sort of compost bin for all other forms of populist activities. This vertical hierarchy is anathema to anthropologists because it is also the basis by which Western culture was privileged over and above all other cultures. Anthropologists such as Friedman have sought to challenge such ethnocentric assumptions, but in his disdain for the populist forms of hybridity he has also reproduced some of the elitist values that are embedded in residentialist conceptions of culture.

Even when anthropologists have adopted a horizontal model of culture and levelled all the criteria for ranking cultural values, this has left the problem of cross-cultural judgement untouched. How do we judge between competing claims of cultural authority when both forms seek to exist in the same place? The answers offered by relativism would be impotent. Friedman's response is equally disabling because it questions the very authority of a minority culture to assume the right to speak as a cultural entity. Friedman's position on diasporic and hybrid culture returns us to the problem about the degree to which a cultural formation needs to be embedded in a specific place and maintain continuous practices in order to develop a coherent and distinctive worldview. Fragments and mutations that have split from the original are, in his view, inadequate forms to provide the basis for a new cultural identity. This test, if applied universally, would in fact disqualify most national claims to cultural autonomy and coherence. Who today can claim to represent a whole and unique cultural identity? While Friedman claims that immigrant societies in places like the United States and the countries of Europe are becoming less multicultural because immigrant communities are losing their distinctive grasp on linguistic and social practices, it does not lead us to the conclusion that these societies are becoming more homogeneous and assimilated. Loss of certain boundaries has not meant the disappearance of cultural differences, but rather the appearance of new forms of mixture and more complex patterns of differentiation. The challenge is to distinguish between compliant and critical hybridity.

Friedman's objection to hybridity theory can also have the

unintended effect of giving succour to the nostalgic fantasies of communitarianism and fuelling fundamentalist ideologies. By stressing that difference presupposes inequality and defining the dynamics of mixture according to the logic of appropriation, it provides ballast for the extremist fears that hybridity inevitably dilutes the strength and contaminates the purity of local culture. This argument leaves little room for manoeuvre in the cultural responses to globalization. Traditional cultural values are under assault not just from the globalizing force of economic liberalism but also from the associated reactions of neo-nationalism and cultural fundamentalism (Hobsbawm and Ranger 1983). As Touraine (2000, p. 166) has noted, we should be mindful of the fact that the logic of capital and the myth of the nation share the same dream of cultural unity.

While I believe that equating the critical role of difference in hybridity with the competitive function of novelty in capitalism is a gross oversimplification, it is necessary to examine the ways hybridity can be promoted as a specific kind of cultural formation and to consider whether this can be distinguished from national and traditional cultural spaces. The examples of hybrid practices by contemporary artists provide a radical challenge to the conventional categories for cultural representation. Friedman's condemnation of hybridity as if it were a masking agent for economic oppression risks introducing economic determinism through the back door of cultural idealism, as it deems that cultural mixture is merely the result of the external force of economic domination and political will. The aesthetic force of cultural mixture is therefore left outside of the field of social change.

Towards a Hybrid Universalism

Charles Taylor's book *Multiculturalism and the Politics of Recognition* (1992) was one of the most comprehensive attempts to address the role of cultural difference in moral outlooks and social systems. Unlike other philosophers, who either ignored or dismissed the significance of cultural difference, Taylor sought to find a place for it within the procedural issues that define the public sphere and, more generally, to link it to the debates on the Enlightenment principles of a common humanity. However, his effort to define the worthiness of different cultures is limited by the same conceptual constraints that were evident in Friedman's residentialist conception of culture. Once again, the validity of a diasporic culture, or the significance of cultural difference, is measured by its degree of attachment to a specific place. Taylor's attempt to reconcile the politics of multiculturalism within a liberal model of universalism is limited by the assumption that culture and identity are bound by relations that formed in a given territory over a significant period of time. This repeats the residentialist view that mobility undermines or fragments cultural formations. In essence, Taylor claims that it is only after a period of settlement that a group can articulate a concept of cultural rights. It is my contention that this is an inadequate basis for defining a system that can accommodate the diverse forms of cultural identity in contemporary society. In this final section I will explore the dynamic role of mobility and ambivalence in the formation of what I call a hybrid universalism.

Amongst the pioneers in this field are Latin American scholars such as Freyre, Oritz and Glissant, who argued that hybridity was crucial for developing a positive language for representing the mixtures that are formed in the violent contact zones of colonialism. These scholars used the concept of hybridity to articulate the critical awareness that is at play when a culture is forged from the uncomfortable dialectic of interdependence and mutual resistance. As Santiago (2002, pp. 30–1) argues, the process of adopting Western civilization in Latin America has been 'one of assimilation and aggressiveness, of learning and reaction, of false obedience'. This perverse relationship between Latin American culture and the culture of colonialism has found one of its most eloquent and powerful expressions in the manifesto of Oswald de Andrade's anthropophagy movement in Brazil. It was neither an attempt at eroticizing its own condition nor an exercise in converting the stigma of miscegenation into a site of positive identification. According to Euridice Figueiredo (2003), it aimed to make explicit both the historical legacy of violent conflict and the persistence of social inequality, and through this struggle with the condition of cultural dependency there is a residual need to find a way 'for their differential insertion into universal totalization'.

The coercive strain, or the ambivalence within hybridity, is thus central to these Latin American representations of cultural identity. A recent attempt to develop a framework for addressing the cultural contradictions of globalization was the symposium 'Créolité', staged by Documenta XI on the Caribbean island of St Lucia. Okwui Enwezor and his curatorial team invited some of the leading writers, scholars and artists to discuss the need for a new conceptual vocabulary that could address both the specific historical formations and the global forces that are shaping cultural identity. The aim of the symposium was not purely a defensive reaction against the structures of neo-nationalism and the homogenizing pressures of globalization, but also an affirmative gesture that sought to create a dialogue between intellectual and aesthetic models which might lead to a new interpretive perspective and construct a new space for the production of social and historical knowledge. This was an ambitious project, and it began with the bold assumption that terms such as 'hybridity' and '*métissage*' were no longer 'adequate as vectors through which to understand and articulate the critical issues of difference and asymmetry of contemporary culture today' (Enwezor 2003b, p. 13). The symposium sought to examine whether the term 'créolité', drawn from three Martinican intellectuals – Jean Bernabé, Patrick Chamoiseau and Raphael Confiant – could be put forward as a concept that could not only describe the consequences of cultural transformation but also provide a new relational perspective, which the Martinicans described as an 'ethics of vigilance, a sort of mental envelope in the middle of which our world will be built in full consciousness of the outer world' (ibid.).

Despite its worthy goals, the symposium did not end with a new consensus over the critical vocabulary or the outline of a cosmopolitan consciousness. In one of the most lucid and comprehensive responses, Stuart Hall examined both the historical conditions of plantation slavery that forged the process of cultural mixture known as creolization and the dynamic creative practices that formed the basis of reflexive self-consciousness that is now defined as créolité. Hall was particularly attentive to the specific conditions of creolization and expressed caution against the potential to overgeneralize the practices of créolité. He stressed that, while the brutal and humiliating conditions of plantation slavery produced an abhorrent social contest, it also created an intense mixture that no longer existed in a 'pure' state but has been permanently 'translated' (Enwezor 2003b, p. 31).

The resulting culture is therefore shaped both by asymmetrical power relations and a critical self-consciousness of the process by which the different cultures relate to each other. Hall noted that, while the process of cultural exchange in the context of colonialism is uneven, the resulting culture of creolization does not entirely reflect the values and objectives of the dominant culture. Even in the most violent interactions, significant transformation occurs to both partners. Transformation is not just initiated by the presence of competing systems of belief; it also occurs *in* the very process of interaction. Hall then considered whether this process could provide the theoretical model for the wider process of transculturation that is evident in all corners of the contemporary world.

Throughout his analysis of the terms of créolité and its relationship to the parallel concepts of diaspora and hybridity, Hall carefully demonstrated that, on a semantic level, all of these terms have shifted widely from their original historical and biological definitions. They have developed along distinctive scholarly and vernacular trajectories and have superseded any of their earlier essentialist or purist associations. Hall was not bothered by the dubious weight of etymological claims to, say, hybridity or the stigma that pinned Creole to an inferior grasp of linguistic competence. On the contrary, he celebrated the signs of innovation and creativity that emerge from the processes of mixture. However, Hall is far more circumspect in relation to the generalizability of the different terms. He recognized that they all refer to aspects of the broad process of transculturation, but in an astute set of observations he outlined the specific conditions under which creolization was formed, and thus qualified it from the different kinds of diasporic attachment, memory and consciousness. He expressed caution against overextending concepts of creolization, and to a lesser extent he was cautious over the universal applicability of diaspora, because they both refer to specific historical circumstances in which communities were formed (Enwezor 2003b, p. 193). Hall's distinction between these terms hangs on the difference between, on the one hand, the excessive conditions of violence and massive disparities of power that shaped creolization and, on the other, the degree of choice that framed both the historical consciousness and the conditions of reception in the diaspora. In Hall's typology, hybridity has the most general application because it is neither bound to the 'specific historical circumstances' of colonialism nor linked to the migration patterns of a particular community. Of the many theoretical definitions of hybridity, Hall acknowledged the influence of the essays written by Homi Bhabha in the 1980s.

Bhabha's main concern was to find a way of representing the impact of a minority within a dominant culture. He was attempting to overcome the assumption that a minority position was entirely damaged by its displacement or inevitably consumed within the new structures. According to the residentialist model of culture, minority cultures were destined to suffer the same fate as a stranger in a cannibalistic society: after being devoured, they were either absorbed or vomited. Between digestion and emission there is little room for negotiation. Bhabha wanted to challenge the cannibalistic underpinning to the residentialist model of cultural difference. He was convinced that the minority position still possessed a degree of agency and that the ongoing journeys of migration provided a vital perspective for understanding the changes of modernity. Bhabha adopted the concept of hybridity to refer to the affirmative presence and ambivalent transformations that occur as a minority claims a space for itself within metropolitan culture. In his writings, hybridity was used to articulate the dynamic for the representation *of* the minorities and the emergence of new cultural forms that result from their participation *in* the dominant culture. He made the bold claim that hybridity was not to be understood as either a shadowy identity that trailed in the absence of an original whole or the transitional phase on the way to some unified entity. Bhabha's use of hybridity was to provoke a paradigm shift in the way we understood the dynamics of transformation. The hybrid forms that resulted from the entry of a minority were more than just partial copies of the past or temporary appendages to the present culture; they were active forces in the field and therefore part of the process of cultural transformation.

Bhabha was not the first to use the concept of hybridity to refer to the dynamics of cultural transformation. In the earlier theories of semiotics and culture developed by Bakhtin and Lotman, the concept of hybridity was also developed to represent the transformative processes of language, culture and knowledge. These authors found evidence of this dynamic at all levels of cultural production and intellectual engagement. However, they also concluded that innovation and improvisation intensify along the border zones of cross-cultural contact. More recently Thomas McEvilley (1991) has argued that the commonality in the methodology of the modernist avant garde and the critical thought in ancient Greek and Egyptian art, and what Michel Serres (1982) calls the problem-solving capacity of scientific knowledge, can be defined as hybridity.

These definitions project hybridity beyond the diasporic and colonial context and utilize it at the most general level of creative and scientific practice. Hybridity is now also used as a methodological concept. The crucial feature in this method is the redirection of an object's trajectory into a 'third space', or the reconfiguration of previous arrangements by the incorporation of a 'third figure'. These switches and shifts always involve movement and realignment. By taking matter out of one place and putting it in another, there is both the disruption and the reordering of the conventional codes and structures. Displacement can lead to either confusion or insight. Hybridity refers not only to the ambivalent consequences of mixture but also to the shift in the mode of consciousness. By mixing things that were previously kept apart there is both a stimulus for the emergence of something new and a shift in position that can offer a perspective for seeing newness as it emerges.

Hybrid art practice is, in my view, a crucial starting point for the urgent task of examining the formations of aesthetic cosmopolitanism. In the past, artists and scholars saw themselves as legislators as they sought to enlighten the minds of the public and reshape the structures of society. Today the position has, as Bauman (1987) noted, shifted to the role of interpreter. Artists and scholars do not just analyse, define and propose, they must also develop collaborative strategies through which knowledge is produced and disseminated in a collective manner. Artists increasingly understand their agency in terms of this interpretative and collaborative modality.

To acknowledge the constitutive force of hybridity would demand that scholars confront the unconscious and ambivalent forces that artists invariably face when they delve deeper into their creative practice. At this level we would have to consider the uncomfortable suspension of moral markers in order to witness the compelling forces that drive some elements of attraction and repulsion in the cultural field. Within this zone we can see that mixtures occur that defy the conventional codes of normative behaviour and cultural propriety. Hybridity cannot therefore be fully explained if the model of interpretation does not allow for both transgressive and relational modes of practice. When driven by this husky desire, hybridity can exceed the boundaries of moral codes and political processes. The vivacious energy of hybridity leads it towards risky encounters. The identity and trajectory of hybridity is driven by the simultaneous desire for both separation and connection. In the spirit of the moving collage it gathers form through a mixture of theft and gift, creation and destruction. The place of hybridity should not be justified in relation to the competitive drive towards maximizing production and the progressivist ideologies of Western modernization, but rather in its capacity to invent a modality for living with difference.

Hybridity thinking compels us to address the complicities and interdependencies in cultural exchange and identity. The mode of thinking that I am proposing does not proceed by making clear-cut and absolute distinctions. It acknowledges that hybridity is dependent on the very things it strives to overcome. Boundaries are a necessary part of the modern world. Any form of identity and hybridity would be meaningless without them. The critical task is not to strive for a utopian space beyond boundaries, but to re-engage the sphere of possibilities that are permitted or excluded by boundaries. Hybridity thinking has been criticized for focusing too heavily on the cultural interventions by diasporic agents and thereby failing to attend to the political inequalities of globalization (Bhabha 1994).[1] Yet these criticisms have not only conflated the critical modality with the commodification of hybrid objects and the co-option of depoliticized hybrid agents; in themselves they also failed to address the very issue of how power and resistance operate throughout the contemporary cultural networks. Without careful attention to the specific ways in which hybridity is constituted, there is the possibility that the hegemonic political and economic forces can exploit the ambiguities of a muted version of hybridity to produce what García Canclini (1995, p. 48) calls a 'tranquillizing hybridization'. This brings us to the crux of the aporia between aesthetics and ethics. Jan Nederveen Pieterse was right when he stressed that hybridity thinking is dependent on the hegemonic forms of border thinking. However, he also noted that this dependency provides a new take on the dynamics of group formation and social inequality (2001, p. 21).

Hybridity thinking is driven by the dual desire of connection and separation. To create something new involves ripping it out of one context, pushing against existing boundaries, and rearranging the order of things. These disruptive acts of mixture can lead to new forms of awareness and construct new networks of agency; however, there are no guarantees that mixture will always entail equality. Hybridity, mobility and difference show us the other side of things, take us to foreign destinations, provide a new perspective on the relationship between aesthetics and the cosmopolitan imaginary.

In a subtle way Kentridge and Durham, as well as Jungen and Julien, are working with the contradictions of hybridity. Where logic would demand an unequivocal answer, they suggest a pause, and then direct attention to the way that opposing views can be held together to form a third. Similarly, we can see how logic of social justice would demand that the rights of difference should be subordinate to equality. But the two terms should not be thrust upon us in the form of a competition. They are in fact co-constitutive. Without one the other is meaningless. For artists, the tension between difference and equality is productive. They do not demand the absolute resolution of one over and against the other. They recognize that holding on to this ambivalence produces what the three Martinican intellectuals Jean Bernabé, Patrick Chamoiseau and Raphael Confiant called a *'nontotalitarian consciousness of a preserved diversity'* (quoted in Enwezor 2002, p. 51). In an age when global power defines itself through the convergence of cultural signs and consolidates legitimacy through the standardization of codes of practice, they stressed that cross-cultural dialogue can only proceed in the dialectic that simultaneously addresses the modalities for representing the persistent and mutating forms of identity, as well as the struggle to transform the universalist frameworks for social justice. Hybridity is always double-edged – pointing to where we have come from and where we are heading. The juxtaposition of different signs and the contrast of alternative perspectives is not only a recurring feature in the composition of artworks but also a strategy that artists utilize in order to provoke new forms of cross-cultural communication. In this context, the work of art exists in the unfinished task of translation. In this paradoxical conjunction of the material manifestation of an object and the endless process of interpretation, the aesthetic function of hybridity becomes more visible. It requires that we witness the simultaneous use of all three levels of hybridity. As a concept, hybridity goes beyond the description of the differences within art and between cultures as it becomes a key part of the translation machine in art and culture.

8

Cultural Translation, Cosmopolitanism and the Void

What is one's own has to be learned just as much as what is foreign.

Holderlin

In his recent publication *The Radicant*, and in his self-proclaimed manifesto that accompanied the exhibition *Altermodern*, Nicolas Bourriaud proposed that the concept of cultural translation was the key to understanding the dynamics of contemporary art. In order to go beyond ethnic essentialism and allow the formation of new intercultural networks, he argued that contemporary artists should maintain a double dialogue with culture. Their artwork is therefore the translation that results from the dialogue with their original culture and the corpus of aesthetic values inherited from modern art (Bourriaud 2009b, p. 165; see also p. 19). This approach, while acknowledging the complementary value of the local culture, reinforces the ground of the modern culture as the one that provides an overarching frame (Enwezor 2009, p. 30)and is therefore vulnerable to the criticism that it establishes an 'apparently symmetrical dichotomy' as a ruse that 'hides a hierarchy' (Ivekovic 2005).[1] Despite Bourriaud's schematic link between cultural translation and contemporary art, he is nevertheless correct in his identification of cultural translation as a central force in the formation of aesthetic cosmopolitanism. Cosmopolitanism usually refers to the social transformation that arises from the mixture of different cultures. In the context of the political impact of migration, these signs of mixture, as I argued previously, are often interpreted through a kinetophobic prism. However, in the recent debates on the cultural consequences of globalization, cosmopolitanism has also been used as a normative concept for addressing a specific orientation towards this process of mixture. Cosmopolitanism therefore includes both a way of being in the world that entails a universalist aspiration for moral connectedness and an emergent social order that extends political rights beyond exclusivist territorial boundaries. However, in order to feel an individual sense of moral connectedness and organize these collective modes of solidarity, there must be a mixture of aesthetic and deliberative modes for comprehending and evaluating the cultural similarities and differences. In this chapter I will focus on the aesthetic dimensions of cross-cultural interaction through the concept of cultural translation.

Cultural translation has been adopted as a key conceptual tool for developing a further understanding of the effects of hybridity in a broad range of contexts, from colonialism to multiculturalism, as well as defining the cultural logic of modernity. This concept has also travelled across a vast range of disciplines. From its origins in linguistics and anthropology to its more recent applications in philosophy and sociology, it has served as a tool for identifying the transformative dynamic that is forged by the interaction of different cultures. By highlighting the productive relationship between dominant and minority partners, it has been used to debunk the myths of cultural purity and absolute autonomy, and thereby widened the conceptual framework within which a broader range of influences are recognized as shaping the imperial, national and global cultural spheres.

Throughout the wide range of uses of cultural translation, one perspective has been dominant. The dynamics of cultural translation have been seen as a form of interaction between different entities. This interactionist perspective views the cultural system as if it operates according to the nexus between boundedness and mobility. Cultural ideas and values are understood as emerging in specific social and historical contexts. They are formed in a bounded place. However, they also have the capacity to travel across their own boundaries and interact with other cultural systems. As bounded cultural entities interact with each other, they draw on the forces of mobility. It is through the continuous process of engagement with the other, the movement of ideas across borders, and the cross-checking of rival viewpoints that cultures are seen as generating new forms that ensure their fitness and viability. This interactionist perspective stresses that, while the integrity and coherence of cultural entities presuppose boundedness, the dependency on mobility also necessitates that all boundaries are semi-porous and flexible. In general, this attention to the interplay that occurs across boundaries has been explained by recourse to the mechanical and biological metaphors of the modern social sciences. Whether it be the anthropophagic concept in cultural theory, linguistic models of dialogue, or the more recent philosophical theory of performativity, the creative force of interaction between rival cultures is represented as a complex sequence that begins with an original moment of encounter and then develops into a process of interpenetration, selection, assemblage and reconfiguration. The process of interaction may not necessarily follow in this precise order. However, even in situations of defensive denial or aggressive withdrawal from the other, this still implies that some part of the other must have travelled across the border and disturbed the culture's internal structure, or the excluded element has the constitutive force to haunt the unity that is predicated upon its absence (Butler 2000b, p. 11). These creative reconfigurations and unruly disturbances are therefore explained by focusing on the interaction that occurs between the state of boundedness and the forces of mobility.

This interactionist perspective has been an invaluable method for explaining how cultural horizons either contract or expand through the contact with foreign ideas and objects. It has highlighted the individual and collective capacity for internal adjustment through an interaction with the other. There is recognition that this process, which reveals the insufficiency of existing cultural structures and necessitates the invention of new points of cross-cultural connection, is often conducted in an atmosphere of ambivalence or agonistic struggle. However, this perspective has two interrelated limitations. First, there is a tendency to subordinate the logic of cultural transformation to an overarching instrumentalist or determinist schema. Second, this perspective rarely notices the function of the void in cultural translation. In order to overcome these pitfalls I will draw on Gerard Delanty's distinction between the interactionist perspective and immanent transcendence (2009, p. 194). Through a series of reflections on the example of the invention of a new visual language in Aboriginal painting, I will also consider how a cosmopolitan theory of cultural translation must address the relationship between creativity and the critical force of the void.

Aesthetics and the Ethics of Kenosis

My starting point is a common scene in an academic forum. The prominent cultural theorist Ihab Hassan (2008b) displayed a reproduction of a painting by the Australian Aboriginal painter Rover Thomas and in all sincerity turned to the audience and asked: 'How would you interpret this painting?' The question provoked a moment of stunned confusion because everyone knew that Hassan already understood how to 'read' the aesthetic and symbolic properties in this painting. This was not the moment in which the invited international guest merely opened the floor so that the audience could inform him with local knowledge. As a participant in the seminar, I felt a nervous energy run through the room. The anxious silence was not just shyness. It was as if a group of strangers was being asked to explain something familiar but for which they lacked words. Suddenly, there was a confrontation with the possibility that neither the art historian's 'good eye' nor the anthropologist's 'access' to the cultural context would suffice as tools for interpreting Rover Thomas's painting. In my view, Hassan's rhetorical question and the anxious silence that it provoked exposed a limit point in the conventional ways of both defining cosmopolitanism and conducting cross-cultural analysis. Hassan, in a number of recent essays, has claimed that much of the cultural turn in literary criticism, and in particular the commentary on multiculturalism and contemporary identity, has now descended into tendentious and narcissistic hype (Hassan 2008a, p. 223; see also Hassan 1996, p. 316).[2] Hassan's frustration with the influence of political and psychoanalytic discourses on identity and cultural creativity has sharpened his attention towards religious concepts and literary expressions of the self–other relationship. As a reaction against the deterministic tendencies that trailed in the wake of the cultural turn, Hassan redirected his focus towards the nihilist tradition in critical thought and claimed that the process of creative transformation is better explained through mystical concepts such as kenosis.

'I'm nobody. Who are you?' Emily Dickinson's probing declaration provides a paradoxical starting point for Hassan's quest for identity. Sceptical of the idealistic claims by humanitarian NGOs, annoyed by the boastful hype of global roaming executives, and repelled by the bile of the leaders of transnationalist jihadism, Hassan turns to an ethical modality of self-dispossession that he claims is rapidly fading from everyday life but 'perdures' in art and theory. The constant in his criticism is the expectation that, at any point in history, 'art may move toward a redeemable imagination, commensurate with the full mystery of human consciousness' (Hassan 1971, p. 258). This expectation remains profoundly disappointed by his review of the literature on cosmopolitanism. Even at its 'genuinely admirable' best, as in the example of Edward Said's attempt to articulate universalism through the dual respect for cultural difference and abiding by a single standard for human behaviour, Hassan considers this to be a variant of wishful thinking and regretfully informs us that such a stance is 'heroically naïve' (1996, p. 316). He concludes that this body of work fails because it adopts an instrumentalist perspective on human subjectivity, and ultimately serves no other function than to lubricate the geopolitical spread of global corporations and collude in the commodification of culture for global consumption.

These are harsh and overreaching judgements. Hassan's rebukes tend to exaggerate the extent to which the debates on cultural identity are framed by either a self-obsessed narcissistic version of identity as a happy consumer or the self-abrogating notion of identity that demands strict codes of loyalty and obedience. However, unlike the critics from both the left and the right who were discussed previously in relation to the status of hospitality in multiculturalism, Hassan does acknowledge a deeper conundrum. The representation of identity is no longer confined to the boundaries of the nation-state but is a matter of contention in both the 'micro'-version of communitarianism and the 'macro'-platforms of transnational fundamentalism. This shift in the social and political contexts of cultural identity therefore compels greater sensitivity towards the wide range of forces that shape contemporary subjectivity. In this quest for an expanded vision of culture and identity, Hassan is once again critical of intellectuals for being prisoners to ideological 'abstractions that demand human blood to maintain them for a higher end' (Coffi 1999, p. 11).

The only trace of a genuine dialogue between the self and other that Hassan identifies is within the nihilist tradition of aesthetic and philosophical thought. But Hassan also knows that this is not enough. He pleas for a social space in which differences can co-exist before they 'flare into rage'. Hassan has already rejected cosmopolitanism as a political ideal that is both too general to sustain the bonds of transnational solidarity and not specific enough to be woven into the fabric of everyday experience. But this leaves his poetic quest for a 'civitas without borders' in an abstract space. At one level it remains as a yearning; at another it adopts the burnt and gritty gaze of an ascetic who decrees that 'You need to see with the "eye of flesh" as well as the "eye of fire"'. Neither a 'bloodied nationalist' nor a 'utopian cosmopolitan', rejecting both liberal tolerance and corporatist cannibalism, Hassan marches through contemporary criticism claiming to have both feet firmly on the ground and daring to pose such unfashionable questions as 'What releases us from blood and belonging? What frees us from implacable self-interest? What gives us to the widest horizon of life?' (1996, p. 228). Hassan proposes that answers to these questions are best grasped through a broader vision of the creative transformation in human consciousness, and he repeatedly reaches for St Paul's use of the term 'kenosis'.

Paul described Christ's 'humbling' of himself in his transformation from God to man as a form of kenosis. By emptying out his divinity, Christ could make space for becoming mortal. For followers of Christ there is a similar expectation. In order to live in a state of grace, they too must clear away their identity and thereby receive the 'flesh' of Christ. By turning to this mystical concept of transubstantiation, Hassan risks dropping deeper into the older traps of idealism and caricaturing the effects of public intellectuals who engage in cultural politics (Clavier 2007, pp. 32–3). It would be all too easy to interpret this spiritual turn as evidence of the poverty of modernist subjectivity and the failure of vanguardist ideologies to produce a meaningful cosmopolitan imaginary. However, rather than accepting the view that a secular vision of cosmopolitanism is 'over' and it is time to get into something else, I will propose that this is a good moment to reflect on the contradictory forces that shape contemporary subjectivity and cultural production. Without glossing the biting critique that Hassan unleashes on the cultural theories of cosmopolitanism, I will seek to recast his annunciation of a terminus as yet another 'way-station' in which oversimplified claims are unloaded and the complexity of cultural translation is revisited.

Translation as Trope for Cultural Transformation

In the second line of her poem 'I'm nobody! Who are you?', Emily Dickinson turns to the reader and poses an equally penetrating query: 'Are you nobody, too?' Hassan is right to claim that the force of nothing, the power of the abyss, the kenotic ideal of self-dispossesion are not issues that feature prominently in the debates on globalization and cosmopolitanism. However, they are not entirely absent from the lineages of critical and cultural theory. At the end of his career the critical theorist Kurt Wolff (1976) proposed the phrase 'surrender and catch' to describe both the state of vibrant oscillation in the self-conscious act of letting go of one's identity and the creative transformation of the self in its encounter with the other. Peter Sloterdijk, a second-generation critical theorist, began his commentary on modern subjectivity with a provocative investigation into 'kinetic nihilism' (Sloterdijk 1998, 2006). The image of being as both nothing and an unfathomable source of energy was also vital to Homi Bhabha's exploration of the 'contingent tension' and 'temporal break' that constitutes hybrid subjectivity in the postcolonial context (1994, p. 191). In each of these sources we find not only comparable accounts of the confrontation of the void and the passage from one state of consciousness to another, but also a common quest to break free of instrumentalist codes of subjectivity. While the trope of translation has been well and truly used – some say 'abused' (Pratt et al. 2010) – as a tool to address the cross-cultural process of adoption and adaptation, I will argue that, in the context of globalization, a new non-mechanistic paradigm is necessary to address the creative function of the void in cultural translation.

Translation is conventionally understood as the process by which the meaning in one language is conveyed in another. It usually involves the discovery of linguistic correspondences between different languages or the transfer of terms from one language into another. The similarity that exists between different languages or the introduction of new terms does not always entail an exact replication of meaning. As corresponding terms are grasped or new ones inserted, there is always an uneven fit. This unevenness or non-equivalence inspires both a lament for what is lost in translation and a celebration of the extension in conceptual understanding through creative improvisation and hybridization. Translation is a process of bringing an element in from the outside that reconstitutes the inside and activates the generalizing capacity for coding and evaluation. Gayatri Spivak describes the shuttling action of translation as an act of reparation. However, she also notes that the subject who performs translation must possess an intimate knowledge of the rules and possible forms of both languages and claims that, in the process of moving between languages, the translator sees their own language as just another language among many, and thereby experiences both the guilty feeling of pricking the narcissistic totality of the mother tongue and initiating the conscious coming into being of ethical responsibility. To move between languages is not only to negotiate the discrepancies between the specific languages, as one idiom refuses to be carried over to the other, but also to reinstate the possibility for transcoding – the generality of the semiotic that Spivak claims can 'appropriate the singularity of the other's idiom by way of conscientious approximations' (2000, p. 15).

At the broadest level, the concept of translation has also been adopted as a meta-concept for addressing the constitutive function of difference in all forms of knowledge production (Derrida 1978, 1998). From this perspective, the conceptual parameters of translation are not confined either to interpretation across linguistic boundaries or to articulation of perception into language, but are extended to address philosophical questions regarding the relationship between the universal and the particular, the process by which transformation occurs in politics, and even the ethical form of intersubjective relations. By claiming translation as a meta-concept, I am not seeking to demonstrate that it only works because there is either a primal linguistic pool from which all languages are derived or an ultimate conceptual horizon at which all meanings will converge. Meaning does not derive from some original source or remain in abeyance until a messianic moment of unity. I do not believe that the continuous iterations of translation will eventually lead to a point of linguistic resolution and ultimate transparency. While the impulse for translation draws from a boundless curiosity over difference and the fundamental desire to communicate with others, the production of meaning is also relatively open-ended. The untranslatable grows out of each new translation. Paul Ricoeur argued that translation proceeds 'in spite of' difference: 'A good translation can aim only at a supposed equivalence that is not founded on a demonstrable identity of meaning. An equivalence without identity' (2006, p. 23). Subsequently, he also quite rightly added that the paradigm for representing translation should be recast beyond the stifling polarity of fidelity/betrayal (2007, p. 24). Therefore a more affirmative perspective would see translation as being produced *through* the encounter with the awesome infinity of difference. Hence the imperfect labour of translating is always a stimulus for both creative modification and conceptual extension.

The concept of cultural translation was first developed to examine the process of cross-cultural interaction in the context of colonialism. It has subsequently been adopted to explore the viability of minority cultures in a multicultural metropolitan setting, to understand the intermingling of a plurality of languages within global media, and to identify the process of transformation that results from the transnational circulation of cultural artefacts. It is extremely effective at highlighting the creative stimulus that is generated by the interaction between the foreign and the familiar in cultural production. By emphasizing the role of mediation between different cultural objects and codes, the concept of cultural translation has become more than a tool for explaining the dynamics of communication; it has also served as a sociological concept to describe the given social forms of mixture and to acknowledge the dynamic feature of hybridization. From this perspective it has in addition facilitated the debunking of essentialist claims that underpin romantic nationalism, ethnic fundamentalism and ethnocentric imperialism. Cultural translation is thus at the core of accounts that seek to demonstrate either the 'vitality' of a pluralist national heritage or the 'developmental' logic of a global culture. Whether it is in the pragmatist accounts of cultural survival or the teleological vision of cultural viability, the concept of cultural translation can also be traced throughout the normative discourses on modernity (Buden and Nowotny 2009).

Many of these accounts of translation and cultural translation share a number of common characteristics and describe their operation according to the interactionist perspective. Languages and culture are seen as being composed of discrete units that have a bounded form. However, the boundaries that surround both the general system and the specific units are never rigid but semi-porous. Mobility is also a constitutive feature of cultural translation. As different units interact with each other, they invariably adjust their internal structures to absorb or repel the presence of the other. This defensive response of rigidity or the creative process of interlinking is never neutral. It can sharpen the processes of differentiation by either reconfiguring the meaning of existing forms, by concentrating on its boundary function, or creating new networks of affiliation through the installation of bridging points. As ideas and objects interact with each other, their original meaning is disturbed and new assemblages are forged through the recombination of the available and foreign units. In some instances, the presence of the foreign can be filtered, to the extent that it becomes almost imperceptible, or persist in a state of residual incommensurability. The force of contact can shear away distinctive edges, twist old forms into new, or produce hybrid combinations. The key feature of this dynamic operation is in the transformation of a bounded cultural unit through the energy that transpires from the conjunction of opposing or previously unrelated units.

The strength of this interactionist perspective on transformation is that it attends to the way innovation occurs through the robust process of mutation, appropriation, assemblage and reconfiguration. It highlights the productive force of collision and intermingling. It also attends to the indissoluble nature of difference in the context in which the other is addressed. However, critics have claimed that this model collapses when the access to the means of representation is unequal (Pratt et al. 2010). I would argue that, while power differentials impair and distort the possibility of cultural translation, this does not prevent all forms of communication. Where this perspective on cultural translation hits a more radical limit is in the extreme instances of colonial rule that entailed the non-recognition of the other as human and imposed a determined blindness towards the value of other cultures. For example, in the British declaration that Australia was *terra nullius*, there was no attempt to excise, transfer or appropriate any indigenous claims to sovereignty, but simply a presumption that there was nothing there to divest of authority. In this situation, the colonial logic was oblivious to any sign of cultural identity, and the Aboriginal people were registered as if they were part of the continent's flora and fauna. This, of course, was a pure legal fiction. In reality early settlers often mingled with and were indebted to Aboriginal communities.

Missionaries set out to convert the so-called wretched of the earth, while writers and painters immersed themselves in a culture which they regarded as superior to any other that they were to witness. However, even if this history of exchange, respect and adoration is reclaimed, the method for explaining cultural innovation still appears inadequate. How can an interactionist perspective address the cultural transactions that occur in a context where the invading culture does not so much appropriate the indigenous culture as simply bypass the process of cross-cultural transcoding and evaluation? While there is much to gain from the interactionist perspective on cultural translation, I will argue that it is not a sufficient basis for explaining the totality of cross-cultural interactions. In particular, I will return to my original example about the difficulty of interpreting contemporary Aboriginal art, given that it emerged in a context where there was little exchange and no genuine cultural recognition, and the subsequent creative force seems to come from the void.

Can There Be Cultural Translation between the Global and the Local?

In his recent book *The Cosmopolitan Imagination*, Gerard Delanty argues that the concept of cultural translation is the key term for grasping the dynamic of transformation in modernity. His conception of cultural translation is mindful of the relativist pitfalls of the interactionist perspective. However, while it stresses the feedback effect generated by the interpretative and evaluative process in cross-cultural exchanges, this account of cultural translation as a form of immanent transcendence also locates the moment of creative transformation at the point in which 'one culture interprets itself in light of the encounter with the other'. Delanty argues that the transformation is marked by two key shifts in perspective. First, the encounter exposes the diversity of ways of seeing the world – the relativization of values. Second, the re-evaluation of prior standpoints then provokes the search for a new normative framework. As one culture adjusts itself from the encounter with the other and sees itself from the foreigner's point of view, it develops the potential to transcend itself and adopt a new kind of universalist perspective and self-understanding that Delanty regards as the 'cosmopolitan condition of living in translation' (2009, p. 196).

This is a significant departure from the interactionist perspective, as it highlights a specific set of normative dimensions of global culture such as human rights discourse and democratic political projects, as well as the expansion of new communication technologies that stimulate the possibility of all culture 'becoming more and more translatable' (Delanty 2009, p. 194). This perspective asserts that a global culture is already in the making, takes a positive view of the encounter between different cultures, and thereby defines global culture as a 'third space', or the medium of translation. Delanty has gone so far as to argue that the intensification in cultural translation is not just an effect of modernity, but also a constitutive force in the formation of modernity. He argues that, in their encounter with difference, cultures can develop both an image of otherness and a means for imagining an alternative social world. This normative quest for an alternative is therefore the driver that is found within cultural translation, modernity and critical cosmopolitanism and also the principle that holds them within a common circuit. According to Delanty, both the self-transformative dynamic of modernity and the creative encounters of cosmopolitanism arise from the double process of translation. Transformation occurs at the level of the particular, as one culture is translated with another, and at a general level, as local culture translates into the third space of global culture. This model of critical cosmopolitanism can be read as a counter to the apocalyptic vision of globalization as a totalizing system that is characterized by its ruthless disregard for boundaries and its pursuit of unfettered mobility (Bauman 2000). It also enriches the sociological accounts on the 'new spirit of capitalism', which reduce the conceptual task of translation to the managerial functions performed by an army of consultants, negotiators and mediators (Boltanski and Chiapello 2007).

From this perspective, cosmopolitanism is not determined by ethical claims for the respect of human differences or political judgements on the just distribution of rewards, but is driven by the process of cultural translation. However, what remains unclear in the interpretation of cultural translation as a form of immanent transcendence is the extent to which the evaluative process presupposes interaction. Does this interaction need to operate in a context of mutuality? Can it still work in situations of profound inequality? Is it conceivable that one culture is capable of developing an evaluative response to another, and to global culture at large, when its own cultural worldview has been annulled or bypassed? And, more generally, if global culture is not only defined by a set of universalistic principles and communicative technologies, but also refers to a mode of becoming that lacks a singular origin, modifies its structure with each iteration, recognizes no absolute boundary and abjures any prescribed direction, then how does this affect the border that distinguishes inside/outside, local/global, self/other, and the nexus between boundedness and mobility (Poster 2008)?

To tease out the need for a new conceptual framework adequate

to representing the relationship between cultural translation, cosmopolitanism and global culture, let me return to the question posed by
Ihab Hassan: How do you interpret this work of art by an Aboriginal
artist? The very existence of Aboriginal artworks seems to defy
all historical projections and thrusts us into the jaws of a cultural
paradox. Contemporary Aboriginal art emerged in a context in which
Aboriginal culture was regarded as obsolete by mainstream society
and the existence of cultural boundaries was not even registered. From
this perspective, Aboriginal culture should have been doomed. Yet the
example of Aboriginal art disturbs this apocalyptic conclusion. Out
of the 'cataclysms' of colonial domination there are now numerous
accounts of the processes by which indigenous groups have adopted
new media to renew traditional cultural forms and have embraced the
communicative technologies of globalization to create new networks
of cultural belonging (Parks 2005). The novel techniques and unique
cultural forms that emerge from these practices are usually interpreted
as evidence of the vitality of cultural translation in the age of globalization.

   While there has been considerable attention paid to the pioneering
role of key individuals and the adoption of new circuits of communication in this process of cultural reconfiguration, hybridization and
innovation, it is not clear how a model of cultural translation can
address the creativity that seemingly arises from a void. How could
there be an interaction, let alone a dialogue, when it was presumed that
Aboriginal communities have lost touch with their own cultural base?
If this is the predicament of Aboriginal people, and they are aware
of their loss of control over both the composition of their own idi-
omatic boundaries and the flows that enable a generalizing system for
exchange, how then do they create for themselves a unique and distinct
cultural language? We need to take a step back and explore how this
cultural production emerged without the 'rub' of rival symbols interacting with each other.

   One must take another view into this creative process and consider
the form of the void – a space in which, at best, only fragments collide,
where cultures do not meet as rivals, but where identification occurs
in the absence of coherent models, and where signs seem to leap out
of their history. In short, I am arguing that, as hybridity emerges
from cultural translation, it is not just evidence of the nexus between
boundedness and mobility but also the creative expression of a paradoxical force: the materiality of the void. Naoki Sakai redefined the
starting point of cultural translation in a similar manner. He shifted
attention away from the interactive dimension, and proposed that
cultural translation is a mode of address that occurs in a field where

the subject is absent and the ground for securing shared meaning is not yet formed. In the commonplace multicultural scene, where a plurality of languages and perspectives cohabit, it cannot be taken for granted that the subject to whom you address yourself can understand you, just as there is no guarantee that their worldview can converge with your own. Sakai is referring to situations where everyone speaks outside of their own language and there is a 'will to communicate despite an acute awareness of how difficult it is'. He defines this social space as a 'non-aggregate community' (Sakai 1997, p. 7). I will now examine the emergence of a process of communication where the aim was not to deliver a pre-existing message to the next generation in a family, or to a like-minded neighbour, or even to a knowable world at large. Rather, I will focus on the act of communication as a mode for both inventing a new addressee and creating the ground upon which such an exchange can occur. I will suggest that the wordless awe that is provoked by contemporary Aboriginal art is due to its presentation of a rear mirror view of the groundlessness of creation and the void to which it gives form.

The Void and Cultural Translation

Cultural translation entails a commitment to imagining an alternative community. The most useful contribution offered by the conceptualization of cultural translation as immanent transcendence is its connection to the driving force of the imaginary. The imaginary is not in contrast to reality; it is the process by which an individual and culture are constituted from the 'unceasing and undetermined image' of the inner void and near infinity of worldly differences (Castoriadis 1997b, p. 3). Cultural translation is both an inventive leap that creates *ex nihilio* and an interactive process that emerges from the 'succulencies' of mixture, fusion and hybridity (Glissant 1997, p. 21). It is motivated by the threat of effacement and the desire to enunciate identity amidst a particular combination of signs. To address this relationship I will now turn to the emergence of the Papunya Tula art movement – one of the crucial moments in the emergence of contemporary Aboriginal art. In the first instance, it is worth grasping some bare details about the context in which the art movement emerged. Papunya was a remote camp in the Western Desert. It comprised a diverse group of displaced people from Pintupi, Anmatyere, Arrente, Luritja and Walpiri. Disease and death were endemic in the camp. The elders were also confronted by the problem of educating an 'out of control younger generation, whose delinquency they blamed not on the alcohol or fast cars in which it found expression, but the breakdown of their own authority' (Johnson 2000, p. 190). In short, this community was more like a cluster community composed of a number of displaced and fragmented settlements. There was no single common language that could be used to span their internal divisions or reach the world at large. Collectively they were also aware that a new global culture threatened to overtake their traditional values and worldview. So how did the elders, while both staring at the abyss in which their respective cultures lay and confronting the dazzling force of global culture, produce a vision that could address the contradictions of their reality?

There is now a prevailing consensus that the emergence of the Papunya Tula painting movement began as a form of reutilization of the traditional designs for the purpose of communicating contemporary stories (Morphy 1998; Healy 2008; see also Bardon 1991). It is widely acknowledged that this provided a social platform upon which the youth could establish a connection with their own heritage while moving within their contemporary reality. As Galarrwy Yunupingu has claimed about the adoption of this practice by numerous other communities: 'Painting has paralleled our political struggles to maintain our culture and our rights to land . . . we paint to show the rest of the world that we own the country, and that the land owns us. Our painting is a political act' (cited in Perkins 2003, p. 58). However, I want to extend the discussion on the politics of art beyond the consideration of cultural barriers that impair the flow of messages, by also facing the question that Derrida asks in his own meditation on translation: 'In what language does one write memoirs when there has been no authorized mother tongue?' (1998, p. 31). According to the curator of indigenous art Vivien Johnson, the story of the emergence of the Papunya Tula movement requires a perspective that notes both the traumatic force of a one-sided collision and the radical leap from near cultural extinction.

> These men embarked upon the disclosure of their cultural traditions to the outside world as art in a sophisticated and radical response to the profound trauma their society was experiencing – precisely as a result of that 'coming in'. We do the founders of Papunya Tula artists a disservice if we do not recognise the necessity that inspired their invention of a painting language based on those traditions and suitable in their own terms for an expanding encounter with that world. (Johnson 2000, p. 188)

'The necessity that inspired their invention' was, in Johnson's terms, the struggle between going out to find a language and the ruptures caused by the languages that were already 'coming in'. This dual struggle corresponds to the torsion that Derrida claimed underpinned translation and which he described as the need to overcome the 'surging wave of anamnesia that the double interdict has unleashed' (1998, p. 31). Paul Carter also frames his account of the emergence of the Papunya Tula art movement by registering the turbulent upheaval that was bobbing up within and pulling down the edifices of their culture. For instance, by noting the coincidence between Papunya Tula and the establishment of the Aboriginal tent embassy in Canberra, Carter (2000) inserts a complex analogy between the political act of representation as an alien within one's own homeland and the aesthetic form of articulating a previously unspoken mother tongue. In both instances, the request for reception within the institutions of their homeland stretches the link between hospitality and translation.

Let us pause to trace out these political and cultural acts of self-representation and thereby consider the role of hospitality in what Derrida claims as the 'law of translation'. According to Derrida, our relationship with language is in a perpetual process of translation. He asserts the relationship between speech and language as a double postulation that can only be bridged through translation: 'We only ever speak one language. We never only speak one language' (1998, p. 7). Both these statements can only be true if language can provide a dual sense of hospitality. Through one entrance language provides both the feeling of being at home in the centre of the world and the opening to other worlds. The Aboriginal emissaries faced a similar task – they needed a language that could hold their sense of homeland and would also be suitable 'for an expanding encounter with that world'. This double postulation of translation introduced a peculiar state of distanciation towards language. On the one hand, the act of invention is neither a process of alienation from a pre-existing state nor a form of resurrection through reconfiguration. By combining Derrida's meditation on translation with Hetti Perkins's claim that tradition and innovation are not mutually exclusive in Papunya Tula (Perkins 2003, p. 61), it is possible to develop a new approach towards understanding the function of alienation and the void in cultural translation.

Alienation from 'one's own' culture is usually seen as a necessary stage in the dialectics of cultural renewal. For instance, in a recent essay by Rey Chow, a Chinese-American cultural theorist, there is a close reading of a scene in which a Chinese-American author reflects on the shifting status of symbols as they move from their original source and circulate as part of a diasporic culture within the dominant culture (Chow 2008, p. 567). Such a reflexive exercise obviously presupposes a capacity for cultural translation, and with great scrupulousness Chow notes how this bifocal translator is seeing 'one's own' culture from the inside and from the outside. Chow does not fail to point out that the act of seeing with the eyes of a stranger also involves a process of distortion and diminution. However, her critique does not suggest that the translator's mourning for the loss of completeness and complicity with the objectification of 'one's own' culture is simply an act of betrayal, for cultural renewal and alienation are entangled in a nexus of disavowal and intercepting.

Similarly, the cultural reflexivity in Papunya Tula did not begin with the artists standing slightly apart from their culture and seeing it as a minority culture that was moving in the dominant culture. Such a stance would presume that their culture was already visible and rebounding against the evaluative mechanisms of the dominant culture. The elders of the Papunya Tula did not undergo this kind of reflexivity because their visual order had not yet been formed. By bringing forth a new visual language, there was no sense in which they were betraying their own culture. Similarly, there was no recoil from the negative gaze of the other or alienation in the sense of experiencing fragmentation or loss of contact with the exquisite state of wholeness. For the Aboriginal artists, the journey through the antinomies of representations includes both a confrontation with what Derrida called the 'abyssal problem' and an ecstatic awakening of the cosmopolitan imaginary.[3] Or, in the words of the Mangkaja artist Jakuna Mona Chuguna:

> There is a word we are thinking of now – ngalkara. It means spreading the word. That is what we want to do with this painting, to let people know . . . I have never lost the idea and feeling for my country, where I came from. It is all still in my brain, it is right there. We have that story all of the time. It is more than my memory, it is mangi (a spirit or essence) that I feel. (Cited in Perkins 2003, p. 66)[4]

If the task of cultural translation involves the articulation of something that is ever present but has no mother tongue, then its relationship to alienation is also beyond the melancholic logic of defacement. The lack does not signify an absence of a cultural repository. On the contrary, Perkins argues that Aboriginal people, irrespective of the extent of their travels or their access to technology, have preserved the capacity to imagine a form of overlap and interplay between different worlds. Aboriginal paintings are often read like maps that reveal the nexus between ceremony and country. However, Perkins also stresses that these paintings push us into the vortex that exists between the many worlds of the Australian landscape, a topology that she has termed 'parallel universes, other worlds' (2003, p. 63).

But let us take another step back, and ask the question How does this process of negotiating antinomies proceed in a void?

Carter's account of this remarkable journey focuses on the role of a stranger who served as a kind of unwitting guide. Geoffrey Bardon was motivated to come to Papunya as a way of gaining access to non-Western graphic symbols and was driven by the ambition of incorporating their symbols into his own visual language. However, upon arrival, he noted that the children had already achieved a dual level of visual dexterity. In the classroom situation, children could draw stories about 'cowboys and Indians' in the conventional Western mode, but outside, when they played in the sand, they drew stories using traditional symbols. Bardon had the perspicacity to recognize that the children were already moving in two worlds. He also noticed that his presence was never neutral, and with the aid of a translator he invited the children, and then collaborated with the elders, to produce traditional designs on Western media. Carter claims that Bardon's breakthrough occurred when he began to collaborate by mimicking their gestures and improvising in pattern design. By engaging in play-acting with the children and the elders, the door was opened to a unique form of cultural crossover. It was only after the collision, the rattle and rumble of signs rubbing up against bodies, that 'the sparks really began to fly' (Johnson 2000, p. 189). As Bardon claimed: 'I was asking the children to understand my language in theirs. I was asking to be understood in their own language' (Carter 2000, p. 250).

Bardon went to Papunya with the aim of incorporating the traditional imagery into a new graphic language for animation, but then found himself acting as a middleman. His aim swerved from seeking to invent his own visual language to facilitating the collective movement of visual codes from one world to the other. While Carter claimed that Bardon 'behaved like a conductor', it was a very peculiar form of direction that he offered. Bardon did not have a score sheet. There was no ideal in his mind. Carter saw him as someone who literally and figuratively jumped into the compositions – humming, dancing, waving, prompting and calling forth something that he did not comprehend and thus could not sense where it would end. But just as suddenly he would command and gesture towards the completion of a work. By engaging the artists in what Bardon called 'talkings-out', the elements of the story would begin to assemble. They did not simply appear in either a random or a predetermined order. It was neither an act of spontaneous creation nor a visualization of traditional mythology. Something else emerged. Bardon explained this creative transformation as a process of putting the archetypes in flow and then punctuating the rhythm of association. This structure produced a near infinite variation of contextual meanings that Bardon defined under the category of hieroglyphs.

For Bardon the mystery of creativity was always expressed in the paradoxes of spiritual incarnation and through an evocation of the capricious force of natural cataclysm. In his own recollections of the time spent at Papunya, he compared his presence to the sight and sound of his Volkswagen Kombi van.

> It seemed at the time my destiny to carry a swag as an itinerant artist-teacher, the van fitted out to meet a vagabond adventure with cameras, paints and canvas, books and dreams. My vehicle was just like the paintings: beautiful, breathing, functional, living entities. I saw both vehicle and paintings as indestructible; a permanent achievement of the mind, like the painter's achievement in recording poetic and epic thoughts of the continent they loved. . . . In daylight my vehicle was perhaps a speck or dot of blue at Papunya. (Bardon 2000, p. 200)

In order to grasp this strange morphing of specks on the horizon, it is worth recalling Norman Bryson's application of the Japanese concept of *sunyata* – 'emptiness', 'radical impermanence', 'blankness' (1999, p. 87). Bryson adopted the concept of *sunyata* to define a perspectival order that does not privilege the subject as an imperious centre. *Sunyata* is presented as a point against which the unity of self is opposed, or even as a zone through which it must pass in order to achieve a higher unity. According to the visual field of *sunyata*, the I/eye is immersed in an indivisible field of 'radical impermanence'. Passing the act of visual interpretation through the conceptual frontiers of *sunyata* therefore provided Bryson with an alternative to the Cartesian perspective.

Carter's commentary on Bardon's practice and theory of creative transformation and his observations of the effect of Bardon's mediation are also framed by a broader theory that highlights the dynamic role of mobility in language and culture. The interaction between Bardon and the artists at Papunya Tula was an instance of the way in which cross-cultural collaboration can deepen what Carter calls the 'grooves' of specific symbols (Carter 1996, p. 356). Implicit in this theory of symbolic transformation is an acknowledgement of the productive force of the encounter with difference and the attendant experience of surrender to the other. Following from Carter's account of the collaboration between Bardon and the men at Papunya, we could proceed with the assumption that the totality of meaning of an artwork is neither fixed in perpetuity within a sacred-secret covenant that precedes the arrival of others nor freely available to all that are curious, but is produced in the relatively open but also stubbornly opaque process of cultural translation.

Carter's attention to the subtle interplay between traditional and cultural codes, the use of different media, and the haptic force of mime and gesture takes us closer to Ihab Hassan's investigation into the relationship between kenosis and creative transformation. Harold Bloom (1973, p. 85), a fellow Gnostic, also adopted the concept of kenosis to explain the creative process. Bloom argues that the artist must undergo an emptying out of the self in order to make way for his or her precursor. However, in the act of self-abnegation, he claims that there is also a critical process of refilling. According to Bloom, as the precursor is admitted into his or her consciousness, the poet undertakes a response that resembles a swerve. The initial force of the swerve serves to make space for the other, but its ongoing trajectory also produces the counter-effect of wiping away the trace of the other. Kenosis is thereby presented as a grounding of the artist's relation and a distanciation from precursors. Bloom is keen to stress that 'This emptying is a liberating discontinuity' (ibid., p. 87).[5]

Bloom's narrative of creative transformation resembles the dynamic of the creative event outlined by Alain Badiou. However, where Bloom uses the process of kenosis to acknowledge the need to empty the self, Badiou offers an even more radical interpretation of St Paul's concept of kenosis (2003, p. 48). Badiou does not see the process of emptying out as either a horizontal approach towards truth or a negotiated encounter with the other, but as an absolute vertical leap out of the void. The act of giving oneself over to Christ is based neither on an intellectual exercise in interpreting the signs of salvation nor on any inherited racial affiliation with divinity; rather, it proceeds from a subjective gesture. It is in this eruptive and singular event that Badiou also sees the grounding of the universal. The significance of Christ is thus not appreciated by following the story of his life, it is not gained by deducing the meaning of his lessons, and it is certainly not the provenance of his fellow tribe. Christ's sovereignty, as an expression of the universal, does not rely on any particular assemblage of evidence. It does not appear in the incremental process of passing from one stage to another. It possesses an authority that is grasped in the flash of its totality, or it is missed entirely. Badiou claims that there is no spectrum that links intellectual deduction and subjective apprehension. In Bloom's account of kenosis and swerve, translation proceeds as a form of negotiated settlement between different signs. By contrast, Badiou's kenotic revelation liberates translation from being the sum of its parts. And so we can now ask, Does the Aboriginal painting that left Hassan speechless find its awesome power through the function of reconfiguration, or does it arise from the sovereignty of the event? Is their meaning dependent on the secondary dialogue with the corpus of modern art? Do they provide a glimpse of mystic truths that defy language?

In my mind, these questions are pointing in the wrong direction. For instance, while there is no shortage of translators, polyglots and bilingual people, their success is not due to a primal source that is yet to be found. Beyond the instrumental need to gain access to another realm or the awareness of the limitations within one's own language, the motivation for translation also draws from a desire to be present and active in the world at large. Translation exists not because there can ever be a precise equivalence between different languages, but from the endless struggle to make your culture viable and extend its visibility amidst the global forces of dispersion. It thrives in the desire to bring your culture into the cosmopolitan dialogue.

It is a commonplace prejudice to assume that the cosmopolitan eye merely skims the surface of other cultures, fails to see the deeper truths, and is unable to grasp the wrinkled textures of indigenous cultures. The flipside of this prejudice is that the wisdom of indigenous cultures is exclusively bound to their time and place and that this 'deep' perspective always lacks a worldly vision. It is my contention that both Carter's account of Bardon's collaboration with the artists at Papunya Tula and Hetti Perkins's vision of the persistence of an Aboriginal cosmology are parallel outlines of an indigenous cosmopolitanism. Bardon could see how the universal nests in the particular, or, to use Bryson's phrase, how the relationship between the universal and the particular is situated on 'a mobile continuum that cannot be cut anywhere' (Bryson 1999, p. 97). Through these examples I have tied the concept of the void to a cosmopolitan theory of cultural translation. Cultural translation is a form of creativity that, as Benjamin (1972) suggested, generates meaning out of the shards of a broken system. The void is not powerlessness but, as Emily Dickinson said, the 'force that renovates the world' (Dickinson 1970, p. 1563).

9

Collaboration in Art and Society

The debates over the cultural consequences of globalization have too often been confined to an unhelpful binary of homogenization or heterogeneity. Just as it would be simplistic to believe that the prevalence of new uniform standards can control the myriad of ways in which ideas are interpreted, so too it would be ridiculous to gather the bubbling articulation of micro-variables as the human faces of globalization. As a force for social change, globalization is not neatly marked in terms of domination or emancipation. However, if the concepts of hybridity and cultural translation are to enable a rethinking of cosmopolitanism beyond the boosterish and apocalyptic visions of globalization, then it will also be necessary to relate these concepts to the political transformations associated with neo-liberalism. In the past two decades, as the world has become more polarized, there has been a radical explosion in activist, dialogical, interventionist and tactical media art practices in almost every corner of the world. These shifts in artistic practice provide a powerful prism for examining the political tensions, paradoxes and contradictions of this era. In this chapter I will focus on the resurgence of interest and the innovations in artistic collectives, and highlight the emergent strategies for self-organization, engagement with issues of control over public space, and the 'hijacking' of new media for global communication.

In 1996 Nicolas Bourriaud proposed the concept of 'relational aesthetics' in order to identify the common artistic practices that were evident in the exhibition *Traffic*. He subsequently claimed that the 'interhuman sphere: relationships between people, communities,

individuals, groups, social networks, interactivity' that existed in the
work of artists such as Pierre Huyghe, Maurizio Cattelan, Gabriel
Orozco, Dominique Gonzalez-Foerster, Rirkrit Tiravanija, Vanessa
Beecroft and Liam Gillick was expressive of an emerging and compelling trajectory within the international scene (Bourriaud 2002b). In
1997 the curators Hans Ulrich Obrist and Hou Hanru launched an
open-ended exhibition called *Cities on the Move*.[1] They proposed a
model in which the exhibition would be reinvented in each location,
and their aim was to face the dramatic changes in urban development
by combining architectural methods for the design of the exhibition
and collaborations between artists and architects. In a subsequent partnership with Charles Esche (2001), who had already suggested that a
distinctive feature of contemporary art was the redefinition of utopian
thinking in the form of what he called a 'modest proposal', Hou Hanru
described the exhibition space of the 2002 Gwangju Biennale as a platform for initiating new ideas and developing critical social relations. By
inviting artists and artistic collectives to create their own spaces within
the framework of the biennale, the two men proposed to shift the focus
of the exhibition from the display of artworks selected on purely aesthetic terms to the making of 'pertinent works' that addressed issues
arising from the specific cultural realities in their own everyday lives.
Hanru and Esche placed faith in the self-organizational and networking skills of the small-scale collectives and were thus willing to devolve
power away from the central role of the artistic director (Esche 2002).
In this small step the biennale project opened itself to the challenge of
creating a dialogue amongst a diverse range of independent collectives,
many of whom were meeting for the first time, but also to the opportunity to engender ongoing and unpredictable encounters. Hence, the
exhibition space was not conceived as a once-and-for-all event, but
more 'like a Pandora's box' (Hanru 2002a, p. 31).

   Reflecting on the intensified patterns of global circulation of artists
and the hybridization of cultures associated with globalization, the
Cuban curator Gerardo Mosquera (2003) proposed that there was a
need for a paradigm shift in the understanding of the circulation of
artists working in the South. He stressed that, in the absence of new
South–South circuits, and given the prevalence of North–South axial
routes, the cultural contours of globalization would continue to reproduce prevailing imperialist inequalities and primitivist stereotypes.
However, Mosquera also suggested that collaborative projects which
were initiated in the South had potential to pluralize both the vernacular and the contemporary meaning of art and culture. Similarly, the
former director of Documenta XI, Okwui Enwezor (2005), claimed
that the emergence of new artistic collectives in Africa and in other

parts of the world was not just a symptom of the crisis in the modernist aesthetic ideology but also representative of a new 'social aesthetic'. The Long March collective in China, dissatisfied with the populist hype of becoming global, developed an alternative model of cultural exchange that its members defined as 'inter-local' (Jie 2005, p. 125). Reflecting on the emergence of socially engaged artistic practices, the British critic Suzi Gablik (1995) argued against the conventional modes of aesthetic appreciation and outlined a new concept of 'connective aesthetics'. A decade later the American academic Grant Kester (2004) continued the examination into artistic experiments with empathic modes of communication and proposed that this emergent approach could be understood as a form of 'dialogical art'. Finally, the Swedish curator Maria Lind (2007) marked this period, in which she saw an upsurge of interest in interdisciplinary practice, a willing immersion into popular culture, and an extension of the affinities with political activist and minority groups, as the beginning of a 'collaborative turn' in contemporary art.

These few examples of artistic practices, curatorial strategies and critical commentary suggest that, in this period, we witnessed not only a spontaneous shift in practice but also the first truly global movement in art. There can be little doubt that these figures were mutually aware of one another's work and ideas. For, even though they live far apart, they participate in a new global public sphere that is comprised of interconnected art schools, cultural events and media networks. However, my concern is not to untangle the anxious web of influence that links each of these nodes to a central artistic pool of reference. My interest lies more in the way each of these critical observations and curatorial strategies is engaged with the critical transformations of neo-liberalism. Political theorists and sociologists have argued that, in the context of neo-liberalism, capital has extended its own terrain by colonizing the lifeworld of consumers. It is my contention that the shift in artistic practice from image production to the initiation of scenes for the replaying of social relations provides a critical perspective on this broader social transformation. For instance, when Bourriaud invokes Duchamp's declaration that in his use of the mass object he discovered a 'kinship with the merchant', this is not simply a commercial boast but a critique of the relation to commodities in the context of capital (Bourriaud 2002a, p. 23). It also reignites the hope that art, even as it relies on the material objects and social relations of everyday life, can also provide either a sudden moment of insight or a slow cumulative process of understanding of 'what it means for something to mean something' (Verwoert 2008, p. 226).

While the prominence of collaborative artistic practices is now unmistakeable, the status of its aesthetic value and the measurement of its social effects is very much in dispute. In particular, there is considerable unease over the similarity between collaborative methodologies in art and the new corporatist ideology that promotes networking. Claire Bishop and Hal Foster were among the first to attack the aesthetic merits of relational aesthetics (Bishop 2004; see also Foster 2003). In the journal *Third Text*, Stewart Martin (2007) described relational aesthetics as the 'aestheticization of novel forms of capitalist exploitation', while in the same issue Rustom Bharucha (2007) went so far as to describe it as a 'pseudo-democratic' neo-liberal appropriation of the creative industries rhetoric of vitality and autonomous performance. These disputes over the status of relational aesthetics culminated in a debate between Bourriaud and Rancière. In *Aesthetics and its Discontents*, Rancière dismissed relational aesthetics for being merely derisive of power and turning art in on itself. He also rejected both the aesthetic value and the political force of artistic strategies that are formed in direct relationship with new social movements. In fact, he goes so far as to describe the effect of relational art as 'undoing the alliance between artistic radicality and political radicality' (Rancière 2009, p. 21). This rather severe judgement is not, as Nicolas Bourriaud (2009a) has counter-claimed, a result of either his failure to see the actual aesthetic choices or his lack of attunement towards the politics of precarity. His criticism comes directly from his link between the aesthetic and political act of division and the distribution of the sensible. Relational art is, in his view, always heading towards some point of convergence, in which the meaning is determined by the rule of ethics. Now an ethical turn in art might not sound so objectionable. However, for Rancière, 'ethics is a kind of thinking in which an identity is established between an environment, a way of being and a principle of action' (2009, p. 110). In short, Rancière rejects relational art because he sees it as being subsumed by a moral imperative to achieve consensus. By giving itself to the service of predetermined social or ethical commitment, it also suffocates its own potential to produce radical dissensus.

It is the combination of humanist ideals of sharing and the market logic of outsourcing that has been a source of considerable critical irritation. The idealism is quickly dismissed as evidence of naïvety, whereas the mercantile spirit is considered as proof that the sole aim of the artist is to exploit others. What is more difficult to register is the possibility that this conjunction does not necessarily lead towards the absolute elevation of one part over the other. Surely the task of the critic is neither to go beyond a dismissal of every principle because of the whiff of artistic opportunism, nor to participate in a premature celebration of the promised utopia, but rather to evaluate the capacity for collaborative art to redefine its aesthetic materiality in the way it 'traverses' the subjectivity of diverse groups of people.

In this chapter I will examine artistic practices that have occurred since the 1990s to argue that the turn towards collaborative and 'community-based' forms of artistic practice is one of the means by which artists participate in the mediation of a cosmopolitan imaginary. I will examine whether the shift from the position of the artist as producer to the artist as a collaborator in the construction of social knowledge not only leads towards consensual representations of other people's reality, but also redistributes agency in the production of social meaning. Drawing from Jacques Rancière's concept of 'the equality of intelligences' and George E. Marcus's recasting of the relationship between the anthropologist and the native as 'epistemic partners', I will propose that, as artists redefine their function as 'context shifters rather than as content providers' (Kester 2004, p. 1), they become more intimately involved in the production and mediation of a cosmopolitan imaginary.

Genealogies of Collaboration

At first glance, much of the art that focused on social relations, political activism and urban interventions in the late 1990s appears to be on a continuum with earlier artistic experiments in community-building, protest actions and street life. Collectives and collaborative art production were a feature of Dadaism, Surrealism and Constructivism in the early parts of the twentieth century, and were then revived in the 1960s in Fluxus, Conceptual, community-based, muralist and feminist art movements. Lucy Lippard (2007) has recently declared that 'the greatest legacy of the 1960s (which took place in the ensuing decades) is the community based arts'. At that time, artists such as the Brazilians Hélio Oiticica and Lygia Clark had already devised techniques for reaching out to new audiences and including them as part of the construction and experience of the work. Oiticica and Clark used the slogan 'individuality within collectivity' to redefine both their affiliation with communities and the process of co-production. They argued against the modernist tradition of art as an autonomous object and promoted the idea that the work of art finds its affirmation in both the active experience of the public and the reclamation of the networks by which objects and knowledge circulate (Enwezor, in Brett 2008). These generous tendencies, which influenced pioneers of conceptual art such as Cildo Meireles and subsequently found expression in the European and American contexts, lead to what Lippard called a 'retreat' from the institutional contexts of art. Community art and public art projects were often motivated by a disavowal of the artwork as a commodity and a rejection of the art institution's separation from everyday life.

In the introduction to the first art historical edited collection of essays on collectivism, Blake Stimson and Gregory Sholette claim that the distinctive feature of the art collectives that emerged across the world in the postwar period was neither the religious promise of redemption nor the economic redistribution of surplus capital, but rather a social agenda: 'taking charge of social being here and now . . . engaging with social life as production, engaging with social life as the medium of expression'. Stimson and Sholette (2007, p. 13) acknowledge that, throughout the twentieth century, internationalist ideals were a prominent feature in the manifestos produced by artists and collective structures were a recurring element in artistic movements. However, they also argue that these precursors of contemporary forms of collaboration were incomplete or partial manifestations, insofar as they failed to develop the organizational potential and articulate a radical voice that would define 'collectivisation as a vital and primary artistic solution'. They concluded that greater emphasis on collaborative and collective practice was precipitated by the socio-political transformations associated with neo-liberalism.

Will Bradley (2007) has also argued that the origins of the shift in artistic practice lie in the ruins of the 'relative defeat of the 68 uprisings'. Bradley claimed that the failure of the left to make a decisive social transformation in this period prompted a loss of faith in vanguardist forms of social organization. However, it also spawned the emergence of social movements that sought to create a vision of society based on non-hierarchical relations. The aim of these new social movements was no longer to be a spearhead formation that led the way for the liberation of all in the future, but rather the embodiment and realization of emancipatory forms that exist in the here and now. The critical approach of the new movements stand in contrast – in fact, Bradley calls it a 'reversal' of the positionality of the earlier vanguardist movement.

Anja Kanngieser (2008) illustrates the difference between modern and contemporary collectives by citing the recurring assumptions in both the Dadaist and Situationist International movements that mainstream art was so complacent and corrupt that it deserved a good 'thrashing'. For most of the twentieth century, artists also presumed that it was their duty to grab the citizen and 'shake him into life'. Through artistic strategies that relied on scandalous provocation, sensory disorientation or moral outrage, they assumed that they could 'coerce the public' into new forms of social action. Underlying this violent reaction to bourgeois art and the contemptuous attitude to the common citizen was the assumption that ordinary concepts and habitual knowledge systems were complicit in processes of mystification, subjugation and alienation. The artist's ability to 'awaken the citizen within us' (Blanchot 1989) implied that they were either already in possession of a clear-sighted perspective or, like the Situationists, that they believed they could invent techniques that would 'teach' citizens how to stop being passive consumers and become self-governing. Similar strategies could be found in the work of conceptual artists such as Hans Haacke, who sought not just to debunk the piety and propriety of cultural institutions but also to unzip the dignity of the elites who sought prestige by their association with the arts. As Lucy Lippard (1973) has noted, the 'escape strategies' employed by conceptual artists were premised on the need to bypass the dependencies upon the mainstream gallery–museum–market system and to relocate art in the midst of the more prosaic sectors of everyday life. However, while conceptual artists in the USA and Europe saw themselves as exercising a form of revolt against the fetishization of the art object, the manner in which they initiated a democratization of aesthetic practice still left many questions hanging. First, if the aim is to change society, is the periphery the best place to start? Second, what kind of insight comes after shock? Third, can there be an open dialogue when members of the public are constructed as ignorant dupes? And, finally, did the dematerialization of the art object encourage the rematerialization of the social process as art?

Neo-Liberalism as Social Context

By the end of the 1980s, there was a substantial shift in the social context and the cultural conditions in which art operates. With the final collapse of Soviet hegemony and the triumph of neo-liberalism, the spaces of civic life in Western liberal states were also dramatically transformed. The primary institutions of socialization – education, welfare and culture – were all systematically subjected to the logic of economic rationalism and increasingly fragmented as a series of private 'service providers' entered the sector. Transnational companies were also utilizing the principles of flexibility, as they began downsizing, outsourcing and restructuring their labour forces into flat cellular organizational modalities and placing greater emphasis on local innovation and autonomous individualism. While these transformations are now commonplace features of discussions on globalization, as is the understanding of attendant shifts in emphasis on consumerism, lifestyle and mediated interactivity for the 'global self', what is less familiar is the connection between these emergent social conditions and the new social practices in contemporary art. As Brian Holmes (2007b) has noted, the slogan used by anti-globalization protestors in London – 'Our resistance is as transnational as capital' – was also expressive of the aesthetic practices which relied on the same digital technologies and information networks as global corporations, but also extended the context and form of social relations.

Mobility and transgression were, for most of the twentieth century, considered to be the critical features of the avant garde. However, in the neo-liberal context, the aim of 'going beyond' the boundaries of convention is no longer seen as a radical gesture but as part of a managerial mindset for negotiating the opportunities of the global world. Hence, the cultural critic Susan Buck-Morss (2003) is quick to suggest that the celebration of mobility and transgression in contemporary art is just a camouflage against the insecurity and displacement that is heightened by neo-liberal principles. The sociologists Zygmunt Bauman (2000) and John Urry (Urry et al. 2006) have a more nuanced vision, as they evoked the ambivalence in the contemporary manifestation of power by claiming that it tends not towards new points of consolidation but towards a perpetual fluidity that involves a process of 'unmooring' from any social base. Writing against the tide of both the fatalistic pronouncements on the end of modernity and the triumphalist paeans to neo-liberalism, Jacques Rancière (2007a) offers a refreshing account of the capacity of art to modify the realm of the 'visible, sayable and possible', or what he calls the 'fabric of the sensible'. Artists, he claims, constantly renew the interface with the political as they alter the tempo, redirect the circulation, juxtapose different elements, or separate units that are normally kept together in everyday life. However, given the transformation of the conditions for the dissemination and reception of art by the complex dynamics of mobility, Rancière also stresses that it is part of the function of art to address the scene in which the public effects of art operate, and the extent to which these effects will inevitably remain uncertain. The emancipatory function of art is thus linked to its paradoxical location: it is both alienated from the hegemonic structures of power and constituted in the flux and interstices of everyday life.

Rancière's perspective on art and politics places greater emphasis on agency and expresses confidence in the emancipatory potential of social interactions. I will adopt his approach in order to question the extent to which the biopolitics of neo-liberalism has monopolized the structures and forms of everyday life. The new work paradigm, which valorizes creativity, self-motivated individuality, and the transformation of dedication to the work ethic from a social duty to a personal lifestyle choice, is central to the Janus-faced condition of flexibility/ precariousness in contemporary society. There is now a greater expectation that change, insecurity and innovation is the dominant feature of working life. In this context, the transgressive and dynamic aspirations of art have been appropriated by the rhetoric of 'thinking outside of the box' that is now at the forefront of corporate ideology. The idealized horizons of creative practice have thus partially merged with the normative expectations in the burgeoning sector of immaterial labour that encompasses creative design, marketing, public communication and cultural industries. This corporatist mimicry of artistic styles, and the correlative means by which artists have adopted the tools developed by corporations, has inspired new forms of political resistance. For instance, during the anti-globalization movements that emerged in the 1990s, artists were engaged in the critique of neo-liberalism, not as members of a mass bloc of unified opponents, but as affiliates that adopted and adapted many of the emergent modes of agency, techniques of practice and codes of communication. In order to clarify the critical role that artists might play in contemporary society, I will now outline four emergent characteristics of collaborative practice.

Four Characteristics of Collaborative Practice

The space of art

One of the most distinctive features of contemporary collaborative practice has been the shift in the mode of institutional engagement. Artists have sought to rethink the site of the museum or the gallery as part of a broader communicational system. The New York collective Group Material used exhibition spaces not as sites for display but as locations for public fora. Lucy Orta claims that her work can bring a certain problem to a point of clarity only when there is open debate among different people. In these collaborations the function of the museum has taken a new focus:

> I don't see museums as spaces any longer, I see them as part of a larger management team which help co-ordinate the various collaborations of the artistic process. . . . I have found that an exhibition can form a role to both reflect upon a subject and raise concerns to another level of debate. (Orta 1999)

A crucial feature of this collaborative practice is the dynamic incorporation of all elements of the museum and gallery structures. This goes against the hierarchical division that separated the role of the artist and curator from public programming and technical 'support staff'. According to Orta, rather than operating following to a romantic model of creative practice, with the artist at the apex of a vertical and sequential chain of command, the preferred mode for developing ideas is by working in an open horizontal sphere. The realization, fabrication and public dissemination of the work occurs in the process of actualizing the idea, rather than through its compartmentalization and distribution in terms of the exclusive categories of creativity, production and promotion.

These horizontal modes of organization and institutional alliances have been a feature of many collectives that were forged during the anti-globalization movement and the global anti-racist networks (Kopp and Schneider 2003). Old museums, cool galleries, or even the networks of new media were no longer the polar extremes of dead and living sites, but nodes that could be utilized for igniting democratic dialogue. As the curator Hou Hanru has argued, art institutions are not fixed into a permanent state, and it is naïve to be automatically opposed to all institutions 'because society itself is already very institutionalized and there is no way for you to get out of it. Therefore, the only thing you can do is to use the existent institutions and change it from the inside' (2002b, p. 15).

The politics of resistance

With the examples of the Danish artist collective Superflex and the South Korean collective Mixed Rice, who work intensively with the existing conditions in local communities and the tools furnished by global experts, the curator Charles Esche has argued that artists are no longer concerned with eschewing the category of art, but rather utilize the various spaces of art to permit new levels of creative exchange. Esche sees these collaborative models as indicative of a new pragmatic politics that is seeking to convert, co-opt and critique institutions from the inside rather than from a distance. By connecting available material and institutional resources to social aspirations, Esche claims that artists now proceed through a methodology that he defines as 'modest proposals' (2005, p. 16).

While there is no illusion as to the perils and polarizations that have been accentuated by neo-liberalism, there has been a fundamental shift in the way artists address their adversaries. Artists who participate in political activism are no longer representing themselves as 'warriors' entering a battlefield in order to eliminate the enemy and capture the ground that is then returned to the oppressed masses. There is now a recognition that the lines of contestation and the affiliations between rival groups in the 'movement of movements' are much more fuzzy (Holmes 2007b). Kester (2004, p. 9) also contends that the parameters of what he calls 'dialogical art' now extend beyond the aesthetic object and include wider forms of public engagement, whereby participants not only respond to artistic initiatives but also shape the communicative process. Hence, Kester argues that these projects tend to raise questions over the boundary of inclusion and exclusion in public dialogue, presenting situations in which people from different social positions or perspectives are invited to discuss common issues. The role of the public is not only switched from that of witnesses of a spectacle to one of participants in a situation, but also extended to their being a constitutive partner actively involved in the whole field of meaning.

Collective authorship

Okwui Enwezor (2005) has noted that, while the earlier historical art collectives tended to be 'based on permanent, fixed groupings of practitioners working over a sustained period', the current collectives are comprised of flexible membership with 'non-permanent course of affiliation, privileging collaboration on a project basis rather than a permanent alliance'. In his analysis of the African collectives Le Groupe Amos and Huit Facettes, he emphasizes that their 'direct actions', which range from creating a network for the transfer of existing skills to utilizing new media techniques for self-governance, are redefining the terms of a public sphere and extending the Western conception of the sovereign subject (Enwezor 2007). He optimistically claims that these 'direct interventions' into specific issues by non-violent means not only create a new space in which the subject is empowered to recognize their ownership of public rights, but also form a 'new politics of the subject' – one which is not bound by the anxieties of authenticity and originality that constrained and ultimately undermined the collectivist spirit in Western modernism.

Vernacular cosmopolitanism and global mobility

In a project called *Liminal Spaces*, artists were invited to address the historical traffic artery that connects Jerusalem and Ramallah, known as Road 60. The curators described the condition of this road as 'prototypical of the alienation, segregation and fragmentation that characterise the Israeli methods of occupation'. They noted the plethora of laws, checkpoints and barriers that have been introduced to restrict the mobility of the Palestinians. The central section of Road

60, which is located within Jerusalem, was relocated and widened in the 1980s to follow the strip of no-man's-land that previously divided the city. What was once planned as a 'boulevard for a united city' became, in reality, a wide buffer zone in the shape of an urban highway. Henceforth the road was transformed into the front line for detaining and diverting Palestinian traffic. During the course of this project, the curators claimed that they needed to repeat that their aim was not 'meant to offer a model for peaceful co-existence' but to provide a 'platform of resistance'.[2]

Superflex's participation in the *Liminal Spaces* project involved a collaboration with the Palestinian Broadcasting Commission to develop an application for Palestine to gain entry into the Eurovision Song Contest. Yael Bartana undertook a photographic documentation of the efforts made by the Israeli Committee against House Demolition to rebuild Palestinian houses. While Bartana sought to record the small gestures of cross-cultural co-operation, Superflex's proposal was premised on the hope that the Palestinians would win and thereby automatically qualify to host the subsequent contest.

These examples from the *Liminal Spaces* project outline the diverse role played by artists within transnational cultural events. They represent a departure from the internationalist exhibitions that either promoted universal commonalities or celebrated cultural differences. These artistic practices and curatorial strategies simultaneously pose the need to identify local civic needs alongside cross-cultural, regional and even global conceptions of human rights, in a way that functions more according to Mouffe's logic of interested agonistic pluralism than the Habermasian notion of deliberative democracy, which is premised on the mutuality of necessarily disinterested subjects. This dual perspective on the interface between the need to have an attachment to specific place and to participate in the broader debates on what it means to be human is influenced by the formation of new transnational social spaces (Doherty 2006). At one level artists have explored the vernacular means by which local communities can bridge seemingly intractable political divides, and at another level they also give voice to fundamental human needs: the right to freedom, to security and to find work that can give dignity to their existence. The slogan 'Our goal is mobility' has provided the banner to many of the collaborative works developed by Schleuser.net (Heuck et al. 2007). This group describe themselves as an artistic enterprise that works as a lobby organization to affirm the rights of human mobility. Their main concern is to shift the perspective of undocumented migrants from the state-centric view that casts them as a threat to social order and to develop an alternative symbolic order for representing the process of border crossing. For instance, at the inaugural International People Smugglers' Convention held in Graz, they organized an interdisciplinary team to create a working platform that could question the public and professional knowledge on human trafficking. Their aim of achieving a deregulation of border management is perhaps the most idealist end of the global transformations that the German sociologist Ulrich Beck (2006) describes as the cosmopolitanization of cultural and social systems.

Protagonist art

Throughout this section I have drawn on a select number of artworks from all corners of the world. This selection gives an indication of the extent to which common characteristics in artistic practice have emerged in different places. Focusing on specific features of their practice has helped sharpen my argument concerning the emergence of distinctive qualities. However, it is also necessary to acknowledge the overlap of many of these characteristics in such artworks. I would now like to turn my attention to the way artists can bring together communities which are stuck in conflicted territories – the violent no-go zones of modern cities that civil and welfare authorities seem incapable of reaching. Such projects provide examples of the way artists not only gain access to rival communities but also participate in the production of non-violent events. In this context I would like to discuss *Nine* (2003), a project by the Panamanian artist Brooke Alfaro. Alfaro approached and, in time, gained the trust of two rival gangs from Panama City. The gangs had been locked in street battles that had resulted in the death of numerous members. For almost a year Alfaro talked with members of the gangs and their families and friends. He then proposed that each gang be videotaped interpreting the same song by El Roockie, a popular rap artist whose lyrics had already bridged the worlds of different parts of the city. After each gang performed their own version, Alfaro arranged for the two videos to be screened simultaneously, side by side, in the contested suburb of Barazza. A street was closed off and makeshift stands were installed for the projectors. With its internal lights turned off and windows covered by bed sheets, an old apartment block was converted into a giant public screen. Spectators from within and outside of the neighbourhood gathered.

In one sense, the event consisted of a spectacle where gang members were elevated into heroic rap stars. But to confine attention to the visual outcome on the screens would be to miss the point. Brooke Alfaro's stated aim in the project was to unify the rival gangs in the brief and temporary moment of the video. In the final image the two gangs appear to march towards each other on the adjacent screens. One guy tosses a basketball in the direction of the oncoming gang. The ball momentarily disappears just as it crosses the gap between the screens and is then caught by a member of the rival gang. The projection ends in darkness. As the contours of the windows and the building began to reappear in focus, I wondered whether this gesture would provoke or diffuse the tension between the gangs. On the street there was a sudden outburst and the crowd shouted 'More!'

Watching the video documentation of this event, I could see that the art was not just the content on the screen but also the experience on the street, which culminated in the uproar of spontaneous pleasure. At the end of the screening the crowd kept shouting 'More!'. This euphoric demand was not just a sign of ecstatic emotion, but also a declaration that the video had migrated from being an artwork made and owned by Alfaro, and headed towards becoming an anonymous and purely temporal public experience that was co-produced by all the participants.

To return to the question of the issue of the status of Alfaro's work as either a recording of the narcissistic self-images of the gang or an intervention into the violent conflict of Panama City, I will now situate this particular event within the broader curatorial philosophy of the festival *ciudadMULTIPLEcity*. The curators, Gerardo Mosquera and Adrienne Samos, sought to offer a new appreciation of the city and art by initiating a series of collaborations between artists and people in which everyone would be an 'active protagonist', while the city would not be treated as a fixed site within which they could engage in deep historical or sustained sociological investigation but be seen as a force field of dynamic energy. The artists were issued with the challenge of conceiving 'simple, direct works that could reach the people' (Mosquera and Samos 2004, p. 31). If the artists could overcome the usual boundaries that channelled the experience of contemporary art into an elite sphere, the curators believed that this would also break the conventional 'linear' relationship and develop a new kind of 'circular' loop that travelled from 'the city toward art and from art toward the city' (ibid., p. 34). To intensify the process of interchange between art and the public, the curators adopted a decentralized methodology, where nothing was predetermined. All the foreign artists commissioned to produce an artwork for the festival were 'adopted' by a local community. They were also encouraged to conduct their research by means of informal workshops with the members of these communities. The effectiveness of the strategy was measured against the extent to which artists and local members of the city could not only transfer their respective knowledge and information but also formulate plausible responses 'to the intricate problems of urban art being discussed in the world today' (ibid., p. 38).

Set against this standard, we can see that Alfaro's project does not exist within the confines of the artist's authorial capacity either to record an event or to intervene in territorial conflicts. Alfaro's initial proposition of gaining the cooperation of rival gangs, and his subsequent success in projecting the two videos, was quickly overtaken by the unruly and spontaneous elements that emerged in the makeshift city square. The total ambience of art emerged from the refashioning of the dilapidated buildings as screens and the performance of the crowd as it gathered, cheered, sung and called out for more. There is no civic law that can compel this response, and the visual documentation that remains of this event, which is its only tangible and durable object, is also paradoxically a trace reminder of something that is ineffable. As the event occurred on the street, it slipped out of the province of the artist's control and merged with the urban dynamics of buildings and people. The inhabitants of Barazza, as well as the outsiders who gathered there, not only witnessed the projection of two videos of rival gangs performing a rap song, but were also engaged in the creation of an ephemeral space with unexpected urban meanings. This did not present a radical new utopian space, but it did provide a glimpse of an alternative view of the relation between local issues of gang rivalry and global questions on art and the city.

Mediation and the Emergence of the New

The shifts in artistic practice and curatorial strategies have occurred in parallel with a radical critique of the methods for textual representation of the social impact of globalization. In particular, George E. Marcus's account of the change in anthropological discourse, from its original role of documenting the form of traditional cultures to its adoption of a new function that he defines in terms of the mediation of the new, can make a break from the residentialist cultural paradigm and provide an alternative conceptual framework for understanding the relationship between culture and mobility (Marcus 2006).

The founding assumption in the ethnographic approach was that all traditional societies possessed a unique cultural system for comprehending the interplay between social and cosmic forces. Anthropologists dedicated themselves to the task of elucidating and representing the specific cultural system that had been formed by a distinct people over a long period of time in a given place. The novel approach that anthropologists pioneered was based on the formation of a double perspective that included the recognition of their own subject position as an outsider and the need to learn social rules and structures from the insider's point of view. However, the limitation of ethnography was, according to Marcus, that its prevailing mode of representation was archival. At best it could describe the experience of 'being there', and at worst it could objectify the subjects of their study into 'exotic others'.

Marcus's reflections on the limitations of ethnography were stimulated by the social impact of mobility on Tonga, the island where he did his own fieldwork. Tongan culture, he noted, was being reshaped by the ongoing effects of migration patterns. Almost all Tongan migrants either maintained contact with, or eventually resettled on, their home island. Marcus also observed that not only were the Tongans in more regular contact with relatives who had migrated to the USA or Australia, they also experienced routine encounters with tourists, commodities and media from distant parts of the world. These changes led Marcus to argue that the central task of anthropology shifted from recording the structures that conferred a unique cultural identity to a more complex method of investigating how a culture is reshaped through its encounter with these complex forms of mobility. At the forefront of this critique was a re-examination of the role of collaboration, which he acknowledged previously 'led a shadowy existence in formal discussions on method'. Marcus became sceptical of the way anthropologists would seek to establish a 'rapport' with their subjects in order to facilitate the data collection that would be subsequently processed and incorporated within the 'authoritative framework' of the final report.

Lu Jie, director of the Long March artistic project in Beijing, has posed a similar reappraisal of the impact of global mobilities and the interaction between insiders and outsiders. At a time when Chinese art was enjoying a meteoric rise in the global art world, he noted that Chinese artists were still complaining of 'floating' along surfaces that did not connect with the specific meaning and context of their work. Hence Lu Jie drew inspiration from the legend of Mao's Long March. Mao's Long March was at first a military retreat by the Red Army into remote provinces in order to evade the forces of the Kuomintang. This also enabled him to extend the ideological message of communism by becoming a 'sower of seeds'. Lu Jie retraced Mao's steps in reverse. He departed from Beijing and headed towards the provinces. Like Mao, he claimed that, when he hit the road, 'it was the road that led us along'.[3] However, while adopting the Maoist principles of interaction with local communities, he disavowed any claim of centralized power and stressed that the project was not a 'top-down' exercise in bringing artists to the people. Unlike the artists who sought to work within and for communities in the 1960s and 1970s, he stressed that his project always involved a 'bidirectional relationship': 'We are not looking to take things to people, and taking things to people is not to say that they are good things which we provide for their entertainment [sic]. We take them there to be tested, and we bring things from wherever we go back with us.' He also stressed that the project was different to the site-specific practices that were common in the 1980s and 1990s. The aim was not to 'parachute' the global artists into exotic sites, nor was the project a 'bottom-up' exercise that sought to 'catapult' the local people into the global scene. Rather, Lu Jie claims that the purpose was to create situations in which different people would co-produce ideas in the context of the 'current moment' and thereby adopt a lateral perspective on the global and local. He describes this perspective as one that is taken from the 'outside towards the inside'.

Marcus was also critical of the tendency towards an unethical appropriation of the knowledge provided by ethnographic subjects and the presumed distinction between the data donated by insiders and the authoritative report generated by the anthropologist. He argued that this hierarchy was based on an untenable illusion that only the outsider possessed the necessary apparatus for the knowledge-making process. What Marcus observed was that in the age of global mobility, with all its attendant complex interactions, there is also a radical transformation in the agency and reflexive capacities of insiders. The insiders see outsiders coming through a jagged prism of interruption, opportunity, invasion and hospitality. Marcus argued that members of a community no longer see themselves as stewards of a specific worldview rooted in a fixed territory, but as agents that are capable of upholding and modifying the residual forms of their cultural identity as it interacts with forces from remote and unknown parts of the world. The critical task of evaluating an idea in a field of rival concepts is no longer the provenance of the outsider. Marcus argues that the consequence of recognizing the insider's agency in the critical knowledge-making process is that it has elevated the function of collaboration, from being a mere step in establishing a 'rapport' for the purpose of a primary data-gathering task to a more complex feedback process in which both insiders and outsiders are tethered as 'epistemic partners'.

According to Lu Jie, the ambition of the Long March project was to create 'incidents' through which people meet, 'set aside' that which is 'already inside' and, through the coincidence of their encounter, 'change their own current attitudes'. Lu Jie was cognizant that such interactions would exponentially widen the range of desires, topics and issues, and that this multitude could not be contained or resolved within the context of an artistic project, and therefore the project was, from the outset, destined to fail at anything other than involving people in the 'problems of our time'. In the absence of a cultural code that has a predetermined mode of assimilating the effects of radical mobility, everyone is engaged in what Marcus calls 'speculative investigation' on the 'breaking up, and morphing of things that are more anticipated or emergent, than present and explicitly conceived'. When the meaning of things is unstable and unpredictable, then the status of documentation will always remain incomplete. Finding answers to the 'problems of our time' is not as simple as excavating and validating pre-existing forms of cultural knowledge. Marcus is pointing to a challenge in the formation of the cultural meanings that emerge from the interaction with global forces, and whose identity is yet to come. Like Lu Jie, he is claiming that the anthropologist/artist can assume a collaborative role in the gestation of new social meanings. If ethnography and collaborative art projects have recognized the need to move on from documenting culture, then this shift not only heightens the ethical obligations of partnership, it also brings them closer to what Rancière called the emancipatory potential in the associational modalities of learning.

Rancière and Marcus share a belief that ordinary people possess the inherent capacities to create meaning from the context of their everyday lives. By entering into this partnership, the artist is no longer in an observational position of exteriority and so somehow detached from the event, but is inserted as a co-partner whose presence will be one of the forces that shapes the process. Rancière's analysis of art as an emancipatory practice is based on the recognition that both the artist and the public assume an active role in constructing the creative meaning. He stresses that the act of perception is always an active engagement with the conditions of spectatorship. Seeing is not a disembodied intellectual exercise that alienates the body. Seeing is on a continuum with acting. This conjunction of the sensorial process with the manifestation of action suggests that the reception of art is always pregnant with political responses. The work of art becomes an intermediary object in the ongoing production of meaning. Just as the artist is not only transmitting an idea but also creating a field for the transmission of ideas, the spectator no longer 'looks at' or 'for' the meaning that is in the work. Rather than art being seen as a destination point for meaning, it is seen as a station that activates the spectator's self-awareness.

Rancière's confidence in the equality of intelligences has nothing to do with the elevation of prior learning or the delivery of a miraculous formula for instant enlightenment. It is drawn from his belief in the inherent capacity that everyone has for learning by means of association. Metaphorical thinking – seeing similarities amongst dissimilarities – is the process by which he claims that everyone learns their mother tongue: 'by looking at and listening to the world around him, by figuring out the meaning of what he has seen and heard, by repeating what he has heard' (Rancière 2007b). It is the activation of this capacity for perceiving, recognizing, relating and discovering connections that provide for Rancière the crucial link between aesthetic experience and political engagement. By showing a non-hierarchical relationship to knowledge, he moves the understanding of collaboration from a one-sided exercise in instruction to a mutual process of problem-solving.

Collaboration of the order that Marcus and Rancière were referring to in the process of collective knowledge-making can finally step out of the shadowy zone in which proprietorial claims were seemingly suspended but then redistributed to an individual. In art criticism, the sceptical and derogatory approaches towards collaboration follow from a deeply ingrained mistrust of collective production. Critical appreciation of collaboration has tended to remain within an instrumentalist paradigm – within which partners are recruited to complete specialized tasks – and the ethics of this relationship are confined to the process of attribution and remuneration for their specific contribution. A more sceptical view of collaboration would stress that all collective actions carry the flaw of inauthenticity as they seek to conceal individualistic motivations and bypass prevailing social divisions. In this paradigm, the humanist ideals of sharing and empathy are forever doomed by the fatal drive that delivers the benefits of collectivism to a cunning individual. Hence, Hal Foster doubts the value of collective collaboration because, in his view, the artists have never undone their privileged authorial status and, more importantly, have failed to acquire the capacity to have a genuine dialogue with the other. Hence, Foster's critique of participatory and site-specific projects which presumed the centrality of the artist's adoption of the 'outsider position' not only reinscribed the classic ethnographic division between participant and observer, but thereby reduced the 'desired exchange of dialogical fieldwork' (1996, p. 197). As Marcus would argue, this is not the way to do fieldwork in a global world and, as Rancière might say, such a low regard for others is not helpful in art. If the potential encounters and possible exchange between the insider and outsider are now bound as 'epistemic partners', or, to put it in Rancière's terms, if participants proceed on the assumption that there is an 'equality of intelligences', then the status of collaboration is no longer balanced on the purity of their idealist motivations, but rather succeeds or fails in relation to the mediation, rather than the description, of a better sense of 'who we are' and 'how we can live together' (Gillick 2007a, p. 130).

Conclusion

My overriding aim in exploring the shifts in artistic practice, curatorial strategies and cultural theory on collaboration has been to reconceptualize the process of creative production through the prism of mediation. The function of mediation is not to catalogue existing facts, or to extract meaning that is suppressed and thereby give aesthetic or intellectual saliency to ideas that are otherwise dispersed or hidden. Mediation requires more than just familiarization with and representation of known and knowable differences. The crucial link between the process of mediation and evaluation of difference in contemporary culture is that it seeks to go beyond the mere inventory and display of differences and to develop new strategies for cultural understandings. In contemporary culture, there is already a surplus of differences that are in competition with each other. The task of mediation is not to develop a criterion through which cultural differences can be ranked by some universal code or to discover a mode of address that can redeem historical damages. Rather, it seeks to create an understanding of new cultural possibilities by allowing each partner to go beyond their own certitudes and participate in collaborative knowledge-making that is not just the sum of their previous experiences.

The discourse on the political significance of art is still trapped in a debate over whether or not it can make a distinctive difference in the overall social context. For instance, Brian Holmes, one of the most optimistic advocates of the affirmative role played by artists in social transformation, argues that the appropriation of the internet, and in general the hijacking of the new communications technology, has inspired the deployment of subversive performances, mobilized information through global networks, initiated new self-organized counter-globalization tactics, enabled collaborative research on emerging issues, encouraged activists to converge on common sites, prompted legal and medical experts to offer support to artists and protestors, and provided the means to document and disseminate accounts of events that would otherwise be ignored or distorted by the mass media. In short, he claims that artists, like all the other participants in the movement of networked resistance, were motivated by the belief that personal involvement at a micro-level would facilitate global change, and thereby realize the paradoxical social democratic and individualist axiom of 'do-it-yourself geopolitics' (Holmes 2007a, p. 275). Holmes describes the scope and effect of these projects as 'tremendous', and makes the further claim that artistic practice is 'one of the keys' to the emergence of a global public sphere, because it is through the opening up of a theatrical space that it simultaneously represents the prevailing social tensions, holds off the urge for group violence and reorders the 'meaning of abstractions that are no longer adequate to the needs and possibilities of life' (Holmes 2007b). While sharing the view that collective practices are more effective in having an impact on the general social fabric, Lucy Lippard (2007) remains slightly more circumspect concerning the prospects for social transformation, and concludes that even the artists engaged in cyberactivism cannot do much more than 'reflect' larger socio-political shifts.

It is my contention that this level of critical attention has a tendency to miss the point of collaborative art practice. Here, the effects of art tend to be registered only to the extent that they appear outside of its own, apparently autonomous, field. Is art only of value when it transforms or reflects the social? This question presumes that art is external to the existing forms of the social and must do something to the social in order to have a viable function. The place and function of art, as always, operates within the social. However, the new collaborative movements have sought to take an active role in social change, not by means of radical intervention or critical reflection, but through the mediation of new forms of cosmopolitan knowledge.

In general terms, I have sought to characterize the function of contemporary art as a form of mediation. The focus on mediation has helped me rethink both the process of creative production and the identity of the artist. Mediation usually refers to the alteration of an object as it is transferred from one context or symbolic order to another. In the transition, meanings can accrue or fragment. By stressing its function, I am not introducing the legal convention of mediation that usually involves the articulation of two rival viewpoints through a third person. There are some parallels to the exercise in which the externality of the third person can also serve as a screen upon which the different parties can project their own interests and thereby explore alternative possibilities for reconciliation. In general, it has to be said that the active role that mediators take in the construction of the 'way out' of any given crisis is underappreciated. I am proposing that we need a more robust and rigorous understanding of the affirmative role that occurs in mediation. In the 1960s, there was a tendency to assume that mediation was another step towards the alienation of the art object. Even more conspicuous was the association of the mediating function of critics and curators as mere parasites and conformists.

As Joseph Kosuth declared, the radical function of conceptual art was to cut out the role of the art critic (Andreasen and Larsen 2007). Gilles Deleuze promoted an alternative view. For him, the primary aim of mediators is to keep things in flow and to encourage others to get past conventional blockages and find new routes. Following on from Deleuze (1990), we can conclude that the work of artistic mediation occurs in the indeterminate space through which people pass and construct their own narratives. By highlighting the role of mediators in the field of cultural production, I have also sought to relocate the 'idealized' position of the artist at the forefront of the engine of social change and move it inside the processes of social production, so that artists see themselves as mediators in the global and local networks of communication. This shift in position also corresponds to a switch in the ambition that many contemporary artists express: a desire to be *in* the contemporary, rather than to be producers of belated or elevated responses.

In this chapter I have argued that, since the 1990s, contemporary artists have become increasingly aware of the pitfalls of making universal claims and the limitations of confining the meaning of their practice to local perspectives. Their attention is focused on the promotion of a cosmopolitan dialogue between different people that can relate local experiences to global processes. Within this context, the artists neither claim to possess a superior knowledge that they will deliver to the public nor aim to extract the raw information from the local context and then develop this into an aesthetic form with global purchase. There are three different ways in which people are increasingly made to feel global: through the substantive forces of socio-economic and geopolitical globalization that exacerbate inequality; through the imaginary forms of equality that are promised by the existing declarations of universal human rights; and, finally, through the collective struggle to achieve a common framework in which it is possible to recognize the rights of all humanity and a place for everyone in a more equal world (Balibar 2002b). In this chapter I have outlined the complex roles undertaken by artists as they shuttle between different social positions, utilize multi-media formats and engage diverse publics. This complex configuration of place, method and attitude, is as David Beech (2005) claims, demanding a new perspective on the artist and their capacity to be 'independent, collaborative, hospitality'.

While these projects are usually documented, the status of the documentary text or image also blurs the conventional distinction between a purely aesthetic art object and a factual document, as well as providing a fundamental challenge to art criticism. However, such collaborative social practices, and even their attendant documentary forms, provoke serious methodological questions for art criticism. How will art history acknowledge the status of the non-durable, site-specific work that passes through the experience of just a handful of people? Whose witness statement will be necessary to validate the artist's intentions and evaluate the projected outcomes of these aesthetic moments?

10

Mobile Methods

Let me illustrate the methodological challenge of aesthetic cosmopolitanism by outlining an artistic project that takes form in a live social setting. In 2004 the curator Marina Fokidis and Lorenzo Romitto, an artist from the collective Stalker, invited me to participate in a 'picnic' on the island of Makronisos that fellow artists were organizing along with the refugees at Lavrio, a camp just outside of Athens. In the evening after this event I recorded the following notes:

> From the windows of Lavrio there is a view of a nearby island called Makronisos. This long island juts out of the sea like the spine of an ancient dolphin. Along the rocky thin line are clumps of green. Oregano grows wild among the thorns. It appears abandoned and lonely. Everyone who stares from the mainland knows that this was the most infamous prison where the political dissidents were confined and tortured into submission. Yet, to this island that no one else wants to go, there is the fantasy that, here, the refugee might come, build a home, stay, and no one will say 'leave'.
>
> Makronisos is the most dreaded name for a Greek island. It means exile, torture and humiliation. And how much more cruel that the mainland was so close, so visible and punishingly beside you. Only the children among the refugees see this island as an open playground. There are a couple of boys, with shaved heads and eyes alert to any chance of a game. They are not orphans, for their parents entrusted the PKK to smuggle them out of the country. The only inhabitants on the island are three Pakistani shepherds. The goats and sheep are everywhere on the island, and wherever there is shelter there are mounds of manure. The shepherds seem to have vanished. Only the rusty Datsun utility truck sits by the edge of the port. After we all disembark one of the artists, Nikos Tranos, and a leader of the PKK

make a speech, in which they announce the self-evident purpose of this event. History needs few words amongst the ruins of abandoned theatres, flattened prison and fragments of walls. Nikos suggests that we announce our presence by clearing a space. He suggests that each person tosses a few rocks onto a common mound. Marina mentions that her father, like all the prisoners, was allocated a heavy rock. They carried these rocks all day, up and down the Sisyphean hills. The rock was numbered, and the prisoners were named after its number. It was almost impossible to distinguish the small pile from the rubble when suddenly the Kurds joined in and the pace gathers, more and more stones quickly flick and clack onto the mound. One smiling man has found a pile of larger rocks. The tossing and throwing is building like a crescendo. When it is over another young man called Mafouz invites me to walk to the peak of the hill. While ascending he tells me that Christians gather rocks to define a place and the Zoroastrians throw rocks to cast out the devil. We speculate whether this clearing and purging are just different ways to speak of heaven.

Assemblages

Such an artistic event has no essence. There is no iconic moment – no gesture which captured the 'spirit' of hospitality, or an object that symbolized the experience of momentary solidarity. It was a day in which one incident clipped onto the next. The participating artists had no doubt that their art was in the whole of the day. There was no predetermined time or specified place that framed the ordinary flow of social activities. The journey to the island was neither the approach nor an exit from a scene. At no point could I distinguish a zone that would resemble a performance space.

The new toll highway to the international airport provides a direct axis that links the ancient port of Lavrio to Athens. Approaching Lavrio there are abandoned mines that resemble a weird hybrid of ancient and industrial ruins. This twisting of time repeats itself inside the architecture of Lavrio. The town now stands somewhere between the remnants of an Ottoman village and a new beach suburb, not quite certain of what to make of its combination of palm trees, pink disco signs and the old grey kafenia with nicotine-stained walls and green formica tables. Flags announce the civic centre. Above the municipal building the Greek blue and white whirrs and whistles in the harbour breeze. Above the adjacent building there is the trooping of Kurdish and Turkish Communist Party flags. In the absence of formal poles they use their antennae to announce the rule of Ocelan. The refugee camp is a former army barracks. Its gates are wide open and the interior holds a volleyball court. A match has just finished. Who wins? Who cares! The players and fans do. Everyday there is a contest. Athens vs.

Lavrio. The men are now standing in the shaded cloisters. They smile as we enter. The women are above on the higher balconies, too busy with other things to notice us.

'We are here to meet Marina', I say.

I am trying to validate our entrance, but it does not seem necessary. It doesn't alter the greeting; their smile is the same. They point to the other side. Marina has been working with these refugees for many months. She stayed there overnight to finalize some discussions about the day's event.

As we enter the building on the other side it is clear that we are in the Kurdish PKK half. Homages to Ocelan, maps of the Kurdish homeland, portraits of martyrs adorn all the walls. On the other side, there are the red flags of the Turkish Communist Party. In the following building there is a mixture of Azerbaijani, Afghan and Iraqi refugees. On all balconies there are satellite dishes.

We can now ask whether it is necessary for art to produce a kind of understanding that is distinctive from other social, creative and critical encounters. In short, is my arrival an opportunity to witness the work that Marina Fokidis does as a curator? Is this process of negotiation, in which she and the artist Lorenzo Romitto are involved, merely part of the preparatory stages for a subsequent event? The usual 'lens' employed in art criticism would render such activity as either a form of social welfare or the necessary fieldwork that would provide an artist with the raw material that is subsequently transformed into an aesthetic product. At best, my role of critic would be to note the context from which the work is derived and then search for the influences that it exerts.

By focusing on the context of art, one does not necessarily dissolve the boundary between art and other social activities. On the contrary, sociologists such as Janet Wolff (1981) and Howard Becker (1982) have critiqued the romantic conception of the artist aloof from social connections, emphasizing the historical causality of creativity and the complexity of the co-operative networks and contexts through which art happens. This materialist sociology of the production of art as work moves by way of demystification and is largely concerned with enumerating the social factors that *affect* art's development. While Wolff, following Anthony Giddens's (1976) conception of the duality of structures, argues that artistic practice is both socially determined and an arena for situated choices, this sociology of art remains tied to the romantic model of the artist removed from social and historical experience, which it worthily attempts to correct. Here, I am interested in formulating a critical disposition that might engage more effectively with art production, which is avowedly – indeed, tactically – embedded in the context and sociability of its making. In the specific encounter between the artists from the collective Stalker and the refugees in the camp at Lavrio, it is impossible to distinguish between background, research, hospitality and art. Art here is not simply rooted in social practices but is itself social praxis. What would previously been seen as social context or a preparatory phase is now also part of the materiality of the total experience.

We find Marina and her friend Iacobo in a back room. As we enter we are immediately invited to join the table. A plastic plate with rice, chicken, salad and yoghurt is placed before us. Some men are eating and talking with Marina and Iacobo while others prepare, serve and clean. Every surface is rough, splintered and chipped, but clean. The leader of the PKK in Greece, the chief, is in the middle of a discussion about cultural politics with Iacobo. Iacobo's views on the significance of an imaginary as opposed to a territorial homeland, on fluid rather than fixed identities, on hybrid instead of essential cultural values, are all received with equanimity. Iacobo can talk and talk, but the chief patiently disagrees, qualifies and explains in a manner that echoes his perfectly ironed shirt and immaculate fingernails. There are no wrinkles, doubts or gaps in his authority. To the chief, an intellectual discussion is tolerable, but politically it must be understood: no culture without nation. Diaspora talk is only a shadow of armed struggle. The seed of the diaspora is not cut free to be something else, but only to reproduce the same tree in a foreign soil. Iacobo has his convictions. He is hanging onto the slivers of convergence and repeats his questions. Marina walks out of the room and the chief drops his attention.

Marina has already achieved her goal. The artists have arranged a boat and a meal for the refugees on the nearby island of Makronisos, and the PKK has agreed that all members of Lavrio should attend. I follow Lorenzo and Mateo as they go next door to deliver a letter to an old man from Azerbaijan. He is incredulous. Not because a fellow countryman has written to him, but that it is from a sailor. How can a landlocked country produce sailors? Yet, this sailor is now stranded on board a deserted ship in Naples? The crew abandoned the ship and he is unable either to depart or disembark. Lorenzo and Mateo tell him how they met him in Naples. The conversation rattles through the corridors of six different languages. Lorenzo and Mateo speak in Italian and English, Theodoris and I translate into Greek. Through the words of an eleven-year-old Afghan boy, who translates into Turkish, the bedridden Azerbaijani listens. Tears well up from in the deep pockets below his eyes. The ship that will take us to Makronisos is sounding its horn. We scuttle around the corner and are amongst the last to board.

'It is just a short trip!' Marina shouts.

'You mean it is that island over there', I interject.

'Yes, just over there. Come on, let's go.'

I always thought Makronisos got its name because it was far from the mainland. The scene from Voulgaris's film 'Stone Years', where two young lovers stare at each other from opposite ends of a ship without their countenance yielding to reveal their embrace, suggested to me that the journey of their exile was towards the far side of Greece, like the winter. Makro also means long. It is also the island that Paris and Helen took refuge on before their escape to Troy.

The captain of our boat is counting heads and shouting for us to keep still. He can see the coastguard hovering at the mouth of the port. The boat is filled beyond its limit. But who will get off, artists or refugees? After a lot of pleading and the promise of a little more money, he agrees to make two trips.

This account of some of the details that surround an experience raises questions about the ambience of art: Where does it begin and end? As artists are increasingly defining their field of practice as the domain of 'existing social realities', it provokes a rethinking of the role of context in art (Nash 2008). I began by describing this as a 'fairly typical art event'. However, it should be clear that this encounter is not quite an 'event' and certainly unlike the 'happenings'. I am not suggesting that the boundary between the organic totality of art and everyday life has suddenly dissolved. For instance, the jagged interplay between political and aesthetic choices was made evident in the installation phase. In a subsequent video by the artistic collective Stalker, a man points to a lake and claims it as his spiritual home. Following the man's gesture, Stalker identified the lake as being in Macedonia. No one can deny this man's claim to his Macedonian identity. However, after the ruins of a grand but short-lived empire, where is Macedonia? Or, rather, which state can claim to be the inheritor of the Macedonian heritage? These political questions of belonging and location and the unstable boundary between aesthetic experience and social event were at the core of Stalker's transnational project called *Via Egnatia*.[1] The artists had travelled along and gathered stories from the ancient road linking Rome and Istanbul. Yeni Tzami, the building in which the video was displayed, was already bristling with contradictions. It was a former mosque built for Jews who had converted to Islam during the Ottoman rule of the Greek city of Thessaloniki. Designed by Vitaliano Poseli in 1902, it nevertheless retained much of the structural form and decorative symbolism of a synagogue. In response to the massive influx of Greek refugees in 1922 it converted into a hostel. After the genocide of the Jewish population by the Nazis it was used as an archaeological museum.

Marina Fokidis, curator of the *Via Egnatia* project in Thessaloniki, and Lorenzo Romitto, one of the founders of Stalker, were conscious of the pernicious way nationalist narratives tend to privilege one collective trauma over all others. And, in the specific case of the video, there was still the dilemma of how to name the place of the lake. They were aware that the act of legitimation, by accepting the words and gesture of the man, or the act of censorship, by deleting the geopolitical reference, would only intensify the rivalry. In order to avoid the artwork being hijacked by a nationalist agenda, it was necessary to find a more subtle interplay between the mediating role of artists and the voices of the storytellers.

The aim of the project was not to resolve geopolitical border disputes but rather, as argued by Marina Fokidis, 'to create a mindscape unfolding between the memories and the actuality, the visitors and the locality, the politics and the sentiment, the producers and the public'. To achieve this 'mindscape' it was necessary to utilize Yeni Tzami as one among many sites in which there was the freedom to listen to contradictory claims of belonging. Fokidis and Romitto could create a platform for each of the different stories being told in the building – Macedonian, Greek, Turkish, Kurdish, Albanian – but it would not work if each identity was confined to a bounded space. The aim, according to Fokidis (personal correspondence, 25 November 2005), was not to hear all the stories in isolation from one another but to create a scheme of 'parallel events' in which all the differences would both come up against each other and produce their 'common space'.

As a participant in the symposium and witness to Stalker's practice, I found myself entangled in the complex process of mediation. In particular I was engaged in the discussion of how to represent cultural longing in a context of geopolitical conflict. We agreed that each voice should find its own space and authority, as well as being positioned in relation to its neighbour. This placed a new responsibility on the respondent to live with the difference in the other's claim, and an obligation on the artists and curators to occupy an intermediate role that enables new possibilities to emerge. This discussion occurred during a parallel performance by Stalker in a home for retired Jewish people. While discussing the legacy of the Ottoman Empire, I found myself staring around the room and noted that the honour boards that lined the walls included figures with Greek, Italian, Sephardic and Ashkenazic names.

Before we left the home, a woman called Victoria Benizelou approached Lorenzo Romitto and expressed her thanks for the work of Stalker. As she was speaking, artists from Italy, France and Greece were still dispersed in various huddles around the room. Pointing to this gathering, she noted: 'What all humans have in common is their mixture.' With emphatic and tender poignancy she then declared: 'It is this mixture that precedes and outlives any narrow national identity.' In her farewell to Lorenzo Romitto, she said: 'From the moment I met you I recognized that you were seeking for community.' I have translated her phrase *psahnaistai yia koinonia* as 'seeking for community'. But I am not sure that 'seeking' captures the radial resonance of the Greek verb, which combines both an outer and an inner journey for self-discovery, and aims towards a state that may never be found. '*Psahnaistai*' refers to both a bittersweet awareness of an endless quest and a restlessness that blows between being and belonging. What appears to have occurred in this mode of engagement is a more diffuse and unpredictable set of relationships between the artists and the refugees. I would prefer to describe the context of these encounters as an 'assemblage'.

Before unpacking this concept, I would like to make a sideways step and address the deep-seated ambivalence that artists have expressed towards the definition of context. The ambivalence oscillates between the dread of decontextualization and the quest for an unbounded relationship between art and its context. In 1971 Daniel Buren observed that the spatial significance of 'the studio as the unique space of production and the museum as the unique space of exposition' needed to be investigated as part of the 'ossifying customs of art' (Buren 1983, p. 61). The following year Robert Smithson decried the 'cultural confinement that takes place when a curator imposes his own limits on an art exhibition' and results in art that is 'politically lobotomised' (Smithson 2000, p. 132). A couple of decades later Rasheed Araeen renewed the desire to escape from prevailing attempts to define the context of art by railing against the theoretical 'prisons' that were 'predetermining and prescribing' the identity and value of non-Western artists within a 'controlled space' (2001, p. 98).

For Buren, the displacement of art from the unique space in which it is produced (the studio) to the museum marks the terms of an alienation complex. The location of art in its primal context – the home of the studio – also forms the limits of the artist's economic and cultural survival. His work cannot remain there, and, yet, when it leaves for the gallery/museum it not only loses meaning, it also loses vitality, for, in Buren's terms, its fate is limited to being in either a 'boutique' or a 'cemetery'. Buren places himself at the edges of this alienated context as he declares: 'The art of yesterday and today is not only marked by the studio as an essential, often unique place of production. All my work proceeds from its extinction' (1983, p. 67). In a similar tone of disavowal, Araeen also protests against the tendency to explain non-Western art that relies primarily on the artist's biographical details and cultural context. In both cases the artists are seeking a context for art which does not remain bound by the primal home, and one which recognizes that its status as an alienated object is a constitutive feature of its identity. Like Smithson, they uphold the view that, as art enters the public domain, its aim is neither to claim an autonomous space nor to find redemption within a ghetto, but rather to establish a direct relation 'with the elements as they exist from day to day' (Smithson 2000, p. 132).

By stressing the relationship with the ephemeral and dynamic elements of the contemporary context in which art is located, these artists sought to overcome the idea that the context could be defined within fixed conceptual, temporal and spatial boundaries. The struggle against these definitions of context were influenced largely by the nationalist and formalist paradigms that dominated most of twentieth-century art history, and, according to Araeen, the same constrictions were evident in the postcolonial theories that putatively deflected attention away from the object of art and towards the culturalist paradigms of hybridity (Zimmerman 2003, pp. vii–viii, 192). However, my interest in the earlier disputes over the definition of the context of art is not confined to the utility of theory for critical appreciation or curatorial framing but, rather, is directed towards the artist's perception of culture as a process of radical mobility. In a context in which visual culture is mediated by a proliferation of digital communicative technologies, criss-crossed by the pathways of peoples from all corners of the globe, and reconfigured by the constant combination of traditional and contemporary modes of practice, it is no longer plausible to define the concept of context as if it possessed a singular set of national traits that are forged in an exclusive setting over a sustained period of time, nor is it sufficient to identify the primacy of formal concerns. Rather, the concept of context is more meaningful if it includes a multi-temporal engagement with the past and the present, a cosmopolitan vision of the cultural horizon, and a specific engagement with social realities (Escobar 2004).

The encounters between the artists and the refugees, the experience of the picnic, the events and performances on Makronisos that I have already described, are now better grasped through the concept of assemblage. The Deleuzian account of assemblage has gained considerable purchase within recent debates on the virtual and causal processes of social transformation (Deleuze and Parnet 2002, p. 69). George E. Marcus and Erkan Saka have argued that, as a 'concept/cluster', assemblage provides a useful 'resource' for addressing the paradoxical but inextricable relationship between the dynamic flows that disrupt and the structural order that emerges in a reconfigured form (2006, p. 102). It alludes to the multiplicity and heterogeneity of agents that intersect and interact within a social space without presuming that this collision of differences leads to either their assimilation into the pre-existing hierarchy or the elimination of their differences.

On the contrary, assemblage allows attention to focus on the critical and creative trajectories that arise from the incorporation of external agents. Hence, Marcus and Saka argue that assemblage can be used to refer to both the states of cognition and the objective relations that emerge in the ephemeral temporality and evanescent reverberations of contemporary social formations.

In the manifesto issued by Stalker there is a similar suggestion that creative energy is generated by the oscillation between dispersal and gathering. The members stress their implication in situations where they confront the limits of their own self-knowledge and the complexity of a territory:

> Stalker is a collective subject that engages [in] research and actions within the landscape with particular attention to the areas around the city's margins and forgotten urban space, and abandoned areas or regions under transformation. These investigations are conducted across several levels, around notions of practicality, representations and interventions on these spaces that are referred to here as 'Actual Territories'. Stalker is together custodian, guide and artist for these 'Actual Territories'. In the multiple roles we are disposed to confront at once the apparently unsolvable contradictions of salvaging through abandonment, of representation through sensorial perception, of intervening within the unstable and mutable conditions of these areas. (Stalker n.d.)

Stalker works by gathering bits of information from historical texts, interviewing people and searching among the debris of abandoned spaces. The members of the collective move throughout the city armed with mobile phones and video cameras. They constantly keep track of one another's movements through SMS. Rather than gathering data for subsequent processing, they focus their effort on determining what can be done in this specific place within the limited time and the available resources. Even in these situations, where the focus is on understanding local concerns, there is a process of connecting with other communities and creating an interlocal network. The use of cameras, and in particular the video recorder, is therefore both an archival tool and a performative device. The artists switch it on and become seriously playful – reporting their fleeting insights in the form of a 'breaking news flash', or posing for group shots in the form of the apostles portrayed by a Renaissance painter. Their discoveries are quickly posted on the web.

The effect is not to submerge art under a political agenda or to provide data for an eventual analysis. The camera is not a recorder of evidence, but a companion in the act of witnessing and a relay device in the interminable network of message-making. Stalker's methodology is different from that of the *flâneur* who would go 'botanizing on the asphalt' of the modern city. It is not the individual epiphanies before the discovery of a hidden architectural gem, but rather a collective remapping of the urban margins. Like the *flâneur*, its members seek to awaken the citizen from their blasé attitude towards the secret folds between the past and the novelty in the present, but, as Nato Thompson observed about political artists in the 1990s, they are desirous of entering the scene physically – 'that is, they place their work into the heart of the political situation itself' (Thompson and Sholette 2004, pp. 13–14).

It is from this perspective that I seek to rethink the status of art that defines its practice as being within the domain of existing social realities, and the emergence of a significant trajectory in art practice that Mark Nash (2008) claims marks a 'documentary turn'. I will argue, though, that the concept of assemblage enables an understanding of the significance of process, whereby the emergence of heterogeneous agents can be articulated without the necessity that their interactions be fixed into thingness or the trace of these interactions be captured into a visual form that can belatedly accrue value as a commodifiable artwork. It is my contention that, yet again, the field of practice has been expanded, and this time the artist's cosmopolitan disposition has greater opportunity for articulation within the process of assemblage. This 'expanded' vision of the context of aesthetic practice is part of a paradigm shift in the understanding of mobility. Through this new prism, it is possible to rethink the relations between local and global through a cosmopolitan frame.

From Diasporic Differences

Within visual studies and art criticism a new set of post-national categories are being utilized to describe a context in which there is a hyper-visibility of non-Western artists and collaborative art practices that involve loose, tactical and international coalitions of artists and participants from a wide range of areas. As Kobena Mercer (2005, p. 7) rightly observed, there is now a 'widespread acknowledgement of multiple identities in public life', and the normative incorporation of multiculturalism has both 'enriched our experiences of art and enlivened the entire setting'. This shift in the grounding of multiculturalism is also confirmed by two key anthologies on contemporary art and culture. In the editorial introduction of *Out There: Marginalization and Contemporary Culture*, Russell Ferguson outlined three aims: first, to establish a relationship between cultural debates and critical theory;

second, to explore representational strategies that affirm cultural identities in complex societies; and, third, to challenge the terms of negotiation that would otherwise continue to make minority cultures invisible (1990, p. 11).

Almost a decade and a half later there appeared a sequel anthology, *Over Here: International Perspectives on Art and Culture*, and while the editors, Jean Fisher and Gerardo Mosquera, express the intention of taking up the legacy of the critique of the condition of marginalization and the possibilities for transformation, they add the following bitter-sweet introductory remark: 'in some respects nothing has changed, but everything has changed' (2004, p. 2). They claim that, despite the mobility of artists from every corner of the world, there is almost no change in the institutional structures of power. However, they also note the emergence of an unexpected level of cultural complexity: 'despite the accusations that globalization has led to artistic homogenization, there have been signs of shifts in the epistemological grounds of contemporary artistic discourses based not in differences but *from* differences' (ibid.).

This slender switch in the use of prepositions is indicative of the broader paradigm shift on the conceptualization of mobility and difference. It recognizes that cultural development can no longer be represented in a teleological narrative that is linear and inevitably Eurocentric. For instance, rather than assuming that the supposed origins of modernism in the West will shape in perpetuity the lineages of influence, they now claim that it is possible to discern a transversal vision of cultural development whereby the local manifestation of modernism carries within it the possibility of establishing a distinctive inflection of the global process. This perspective abandons the Eurocentric hierarchy of cultural validation and adopts an understanding of the horizontal process by which an idea spreads and mutates as it connects with specific locales. Fisher and Mosquera adopt the metaphor of 'cultural corridors' to describe the formation of common links across diverse sites and to stress the multi-directionality of the traffic.

While the original anthology *Out There* examined the extent to which 'the other' can appear in the centre, and whether the centre is capable of accepting difference, in the sequel volume, *Over Here*, the call for recognition moves beyond the framework of either a self-confirming mirror or a redemptive accommodation with otherness, as it summons an approach to an elsewhere that, as in the game of hide-and-seek, is both nearby and separate. The power of the metaphor of 'cultural corridors' does not arise from its one-way access to the centre, but in its facilitation of transversal traffic. Hence, the aim is not a validation of the minority as a worthy equal within the centre's cultural hierarchy, but the creation of networks *from* which cultural differences move and interact with each other.

When the artists in the Stalker collective redefine their practice as an open conversation and explore the ways in which strangers can meet, this is expressive of both a political commitment to the belief that art can make a social difference and a fascination with the conditions for cosmopolitan dialogue, or what Mica Nava (2007, p. 14) described as 'performing mutuality'. This fascination occurs both at a semiotic level – that is, the potential for art to contain both particularistic and universal meaning – and at a social level – with the possibility of artists being connected simultaneously to local and global cultural networks. Cosmopolitanism is not just about private consciousness; it is also a social activity of mutual respect and a shared commitment in developing inclusive and hybrid rituals.

My own role as a participant in the assemblage of artists and refugees at Makronisos was also motivated by this kind of 'visceral cosmopolitanism'. But as a critic I am left struggling to give due form to the experience of that day. I am aware that the artists do not presume that their work will have a significant political impact – the mass media did not report it, nor did the politicians who debate migration policies notice it. Art criticism would normally gloss such activity as mere social activism or relegate it to the fringe of 'community art'. However, part of my attraction to the work of collectives such as Stalker is that success and failure is not registered within these conventional institutional markers. Their practice is not exclusively funnelled by the imperative of the art market. As a collective, they appear to be uninterested in populist media hype and, most refreshingly, interpersonal relations are not dominated by a self-promoting art personality. Their approach and conduct is, to use the critical phrase proposed by Charles Esche (2005), 'modest'. Attention is concentrated on the lived experience of interaction. What matters for them is the subtle transformation that occurs through these experiences. However, in the absence of a fixed object, is it sufficient for the critic to focus on the multiple documentary traces that trail in the wake of such assemblages? How does art criticism, which has tuned its analytic skills to the interpretation of an image, suddenly turn to address the temporality of an ephemeral spatial manifestation – what Pierre Huyghe (2008) recently called the art that appears as an 'apparition'?

When Victoria Benizelou recognized that Stalker was 'seeking for community', she was also touching on an attitude towards others that Norberto Bobbio described as 'meekness'. She expressed thanks not only for the smiling generosity that was expressed by the artists, but also for the way in which their attention to the small details of everyday life created an atmosphere of surprising connection with the residents in the Jewish home. These meek amd modest gestures initiated by Stalker are expressive of both a deep interhuman connection and the formation of a temporary community. The meek, according to Bobbio, also find hope in the fragments of the past and in the fleeting hints of recognition with the other. Bobbio is clear that meekness must not be confused with the sadness of humility or compared to other passive states such as modesty, submission or resignation. On the contrary, he asserts that meekness revels in its capacity to survive and remain calm in the face of adversity, and is untouched by the tendrils of vengeance and fury. Meekness, he insists, is a unilateral social virtue: it does not expect reciprocity. A meek person does not brighten their kindness, curiosity and concern in proportion to the other's power. Bobbio praises the meek not for their display of a superior form of good will but for the way in which they behave as if their generosity simply exists, like a constant pulse. It continues even when every gesture goes unnoticed. For, as Bobbio states: 'The meek are cheerful because they are inwardly convinced that the world to which they aspire is better than the one they are forced to inhabit' (2000, p. 31).

Benizelou recognized that the gift offered by the members of Stalker was not just the service of a civic duty but was also inspired by the aesthetic experience of cosmopolitanism. It was not just the offering of a service to the other, which in all its kindness would still imply an outstanding obligation for compensation, but rather an open gesture in which both find recognition. While art practices that aim to initiate social relationships in public spaces and explore cultural modes of exchange that resist capitalist codes have been a powerful presence in the contemporary art scene since the 1960s, critical discourse has been rather slow to respond. For instance, only in the last decade has the concept of the everyday been developed into a critical tool for addressing the 'lure of the ordinary' in contemporary practice (Johnstone 2008). Similarly, while there is a longstanding tradition of monographs that explore the complex affiliations that artists developed with other people, novel symbols and foreign ideas, the actualization of the lived forms of this cosmopolitan disposition has remained undertheorized. Cosmopolitanism and the cultural elements that form an assemblage, when they were acknowledged, were invariably relegated to incidental or background information in the pursuit of formalist aesthetics or socio-political questions. Critical discourse continues to focus on the belated documentary traces or the objects that are the product of the collaborative process. While criticism remains preoccupied with aesthetic objects, this not only defers the investigation into the social space and interpersonal relations that are undisputably part of the materiality of art, but it also delays the development of new techniques of spatial observation and critical concepts for evaluating the subjective states of empathy, trust and reciprocity. It is my contention that a closer examination of the sociological and philosophical theories that have influenced the debates on the social context of art will take us only part of the way towards representing the albeit incomplete, but nevertheless generative, force of cosmopolitan imaginary.

I have already suggested that a more fruitful path can be found through the approach outlined by Gerald Raunig (2007, p. 17). He claimed that the revolutionary aim to achieve a fusion of art and life, or even the diffusion of art into life, neither assists in bringing the revolution closer to hand nor enlivens the experience of art. Raunig argued that the revolutionary role of art is neither to capture the essence of the ordinary nor to merge within the complex web of everyday life, and thereby offered an alternative view that art always retains its emergent and distinctive self-presence as it moves through social spaces and interacts with other elements. This process of interaction between the aesthetic and the political does not result in a state in which one is subordinate to the other, or even a synthesis of the two, but in the formation of a complex structure that resembles an assemblage.

Raunig's presentist, rather than future-oriented, vision of art and politics is also shaped by his conviction that the experience of participating with art collectives will frame the outlook on its aesthetic and political realities. His perspective bears closer alignment with the strategic utilization of social meanings and embodiment of the existing realities expressed by collectives such as Stalker. As is the case with my justification of the function of the 'notes from my diary', with which I narrated my own presence in the assemblage at Makronisos, Raunig insists that it is not possible to appreciate what happened without 'being there'. Like Brian Holmes, he claims that he only writes about collaborative art events in which he was an active participant (Holmes 2007a, p. 290). This methodological principle is not elaborated upon in any detail. However, Raunig does suggest that the canonical art historical methodologies, which focus on 'auratic' objects or on belated documentary traces, are likely to dismiss collaborative art projects as mere 'activism' and thereby fail to register them as a worthy subject of study.

Stalker stresses that collective and collaborative practice offers an intimation of community. However, while being open to the needs of the other, it does not propose a new structure that can accommodate difference:

It is a process where the producers and receivers play a common game; that's the reason why we have never conceived Stalker as a group but as an inter-related and open system that is growing and emerging through its actions and through all the individuals that operate with (for and among) Stalker. A reality without one physical body, not even one of the persons who gave life to it. 'We' have always been an entity, which comprises of 'others' who – without pretending to be us – participate in the activities of becoming us in their/our practice. This way Stalker could be anyone. Stalker is a desiring community where no one belongs and where individuals encounter each other. It is an unstable entity, a temporary community, which is founded on possibilities, on desire, on intention, on promise and waiting. (Fokidis 2005, p. 282)

Stalker cannot offer itself as a model for community-building. In Lorenzo Romitto's description of the operation of the artists' prac-tice as an 'inter-related and open system', 'a desiring community', 'a temporary community', there are echoes of Giorgio Agamben's (1993) concept of the 'coming community'. According to its own logic, such a community could not address the social needs for continuity and coherence that come with more stable forms of dwelling. When Stalker arrives in a specific location, and even when it has stayed long in one place, the members do not present a new blueprint for community-building. There is no predefined structure with its own rules, explicit codes of conduct, set goals and mechanisms for regulating exclusion. There is simply the optimism that the communal system will emerge in the encounter with the other. For, as Francesco Careri states, Stalker lacks any fixed form of identity: 'Stalker is something that transpires, a moment that we share, it's a situation' (Careri 2004, p. 28). The empha-sis is not on claiming the city in the name of cosmopolitanism, but on the co-production of perspectives and social relationships for a coming community. The function of practice is neither the production of iconic objects nor the construction of a new social hierarchy, but simply the art of mediation.

If Stalker does not offer an objective alternative, then we must look more closely at the faith of its members that something else comes from the fleeting encounters between strangers. This refusal to build the monument for the cosmopolitan city raises even more questions about the meekness of cosmopolitan agency. If the work of art is not completed in the construction of an object, but realized only in the unending experience of a coming community, then is there nothing more than the savouring of exquisite moments of novelty – or is this intimation also a form of nostalgia for a different future with others? Where can we find the traces of this elusive cosmopolitanism? In Stalker's manifesto, and to a certain extent in their practice, we can see that the juxtaposition of cultural differences, and the invitation for different people to come together, is driven by a desire to gain a glimpse of a cosmopolitan community that is always in the process of becoming.

The glimpse is of something that lies hidden. I am not suggesting that the function of art is to uncover forgotten or ignored states. Stalker's conception of an 'Actual Territory' does not refer to a fixed entity. There are better tools for excavating and classifying the remains of the past. Art should not be confused with these acquisitive methods that seek to capture the truth. The glimpse that art offers is less stable; it is more like the flickering recognition of a potential for change. Stalker gives us no hint of how the creative power of art 'becomes at the same time, homeland, self-belonging, attachment to clan and cosmic effusion' (Guattari 1995, p. 107), but it does warn that the glimpse will never reveal itself if one code serves as the pervasive screen through which everything else must pass. Without hospitality there is no hint of cosmopolitanism (Papastergiadis 2007e). However, as Derrida reminds us, hospitality must exist alongside the counter right of sovereignty (Derrida and Dufourmantelle 2000).

What is the difference between art and politics? I have been arguing that artists do not deliver documents which reveal the condition of cosmopolitanism, but, rather, that they take an active role in the mediation of its emergence. This is not an exercise that can be conducted through solitary reflection and experimentation. Artists now seek to come closer to a community not simply to reveal its secrets but to realize the inherent desire for conviviality. Mediation is the process of working out the next step for living together in times when the perplexity of difference is almost overwhelming. It is not just a revelation of the inner truth of a personal identity or an outline of the broader social structure, but the action of putting together different sets of interests so that they can work on each other simultaneously and thereby create what Lu Jie (2005, p. 125) calls a 'social montage'. As another small step in the outline of a cosmopolitan methodology for art criticism, I conclude with a diary passage on the awkward and sometimes mute gestures that bring us closer to the task that the artist Jimmie Durham (2004, p. 119) described as 'humanity . . . trying to talk to itself'.

Around the island we observe a variety of movements. Lorenzo and Matteo have gathered a small group, and they find a spot behind the old theatre to place a concrete plaque that had been inscribed by a former prisoner. Amongst the broken columns of the ruined church, refugees and artists are being positioned for a performance. An artist suggests that some of the refugees join her in healing chant, but within a few minutes the levity of the gesture collapses as the refugees are unable to suspend a sudden outburst of giggling. From above, the grid of the camp's foundations is barely visible.

The one remaining wall is, for this day, converted into a table. All along the twenty metre wall a sheet of paper has been laid down, like a long tablecloth. The space is divided: bread, cheese, olives, tomatoes, cucumbers, water and wine . . . bread, cheese, olives, tomatoes, cucumbers, water and wine . . . bread, cheese, olives, tomatoes, cucumbers, water and wine . . . The men from Lavrio squat on their haunches. I stand on the lower side of the wall. We are facing each other at eye level. Quietly and jokingly, squinting in the sunlight and hungry from the sea, we eat together.

Epilogue: The Coming Cosmopolitans

As Cavafy, an Alexandrian cosmopolitan poet, foretold in the poem 'Ithaka' – the homecoming is made 'marvellous' only after the traveller has confronted the 'monsters' that lurk in his own consciousness and abandoned the expectation that the homeland is as 'perfumed' as the experience of the journey. In this poem he strips away the sentiment of the home as the ultimate destination. The only satisfaction that Cavafy promises is the dry contentment that Ithaka gives the traveller a starting point. However, knowing the homeland, in all its bareness, makes the return no less irresistible. Ithaka is what it is, and it is not the whole world (Cavafy 1984, p. 29). The psychoanalyst and philosopher Julia Kristeva also passed on a similar piece of advice when she stressed the need for an inward investigation of the strangeness that occurs at the borders of the self, and noted that a characteristic feature of cosmopolitans is that they 'give up hunting for the scapegoat outside their group' (Kristeva 1993, p. 51; see also Girard 1980, p. 22). In George Orwell's willingness to trade imperial attachments for an understanding of the whole world, the contemporary cultural theorist Paul Gilroy (2004, p. 88) finds an expression of cosmopolitanism that is not 'a devaluation of love, but its transmutation into the fragile, emergent substance of vital planetary humanism'.

Who would dare to be a cosmopolitan today? There are three reasons that are commonly proposed. First, there is a belief that the aggregation of all cultural perspectives would expand and strengthen our *human consciousness*. Second, there is the hope that a common political and legal framework would overcome traditional conflicts and promote *transnational solidarity*. Third, there is a presumption that all cultures are fundamentally the same – or, put another way, the global is just the local writ large, and a *universal culture* is an extrapolation from all the specific cultures. Cavafy, Gilroy and Kristeva's cosmopolitans, as well as artist collectives such as Stalker and transnational aesthetico-political movements like No One is Illegal, go beyond a merely defensive vision of cosmopolitanism, as they challenge us to think of globalization as a tool that brings the world to our home and an opportunity to think about the kind of world in which we want to live.

My journey through the artistic practices of cosmopolitan dialogue has led me to observe that, while they do not have the answers to the issues that we face in the world, artists have developed techniques for finding the questions with which they can cross-examine the perplexity of our common condition. This collaborative methodology has shifted the emphasis of contemporary art practice from what Hsu (2005, p. 76) called the 'cultural representation' of difference to the mediation between the jostling differences that co-exist in our midst. The aim of this kind of practice could be described as both interventionist and meek in equal measure. It does not point towards new transcendent categories or a new hierarchy that can be superimposed above all others. The only hope that it offers is to create a framework in which we can engage with the plurality of differences without the violent annihilation of the other.

These artistic methodologies stand in stark relief to those executed in the mainstream debates on cultural identity. Social scientists and political commentators who have been stuck in the residentialist mindset have been reluctant to acknowledge the cosmopolitanism that is always already in our midst. They assume that culture has to be fixed to be real. They do not have the tools to count the ways in which transnational mixtures shape our everyday life. As a consequence they do not tell the whole story of who we are, and, increasingly, this way of seeing recognizes less and less of who we are becoming. Seeing the reality of cosmopolitanism is difficult. The pathos of cosmopolitanism is often justified by the lack of place. Cosmopolitanism is reduced to a general dreaming because it is somehow removed from the messy process of building a specific place in the world. It is often presented as being in opposition to any specific attachment to place, without sovereignty and therefore not part of reality. The etymological links between the real, the royal and the estate are not coincidental. They reflect the residentialist association between power and place.

Find the gesture of hospitality and there lies the place of cosmopolitanism. Cosmopolitanism does not wait for emperors to impose forced marriages, nor does it descend like the grace of a higher deity. It starts in every small gesture of reciprocity. If it is seen as part of the drive to achieve sociality and an ideal that emerges from the middle of critical consciousness, then we could argue that everyone is potentially a bearer of cosmopolitanism. Hospitality on the basis of no expectations may sound rather idealistic, but it also rests on the more pragmatic principle that one should receive a stranger with the presumption that he or she may be a god in disguise. I would like to propose that art keeps open the mystery of the stranger's identity. Hence, Norberto Bobbio's (2000) concept of meekness is very useful for explaining the state of being that is necessary when we think of the relationship between an artist and the other. Meekness, in his definition, does not imply passivity or resignation, but refers to a way of relating to the other that is not bound by instrumental calculations of fear and benefit. You are open to the other because this is the only way towards mutual understanding. Cosmopolitanism has been all too easily dismissed as an impossible utopia, and cosmopolitans have been denigrated because they supposedly live without roots. This is an abuse of the loyalty test. Our understanding of cosmopolitanism also suffers because it has been kept separate from the debates on multiculturalism. Cosmopolitanism has been distanced from multiculturalism because, while philosophers and cultural theorists have represented the former as the intellectual effort to transcend national categories, public policy analysts that advise state bureaucracies have tended to reduce the latter to a political strategy for managing minorities within a nation-state. The neat conceptual boundary that separates multiculturalism from cosmopolitanism severs the more expansive visions of both concepts.

Cosmopolitanism and multiculturalism are co-constitutive. One needs the other for each to come into being. Cosmopolitanism without multiculturalism is just an ivory tower. Multiculturalism without cosmopolitanism becomes a nasty ghetto. Putting them together gives politics a whole new agenda. The challenge of developing a new conceptual framework that can embrace mixture and mobility has so far been averted by separating the philosophical debates on rights and ethics from the political challenges of negotiating cultural boundaries and social obligations. By maintaining a view on cosmopolitanism as if it were a spectral dreaming and reducing multiculturalism to a slimy avenue of opportunism and appeasement, both are effectively excluded from the central arena of politics. For instance, if cosmopolitanism is always in an immaculate state of self-realization, then it has no need for a political agenda. It is always already being itself and requires nothing from politics. It can somehow exist without any dependence on the state, and is therefore elevated to a nebulous zone that is above politics. On the other hand, multiculturalism is excluded from politics because it is presumed that, if one set of grievances are recognized as valid, this opens the floodgates to an infinite set of claims. Its agenda spirals into an endless competition for the position of victim. However, both of these views ignore the fundamental challenge of living with difference, which, as Balibar (2002a, p. 148) argued, involves the invention of new kind of hybrid universalism.

Cosmopolitanism is not without risks. Immanuel Wallerstein suggested that radicals should be 'forcing liberals to be liberal' (2003, p. 239). This injunction is a sign of the timidity and defensiveness that prevails on the left. The adoption of the 'clash of civilizations' thesis by almost all the mainstream Western political parties has produced a culture of fear that delivers both cosmopolitanism and multiculturalism to the realm of melancholic zombie concepts. In this zeitgeist, cosmopolitanism is the spirit that drifts without a body, and multiculturalism is searching for life in a dying body. A contemporary perspective would not aim to standardize humanity or appeal to unity via the annulling of differences. It would offer a new model of co-existence in which rival claims could negotiate their local or regional differences without being confounded by nationalist categories. Looking for human bonds that do not depend on either the attraction towards cultural equivalence or an instrumental duty of reparation invokes an investigation into the question What is it to be human without any formal and fixed markers? Agamben (1993, p. 85) touched upon the emergence of such an aesthetico-ethical form of belonging that defies the state's structures and generates a 'coming community' in which 'humans co-belong without a representable condition of belonging'.

In this book I have sought to bring together different reactions to the politics of fear. The evidence of protest, disapproval and resistance abounds. But what does it add up to? One of the striking features in the contemporary political landscape is the simultaneous collapse of support for formal political structures and an absence of a centralized oppositional politics. In the networked society, most of the voices and images of resistance remain isolated from one another. They have not coalesced into a new social movement. The voices of cosmopolitan hope are weak. Is this weakness like a sign of flickering pulse that is doomed to fade? Or does it mean that, in all its multiple, uncertain and complex variety, this emergent form of community is a force that will gather momentum and create new social and political identities? To be able to reckon with these questions, we need to construct new frameworks within which the contemporary forms of belonging and solidarity can start to make sense. The divisive territorial units, the exclusive appeals of blood, and the purist ideological visions that shaped the conditions of being in the nineteenth and twentieth centuries have little to offer the world in which are already moving. We have become accustomed to think of this world as a networked space. Indeed, there are now countless virtual and real lines that criss-cross each other and connect points that are separated by vast distances. Bruno Latour has often noted that the image of the network is everywhere. It has become the ambient form of our contemporary society. However, after reflecting on an artwork by Thomas Saraceno, *Galaxies Forming along Filament, Like Droplets along the Strands of a Spider's Web* (2009) Latour (2011) proceeded to perform an auto-critique of his actor-network theory. Saraceno's installation was comprised of a cosmic arrangement of elastic connectors that cut across all the dimensions of a room and entangled themselves in spherical structures. In this artwork, Latour saw both the vitality of networks and the necessity of nested spaces. He took pleasure in pointing out that the lines of the networks and the entangled structure were made of the same elastic material. Their only difference was the density and patterning of the lines. As Latour pondered over the hierarchy of the global elastic connectors and the topology of the knotted structures, he took inspiration from Peter Sloterdijk's vision of the sphere as the opposite of the network, and concluded that this artwork provided a more robust vision of the stitching together that occurs in social spaces. Perhaps the image of these knotted spaces as spheres is too neat and exaggerates the extent to which it can yield a hermetically sealed condition. I prefer to imagine the relationship between the network and the nested structures as being on a continuum between lines and clusters.

The cluster is a space for living and communication. It emerges as a radial point that consolidates the incessant processes of communication between inside and outside. The inside of a cluster comes from the gathering together of the outside lines. The inside of the cluster is not in opposition to the externality of networks, but rather it is the reorganization of the lines of connection. It turns the thin edges of a network into a thick environment of nested possibilities. It assembles an experience of interiority out of folding together previously and newly acquired exteriors. This image of the cluster is one that I have relied upon when thinking of the social spaces created in artistic encounters. These spaces are formed as different people come together to consider the interconnection between local and global forces. As lines in the network converge they do more than just enable movement; they also create a shape and a structure. The shape at first appears as a series of knots. As this becomes more organized it can resemble a woven pattern. The density and repetition of specific lines means that certain sequences not only gain definition, they also begin to concen-trate energy within a bounded form. These clustered spaces are thus more like semi-permeable environments that gain shape only through the intensity of traffic. Artists have fastened onto the emancipatory potential of networks. However, they have also pointed out that no one lives in a network alone. The network is just a line of possibility between different points. This line is as thin or as thick as the traffic that it transmits. Where the lines of communication begin to gain density there is the emergence of shared ground. At these points of attraction and interest there is a clustering of activity and engagement. If there is anything to learn from the aesthetic forays into the ideas of home and the stranger, hospitality and cosmopolitanism, it revolves around the belief that the imagination can yield an alternative sense of place, create new modes of relating to others, and present another way of seeing the world as a whole.

Notes

Introduction: Waiting for the Barbarians

1 ARS Kiasma is an annual international art exhibition run by the Kiasma Museum of Contemporary Art, Helsinki.

2 Throughout this book I have used the term 'refugee' to bridge the quasi-legal and moralistic distinctions between different kinds of asylum seekers. I have also used the term 'migrant' in a generic way because I believe that the distinctions that are promoted in the popular discourse have at best a spurious conceptual basis and are usually a matter of conveniently reducing complex forms of connection to and complicity with the forces that compel people to move.

3 For a more detailed analysis on the refugee crisis in Australia, see Papastergiadis (2007d), pp. 371–91; Papastergiadis (2007a), pp. 52–71; and Papastergiadis (2006b), pp. 429–42.

4 *Borderpanic* was curated by Zina Kaye and Deborah Kelly in conjunction with Performance Space and Museum of Contemporary Art, Sydney, and Next Five Minutes 4, Amsterdam, September 2002 (see www.h-net.org/announce/show. cgi?ID=131198).

5 Rancière retains an abiding belief that the measure of revolutionary aesthetics and politics is found in their expression of a 'common humanity' (2004, p. 27). For him, equality is not a political ideal that must be defended or attained, but rather a pre-political condition – a human capacity that enables strangers to become mutually intelligible. In categorical terms he states art is the implementation of equality (ibid., p. 53).

Chapter 1 Ambient Fears

1 In 1985 Ronald Reagan declared a national emergency because of the threat of the Nicaraguan military. He warned Americans that they were only two days from Texas.
2 The original code name for the battle was 'Operation Infinite Justice'. It was replaced by the name 'Enduring Freedom' because, as Muslim clerics noted, only God could execute infinite justice.

Chapter 2 Kinetophobia, Motion Fearness

1 This antagonistic view of cross-border relations is most powerfully exemplified in the construction of a 3,200 km wall along the border between the USA and Mexico, at an estimated cost of $US8 billion (www.bbc.co.uk/2/hi/ameri cas/4407558.stm).
2 The 'cliff' of a 30 per cent wage differential that was, in the 1950s, the famous benchmark for explaining the point at which a migrant got motivated to move is now dwarfed by the height of the differential that separates the income levels between the North and the South. See Massey et al. (1998), p. 8.
3 See for instance, https://www.imap-migration.org. This map was developed in co-operation with the leading agencies involved in the surveillance of migration pathways, and it exists in two versions, one which is publicly available and another that 'contains detailed information restricted to representatives of the partner states and partner agencies' (http://www.icmpd.org/10.html).
4 On the range of collective art projects that respond to the militarization of migration, see Biemann and Holmes (2006).
5 The term 'transmigrant' refers to someone who crosses borders on a recurring basis and is not subject to the restrictions faced by itinerant and seasonal migrants.
6 A 2006 study of media reports on asylum seekers found that, along with many common words that evoke an embodied sense of disgust – such as 'crime', 'dirty', 'cheat', 'burden', 'ruthless', 'ruin' – words were used to represent migration that carry connotations of uncontrolled and dangerous flows: 'wave', 'flood', 'influx', 'mob', 'horde', 'rampage', and 'disorder'. Tyler (2006), p. 191. See also Žižek (2002).
7 Douglas Massey and J. Edward Taylor argue that, in the USA, there is a historical correlation between growth in trade and immigration, and also between the recent restrictions on immigration and the decline of rates of trade between the USA and the rest of the world; see Massey and Taylor (2004), p. 377. Similar arguments have been made in relation to the UK and Australian economies: Sriskandarajak et al. (2008); Murphy (2000), p. 159.
8 For a critical evaluation of the concept of mobility in the humanities and social sciences, see Cresswell (2006).
9 The Large Hadron Collider in Geneva commenced its experiments on 7 September 2008.

Chapter 3 Hospitality and the Zombification of the Other

1 This quotation is taken from a documentary film entitled *Hope: A Documentary Film about Amal Basry and the SIEV X Disaster*, directed by Steve Thomas (Flying Carpet Films, 2007).
2 All references to the Fadaiat project are drawn from the Fadaiat book, available at http://fadaiat.net/english.html.
3 For examples of this new discourse, see Basch et al. (1994) and Chambers (1994).
4 Refugee Week was launched at the Carillo Gantner Theatre, University of Melbourne, on 19 October 2006.

Chapter 4 Aesthetic Cosmopolitanism

1 Groys, B. (2008), p. 151. Groys is not alone in this reflex form of economic determinism in the face of cultural difference. The most influential essay in this field is still Žižek (1997).
2 Guattari makes an explicit link between creativity and cosmopolitanism. He defines art as a 'creation in a nascent state, perpetually in advance of itself' – that is, a gesture that does not intersect with the preset rhythms or fall into the available spaces of its own time and place. This movement, he adds, 'becomes, at the same time, homeland, self-belonging, attachment to clan and cosmic effusion' (1995, p. 107).

Chapter 5 Aesthetics through a Cosmopolitan Frame

1 Rancière makes a similar move in Rancière (2007a), p. 259.

Chapter 6 The Gobal Orientation of Contemporary Art

1 Brian de Palma's aptly named film *Redacted* (2007) was, in his words, a sequel to his earlier film *Casualties of War* (1989). However, the key difference between the two films is that the story of abuse in the Vietnam War is told through the flashback memories of a central character, whereas the Iraq War is represented through innumerable stories found on the internet.
2 This was the theme of the 2008 Brighton Photography Biennial, *Memory of Fire: The War of Images and Images of War*, curated by Julian Stallabrass.
3 It is worth comparing this use of the banner with the more disjunctive use of the form by Thomas Hirschhorn. Hirschhorn created a banner 18 metres long that was composed of images of dead bodies from the Iraq War. All the images were drawn from the most proximate of sources – the internet – and yet his title of his work, *The Incommensurable Banner* (2008), suggests that, by putting these images together, he has not necessarily helped make sense of the event.
4 'There are no photographs, no videos of his works – they are saved exclusively in the memory of the participants. It is possible to buy a "Sehgal" – but only in the presence of a notary, with whom one negotiates how and where the piece is

to be executed' (Sebastian Friezel, 'Ceci n'est pas le vide', www.signandsight. com/features/203.html).

5 For a critique of the failure of the art world to engage with the interplay between the aesthetic and political dimensions of Documenta XI, see McEvilley (2002), p. 82.

6 See, for instance, Hans Haacke's New York poster project commemorating 9/11 (2002), Steve McQueen's *Gravesend* (2007) and Multiplicity's *Solid Sea 03* (2003), in which contrasting video footage is provided of journeys taken along the Israeli and Palestinian corridors that link Hebron and Nablus. Needless to say, the Palestinian route is via numerous checkpoints, along broken surfaces, and takes five times as long.

7 For a detailed discussion of the thematic of exile in Duchamp's life and practice, see Demos (2007).

8 Partha Mitter defines the virtual cosmopolitan as a 'native of the peripheries, . . . who is intellectually engaged with the knowledge system of the metropolis . . . proficient in their own language and who has no lack of confidence in tackling the whole of the world of the intellect' (Mitter and Mercer (2005), p. 38).

9 Of course, the 'clash of civilizations' thesis is imbued with anthropomorphic capacities, but these attributed characteristics of movement and collision are not just a case of misreading the inherent cultural content of, say, the Muslim civilization, but also part of an essentialist strategy to imply both that the other possesses a self-contained and unified identity and that there is a fixed moral boundary between us and them. There cannot be a clash between elements unless they are already positioned as discrete entities that are driven by antagonistic forces. Hence the adoption of the 'clash of civilizations' thesis was both an effort to cleave apart elements that were already caught in each other's orbit and a denial of a long history of mutual interdependence and co-existence. It is my contention that the so-called problems between different cultures is a product not so much of their absolute distance from each other as of their proximities and entanglements, which generate border disputes. If we are to recognize that there are differences between neighbours, does this imply that they are inevitably locked in an antagonistic battle of mutual destruction, or is there another option – that through negotiations new forms of settlement can be found in which both parties can not only survive but also develop fresh understandings of each other?

Chapter 7 Hybridity and Ambivalence

1 The earliest critic was Parry (1987), followed by Young (1995).

Chapter 8 Cosmopolitanism, Cultural Translation and the Void

1 Ivekovic makes a strong claim for translation as the 'original mother tongue of humankind', which has profound implications for cosmopolitan theory.

2 I would like to thank Berndt Clavier for his discussion on Hassan.

3 See Derrida (1998), p. 25, where he describes the property of language as possessing a 'structure of alienation without alienation'. In a later passage he
   prompts translators 'to invent your language if you can or want to hear mine
   . . . Compatriots of every country, translator – poets, rebel against patriotism.
   . . . Each time I write a word, a word that I love and love to write, in the time of
   this word, at the instant of a single syllable, the song of this new International
   awakens in me' (ibid., p. 57).
4 See also Papastergiadis et al. (2007), Papastergiadis (2006).
5 This desire to clear away the influence of others and even the trace of the self is
   also expressed by the painter Philip Guston in a story once told to him by John
   Cage: 'When you start working, everybody is in your studio – the past, your
   friends, enemies, the art world, and above all, your own ideas – all are there. But
   as you continue painting, they start leaving, one by one, and you are left com-
   pletely alone. Then, if you are lucky, even you leave' (Guston, quoted in 'The
   Philadephia Panel', *It Is*, 5, spring 1960, pp. 36–8).

Chapter 9 Collaboration in Art and Society

1 *Cities on the Move* opened in 1997 at Vienna's Secession and toured for three
   years, to CAPC in Bordeaux, MoMA PS1 in New York, the Louisiana Museum
   in Denmark, the Hayward Gallery in London, and the Kiasma Museum of
   Contemporary Art in Helsinki, and closed in Bangkok in 1999.
2 *Liminal Spaces*, curated by Eyal Danon, Galit Eilat, Reem Fadda and Philipp
   Misselwitz, has a website at www.liminalspaces.org. See also the comparable
   project by the Italian collective Multiplicity, *The Road Map* (2003), discussed in
   Multiplicity (2005).
3 www.longmarchspace.com/publication/list_publication.html?locale=en_US.

Chapter 10 Mobile Methods

1 *Via Egnatia* – a path of displaced memories – is a project by Osservatorio
   Nomade, Stalker (Rome), Autogeree (Paris), and Oxymoron (Athens).
   Marina Fokidis curated the conference and installation of works in the Yeni
   Tzami archaeological museum in Thessaloniki. The conference and exhibition were held between 3 and 17 February 2005. In his opening speech, Charis
   Aidonopoulos, the deputy mayor of Thessaloniki, acknowledged that the time
   was right to invite artists and scholars to discuss such vexed historical issues as
   the plight of refugees and the need for a way out of the impasses of 'national
   thinking'.

References and Bibliography

Ackerman, H., and Gauthier, J. (1999) 'The ways and nature of the zombi', *Journal of American Folklore*, 104(414), pp. 466–94.

Agamben, G. (1993) *The Coming Community*. Minneapolis: University of Minnesota Press.

Agamben, G. (1998) *Homo Sacer: Sovereign Power and Bare Life*, trans. D. Heller-Roazen. Stanford, CA: Stanford University Press.

Agamben, G. (2000) *The Open: Man and Animal*, trans. K. Attell. Stanford, CA: Stanford University Press.

Agustin, L. (2006) 'The disappearing of migration categories: migrants who sell sex', *Journal of Ethnic and Migration Studies*, 32(1), pp. 29–47.

Aijaz, A. (1992) *In Theory*. London: Verso.

Anderson, B. (1983) *Imagined Communities*. London: Verso.

Andreasen, S., and Larsen, L. B. (2007) 'The middlemen: beginning to talk about mediation', in *Curating Subjects*, ed. P. O'Neil. London: Open Editions, pp. 20–30.

Ang, I. (2001) *On Not Speaking Chinese*. London: Routledge.

Anthias F., and Lazardis, G. (eds) (2000) *Gender and Migration: Women on the Move*. New York: Berg.

Appadurai, A. (1996) *Modernity at Large*. Minneapolis: University of Minnesota Press.

Appiah, A. (2006) *Cosmopolitanism*. New York: W. W. Norton.

Araeen, R. (2000) 'A new beginning: beyond post-colonial cultural theory and identity politics', *Third Text*, 14(50), pp. 3–20.

Araeen, R. (2001) 'Re-thinking history and some other things,' *Third Text*, 15(54), pp. 93–100.

Asad, T. (2007) *On Suicide Bombing*. New York: Columbia University Press.

Austin, J. (ed.) (2003) *From Nothing to Zero: Letters from Refugees in Australia's Detention Centres*. Melbourne: Lonely Planet.

Babcock, E. (2006) 'The transformative potential of Belizean migrant voluntary associations in Chicago', *International Migration*, 44(1), pp. 31–53.

Backhouse, M. (2003) 'Suspension of disbelief the key to these spaces', *The Age*, 3 January.

Badiou, A. (2003) *Saint Paul: The Foundation of Universalism*, trans. R. Brassier. Stanford, CA: Stanford University Press.

Bailey, O. G., Georgiou, M., and Harindranath, R. (eds) (2007) *Transnational Lives and the Media: Re-imagining Diaspora*. New York: Palgrave Macmillan.

Balibar, E. (1994) *Masses, Classes and Ideas*, trans. J. Swenson. New York: Routledge.

Balibar, E. (2002a) *Politics and the Other Scene*. London: Verso.

Balibar, E. (2002b) 'The three concepts of politics: emancipation, transformation, civility', in *Politics and the Other Scene*. London: Verso, pp. 1–39.

Balibar, E. (2007) 'On universalism: in debate with Alain Badiou', trans. M. O'Neill, http://eipcp.net/transvrsal/0607/balibar/en.

Balibar, E., and Wallerstein, I. (1991) *Race, Nation, Class*. London: Verso.

Bardon, G. (2000) 'The money belongs to the ancestors', in *Papunya Tula – Genesis and Genius*, ed. H. Perkins and H. Fink. Sydney: Art Gallery of New South Wales.

Bardon, J. (1991) 'Interior: a monograph concerning hieroglyphs in Australian art, and their perspectives', in *Revolution by Night*. Sydney: Local Consumption, pp. 227–36.

Barnett, T. (2004) *The Pentagon's New Map*. New York: Putnam.

Basch, L., Glick Schiller, N., and Szanton Blanc, C. (1994) *Nations Unbound*. New York: Gordon & Breach.

Baudrillard, J. (2004) *The Gulf War Did Not Take Place*, trans. P. Patton. Sydney: Power.

Bauman, Z. (1987) *Legislators and Interpreters*. Cambridge: Polity.

Bauman, Z. (1991) *Modernity and Ambivalence*. Cambridge: Polity.

Bauman, Z. (2000) *Liquid Modernity*. Cambridge: Polity.

Bauman, Z. (2001) *Community*. Cambridge: Polity.

Bauman, Z. (2002) *Society under Siege*. Cambridge: Polity.

Bauman, Z. (2006a) *Liquid Fear*. Cambridge: Polity.

Bauman, Z. (2006b) *Liquid Life*. Cambridge: Polity.

Bauman, Z. (2007) *Liquid Times: Living in an Age of Uncertainty*. Cambridge: Polity.

Beck, U. (1999) *World Risk Society*. Cambridge: Polity.

Beck, U. (2002) 'The cosmopolitan society and its enemies', *Theory, Culture & Society*, 19(1–2), pp. 17–44.

Beck, U. (2006) *Cosmopolitan Vision*. Cambridge: Polity.

Becker, H. (1982) *Art Worlds*. Berkeley: University of California Press.

Beech, D. (2005) 'Independent collaborative hospitality', *Variant*, 2(22), p. 16.

Belting, H., and Buddensieg, A. (eds) (2009) *The Global Art World: Audiences, Markets and Museums*. Ostfildern-Ruit: Hatje Cantz.

Benjamin, W. (1972) 'The task of the translator', in *Illuminations*, trans. H. Zohn. London: Fontana, pp. 69–82.

Bhabha, H. (ed.) (1990) *Nation and Narration*. London: Routledge.

Bhabha, H. (1994) *The Location of Culture*. London: Routledge.

Bhabha, H. (1996) 'Unsatisfied: notes on vernacular cosmopolitanism', in *Text and Nation*, ed. L. Garci-Morena and P. C. Pfiefer. London: Camden House.

Bhagwati, J. (2003) 'Borders beyond control', *Foreign Affairs*, 82(1), pp. 98–104.

Bharucha, R. (2006) *Another Asia*. New Delhi: Oxford University Press.

Bharucha, R. (2007) 'The limits of the beyond: contemporary art practice, intervention and collaboration in public spaces', *Third Text*, 21(4), pp. 397–416.

Biemann, U., and Holmes, B. (eds) (2006) *The Maghreb Connection: Movements of Life across North Africa*. Barcelona: Acta.

Binswanger, D. (2005) *Die Weltwoche*, 10 November, quoted at www.signandsight.com/features/491.html.

Birnbaum, D. (2008) *The Hospitality of Presence: Problems of Otherness in Husserl's Phenomenology*. New York: Sternberg Press.

Bishop, C. (2004) 'Antagonism and relational aesthetics', *October*, 110, pp. 51–79.

Bishop, C. (2006) 'The social turn: collaboration and its discontents', *Artforum*, February, pp. 178–83.

Blanchot, M. (1989) 'Everyday speech', *Yale French Studies*, 73, pp. 12–20.

Bloom, H. (1973) *The Anxiety of Influence*. New York: Oxford University Press.

Bobbio, N. (2000) *In Praise of Meekness*, trans. T. Chataway. Cambridge: Polity.

Boltanski L., and Chiapello, E. (2007) *The New Spirit of Capitalism*, trans. G. Elliott. London: Verso.

Borjas, G. (1989) 'Economic theory and international migration', *International Migration Review*, 23(3), pp. 209–37.

Bourke, J. (2006) *Fear: A Cultural History*. London: Virago.

Bourriaud, N. (1996) 'An introduction to relational aesthetics', in *Traffic*, ed. N. Bourriaud. Bordeaux: CAPC Museé d'art contemporain.

Bourriaud, N. (2002a) *Postproduction: Culture as Screenplay*, trans. C. Schneider. New York: Lukas & Sternberg.

Bourriaud, N. (2002b) *Relational Aesthetics*, trans. S. Pleasance and F. Woods Dijon: Les Presses du réel.

Bourriaud, N. (2009a) 'Precarious constructions: answer to Jacques Rancière on art and politics', *Open: Cahier on Art and the Public Domain*, 17, p. 23.

Bourriaud, N. (2009b) *The Radicant*, trans. J. Gussen and L. Porten. New York: Lukas & Sternberg.

Bowen, J. R. (2006) *Why the French Don't Like Headscarves: Islam, the State and Public Space*. Princeton, NJ: Princeton University Press.

Boyle, F. (2001) 'No war against Afghanistan!', speech at Illinois Disciples Foundation, 18 October, www.ratical.org/ratville/CAH/fab112901.pdf.

Bradley, W. (2007) 'Introduction', in *Art and Social Change*, ed. W. Bradley and C. Esche. London: Tate in association with Afterall, pp. 9–24.

Brah, A., and Coombs, A. (2000) *Hybridity and its Discontents*. London: Routledge.

Brenner, N. (2004) *New State Spaces: Urban Governance and the Rescaling of Statehood*. Oxford: Oxford University Press.

Brett, G. (ed.) (2008) *Cildo Meireles*. London: Tate.

Bryson, N. (1999) 'The gaze in the expanded field', in *Vision and Visuality*, ed. H. Foster. New York: New Press.

Buchler, P., and Papastergiadis, N. (eds) (1996) *Ambient Fears*. London: Rivers Oram Press.

Buck-Morss, S. (2003) *Thinking Past Terror*. London: Verso.

Buden B., and Nowotny, S. (2009) 'Cultural translation: an introduction to the problem', *Translation Studies*, 2(2), pp. 196–219.

Bull, M. (2007) 'Vectors of the biopolitical,' *New Left Review*, 45 (May/June), pp. 7–25.

Buncombe, A. (2001) 'Bush rejects Taliban offer to surrender bin Laden', *The Independent* 15 October, p. 1.

Burbach, R., and Tarbell, J. (2004) *Imperial Overstretch: George Bush and the Hubris of Empire*. London: Zed Books.

Burchill, D. (2006) 'Where I'm calling from', *Australian Literary Review*, 6 September, p. 4.

Buren, D. (1983) 'Function of the studio', in *Museums by Artists*, ed. A. A. Bronson and P. Gale. Toronto: Art Metropole.

Burgin, V. (1986) *The End of Art Theory*. London: Macmillan.

Burnside, J. (2002) 'Refugees: the Tampa case', *Postcolonial Studies*, 5(1), pp. 17–28.

Butler, J. (2000a) 'Competing universalities', in *Contingency, Hegemony, Universality*, ed. J. Butler, E. Laclau and S. Žižek. London: Verso, pp. 136–81.

Butler, J. (2000b) 'Restaging the universal', in *Contingency, Hegemony, Universality*, ed. J. Butler, E. Laclau and S. Žižek. London: Verso, pp. 11–43.

Butler, J. (2004) *Precarious Life*. London: Verso.

Byrne, D. (1998) *Complexity and the Social Sciences*. London: Routledge.

Capra, F. (1996) *The Web of Life*. New York: Anchor Books.

Careri, F. (2004) *Stalker: exposition du 5 février au 23 mai 2004*. Bordeaux: CAPC – Musée d'art contemporain; Lyon: Fage Editions.

Carroll, J. (2002) *Terror: A Meditation on the Meaning of September 11*. Melbourne: Scribe.

Carter, P. (1996) *The Lie of the Land*. London: Faber & Faber.

Carter, P. (2000) 'The enigma of a homeland place: mobilising the Papunya Tula painting movement 1971–1972', in *Papunya Tula: Genesis and Genius*, ed. H. Perkins and H. Fink. Sydney: Art Gallery of New South Wales.

Cash, J. (2004) 'The political/cultural unconscious and the process for reconciliation', *Postcolonial Studies*, 7(2), pp. 165–75.

Castells, M. (1989) *The Informational City*. Oxford: Blackwell.

Castells, M. (1996) *The Rise of Network Society*. Oxford: Blackwell.

Castles, S. (2004) 'The factors that make and unmake migration policies', *International Migration Review*, 38(3), pp. 852–84.

Castles, S., and Kosack, G. (1973) *Immigrant Workers and Class Structure in Western Europe*. Oxford: Oxford University Press.

Castles, S., and Miller, M. (2003) *The Age of Migration*. New York: Palgrave.

Castoriadis, C. (1997a) *The Castoriadis Reader*, trans. D. Curtis. Oxford: Blackwell.

Castoriadis, C. (1997b) *The Imaginary Institution of Society*, trans. K. Blamey. Cambridge: Polity.

Castoriadis, C. (1997c) *World in Fragments*, trans. D. Curtis. Stanford, CA: Stanford University Press.

Caterson, S. (2007) 'The words on terror', *The Age*, 15 December, p. 7.

Cavafy, C. P. (1984) 'Waiting for the barbarians', in *Collected Poems*, ed. G. Savidis, trans. E. Keeley and P. Sherrard. London: Hogarth Press.

Chambers, I. (1994) *Migrancy, Culture, Identity*. London: Routledge.

Chaudhuri, A. (2009) 'Cosmopolitanism's alien face', *New Left Review*, 55(Jan/Feb), pp. 89–106.

Cheah, P. (2003) *Spectral Nationalism*. New York: Columbia University Press.

Cheah P., and Robbins, B. (eds) (1998) *Cosmopolitics: Thinking and Feeling beyond the Nation*. Minneapolis: University of Minnesota Press.

Cheetham, M. (2009) 'Theory reception: Panofsky, Kant, and disciplinary cosmopolitanism', *Journal of Art Historiography*, 1(December), pp 1–13.

Chiswick, B. (2000) 'Are immigrants favourably self selected? An economic analysis', in *Migration Theory*, ed. C. Brettell and J. Hollifield. London: Routledge, pp. 61–76.

Chomsky, N. (2001) *September 11*. Sydney: Allen & Unwin.

Chow, R. (2008) 'Translator, traitor, mourner (or dreaming of intercultural equivalence)', *New Literary History*, 39(3), pp. 565–80.

Clark, T. J. (1982) *Image of the People: Gustave Courbet and the 1848 Revolution*. Princeton, NJ: Princeton University Press.

Clavier, B. (2007) 'Hassan: the disenchantment of skepticism', in *John Barth and Postmodernism: Spatiality, Travel, Montage*. New York: Peter Lang.

Coffi, F. (1999) 'Postmodernism, etc.: an interview with Ihab Hassan', *Style*, fall, p. 11.

Comaroff, J., and Comaroff, J. (1999) 'Occult economies and the violence of abstraction: notes from the South African postcolony', *American Ethnologist*, 26, pp. 279–301.

Comaroff, J., and Comaroff, J. (2002) 'Alien-nation: zombies, immigrants and millennial capitalism,' *South Atlantic Quarterly*, 101(4), pp. 779–805.

Corey, R. (2004) *Fear: The History of a Political Idea*. Oxford: Oxford University Press.

Creed, B. (2003) *Media Matrix: Sexing the New Reality*. Crows Nest, NSW: Allen & Unwin.

Cresswell, T. (2006) *On the Move*. London: Routledge.

Cubitt, S. (2008) 'Indigenous, settler and migrant media', *Third Text*, 22(6), pp. 733–42.

Danto, A. C. (1992) *Beyond the Brillo Box: The Visual Arts in Post-Historical Perspective*. New York: Farrar, Strauss, Giroux.

David, C., and Chevrier, J.-F. (eds) (1997) *Politics, Poetics: Documenta X, the Book*. Ostfildern-Ruit: Hatje Cantz.

Davis, M. (2001) 'The flames of New York', *New Left Review*, 12 (Nov/Dec), pp. 34–50.

Delanty, G. (2009) *The Cosmopolitan Imagination.* Cambridge: Cambridge University Press.

Deleuze, G. (1990) 'Mediators', in *Negotiations, 1972–1990.* New York: Columbia University Press, pp. 125–34.

Deleuze, G., and Guattari, F. (1983) *Anti-Oedipus,* trans. R. Hurley. Minneapolis: University of Minnesota Press.

Deleuze, G., and Parnet, C. (2002) *Dialogues II,* trans. J. Tomlinson, B. Habberjam and E. Albert. New York: Columbia University Press.

Demos, T. J. (2007) *The Exiles of Marcel Duchamp.* Cambridge, MA: MIT Press.

Derkson, J. (2001) 'Prototypes for new (spatial and temporal) understandings', in *ARS 01: Unfolding Perspectives,* ed. M. Jaukkuri. Helsinki: Museum of Contemporary Art [exhibition catalogue], p. 101.

Derrida, J. (1978) *Writing and Difference,* trans. A. Bass. Chicago: Chicago University Press.

Derrida, J. (1998) *Monolingualism of the Other, or, The Prosthesis of Origin,* trans. P. Mensah. Stanford, CA: Stanford University Press.

Derrida, J., and Dufourmantelle, A. (2000) *Of Hospitality,* trans. R. Bowlby. Stanford, CA: Stanford University Press.

Devetak, R. (2005) 'The Gothic scene of international relations: ghosts, monsters, terror and the sublime after September 11', *Review of International Studies,* 31, p. 622.

Dickinson, E. (1970) *The Complete Poems of Emily Dickinson,* ed. T. Johnson. London: Faber & Faber.

DIMA (Department of Immigration and Multicultural Affairs) (1995) *Business Temporary Entry: Future Directions. Report by the Committee of Inquiry into the Temporary Entry of Business People and Highly Skilled Specialists.* Canberra: Australian Government.

Doherty, C. (ed.) (2004) *Contemporary Art: From Studio to Situation.* London: Black Dog.

Doherty, C. (2006) 'Landscapes of mobilities', in *Places of Departure,* ed. E. Cavusoglu. London: Film and Video Umbrella.

Duffield, M. (2001) *Global Governance and the New Wars: The Merging of Development and Security.* London: Zed Books.

Dumment, M. (2001) *On Immigration and Refugees.* London: Routledge.

Durham, J. (1993) *A Certain Lack of Coherence: Writings on Art and Cultural Politics,* ed. J. Fisher. London: Kala Press.

Durham, J. (2004) 'Stones rejected by the builder,' *Jimmie Durham.* Milan: CHARTA.

Eco, U. (1989) *The Open Work,* trans. A. Cancogni. Cambridge, MA: Harvard University Press.

Eco, U. (2001) *Five Moral Pieces,* trans. A. McEwen. London: Secker & Warburg.

Eco, U. (2007) *Turning Back the Clock,* trans. A. McEwen. Orlando, FL: Harcourt.

Eno, B. (1996) *A Year with Swollen Appendices: Brian Eno's Diary.* London: Faber & Faber.

Enwezor, O. (2002) 'The black box', *Documenta XI, Platform 5.* Ostfildern-Ruit: Hatje Cantz.

Enwezor, O. (2003a) 'Documentary/verite: bio-politics, human rights and the figure of "truth" in contemporary art', *Australian and New Zealand Journal of Art*, 4(2), pp. 11–42.

Enwezor, O. (ed.) (2003b) *Créolité and Creolization: Documenta XI, Platform 3*. Ostfildern-Ruit: Hatje Cantz.

Enwezor, O. (2003–4) 'Mega-exhibitions and the antinomies of a transnational global forum', *MJ-Manifesta Journal*, 2, pp. 6–31.

Enwezor, O. (2005) 'The artist as producer in times of crisis', in *Empires, Ruins + Networks: The Transcultural Agenda in Art*, ed. S. McQuire and N. Papastergiadis. Melbourne: Melbourne University Press, pp. 11–51.

Enwezor, O. (2007) 'The production of social space as artwork: protocols of community in the work of Le Groupe Amos and Huit Facettes', in *Collectivism after Modernism: The Art of Social Imagination after 1945*, ed. B. Stimson and G. Sholette. Minneapolis: University of Minnesota Press, pp. 223–52.

Enwezor, O. (2008a) 'A space of encounter: interview with Victoria Lynn', *Art and Australia*, 46(2), pp. 216–17.

Enwezor, O. (2008b) *Archive Fever: Uses of the Document in Contemporary Art*. New York: Steidl/ICP.

Enwezor, O. (2009) 'Modernity and postcolonial ambivalence', in *Altermodern: Tate Triennial*, ed. N. Bourriaud. London: Tate.

Enzensberger, H. M. (1994) *Civil War*. London: Granta.

Esche, C. (2001) 'Modest proposals, or, Why the choice is limited to how wealth is to be squandered', in *Berlin Biennale*, ed. S. Bos and A. Fletcher. Berlin: Berlin Biennale.

Esche, C. (2002) 'We won't use guns, we won't use bombs, we'll use the one thing we've got more of, that's our minds', in *P A U S E*, ed. C. Esche, H. Hanru and S. Wan-kyun. Gwangju, South Korea: Gwangju Biennale Press.

Esche, C. (2005) *Modest Proposals*. Istanbul: Baglam.

Escobar, T. (2004) *El arte fuera de sí*. Asunción, Paraguay: Fondec, pp. 21–94.

Faist, T. (2000a) *The Volume and Dynamics of International Migration and Transnational Spaces*. Oxford: Clarendon Press.

Faist, T. (2000b) 'Transnationalism in international migration: implications for the study of citizenship and culture', *Ethnic and Racial Studies*, 23, pp. 188–222.

Ferguson, B. W., and Hoegsberg, M. M. (2010) 'Talking and thinking about biennials: the potential of discursivity', in *The Biennial Reader*, ed. E. Filipovic, M. van Hal and S. Øvstebø. Ostfildern-Ruit: Hatje Cantz, pp. 360–77.

Ferguson, R. (ed.) (1990) *Out There: Marginalization and Contemporary Culture*. New York: New Museum of Contemporary Art; Cambridge, MA: MIT Press.

Figueiredo, E. (2003) 'Yes we have bananas: (how to represent Brazil and Brazilians)', paper presented at the conference Transcultural/Translators: Meeting Race, Indigeneity and Ethnicity in Four Nations, Villa Serbelloni, Bellagio, August.

Fischer-Lichte, E. (2008) *The Transformative Power of Performance: A New Aesthetics*, trans. S. Iris Jain. London: Routledge.

Fisher, J., and Mosquera, M. (eds) (2004) *Over Here: International Perspectives on*

Art and Culture. New York: New Museum of Contemporary Art; Cambridge, MA: MIT Press.

Fisk, R. (2005) *The Great War for Civilisation: The Conquest of the Middle East*. London: Fourth Estate.

Flynn, D. (2005) 'New borders, new management: the dilemmas of modern immigration policies', *Ethnic and Racial Studies*, 28(3), pp. 463–90.

Fokidis, M. (2005) 'The site as textile of paths and relations: netting the Egnatia: a dialogue between Marina Fokidis and Lorenzo Romitto', in *Empires, Ruins + Networks: The Transcultural Agenda in Art*, ed. S. McQuire and N. Papastergiadis. Melbourne: Melbourne University Press.

Foster, H. (1996) 'The artist as ethnographer', in *The Return of the Real*, Cambridge, MA: MIT Press.

Foster, H. (2003) 'Arty party', *London Review of Books*, 25(23), pp. 21–2.

Foster, H. (2004) 'An archival impulse', *October*, 110, pp. 3–22.

Freud, S. (1948) *Inhibitions, Symptoms and Anxiety*, trans. A. Strachey. London: Hogarth Press.

Friedman, J. (1999) 'The hybridization of roots and the abhorrence of the bush', in *Spaces of Culture: City, Nation, World*, ed. M. Featherstone and S. Lash. London: Sage.

Friedman, T. (2001) 'Foreign affairs: smoking or non-smoking', *New York Times*, 14 September, p. A27.

Friedman, T. (2002) 'A failure to imagine', *New York Times*, 19 May.

Furedi, F. (2005) *The Politics of Fear*. London: Continuum.

Gablik, S. (1995) 'Connective aesthetics: art after individualism', in *Mapping the Terrain: New Genre Public Art*, ed. S. Lacy. Seattle: Bay Press, pp. 74–87.

Gallagher, C. (1989) 'The bio-economics of our mutual friend', in *Fragments for a History of the Human Body*, ed. M. Feher, R. Naddaff and N. Tazi. New York: Zone.

García Canclini, N. (1995) *Hybrid Cultures*. Minneapolis: University of Minnesota Press.

Garnaut, J. (2006) 'Costello to violent Muslims: get out', *Sydney Morning Herald*, 24 February, p. 1.

GCIM (Global Commission on International Migration) (2002) *International Migration Report 2002: Migration in an Interconnected World: New Directions for Action*. Geneva: GCIM; available at: www.gcim.org/en/finalreport.html.

Geczy, A. (2003) 'Focussing the mind through the body: an interview with Mike Parr', *Artlink*, 23(1).

Geddes, A. (2000) *Immigration and European Integration: Towards Fortress Europe*. Manchester: Manchester University Press.

Giddens, A. (1976) *New Rules of Sociological Method*. London: Hutchinson.

Gillick, L. (2000) *Renovation Filter: Recent Past and Near Future*. Bristol: Arnolfini Gallery.

Gillick, L. (2007a) 'For a functional . . . utopia? A review of a position', in *Curating Subjects*, ed. P. O'Neill. London: Occasional Table.

Gillick, L. (2007b) 'Is there anything for art to say about Iraq?' *The Guardian*,

Art & Design Blog, 22 May; available at: www.guardian.co.uk/artanddesign/artblog/2007/may/22/isthereanythingforarttos?INTCMP=SRCH.

Gillick, L. (2010) 'Contemporary art does not account for that which is taking place', http://e-flux.com/journal/view/192.

Gilroy, P. (1993) *Black Atlantic*. London: Verso.

Gilroy, P. (2004) *After Empire: Melancholia or Convivial Culture?* London: Routledge.

Girard, R. (1980) *The Scapegoat*, trans. Y. Freccero. Baltimore: Johns Hopkins University Press.

Girard, R. (2001) 'What is occurring today is a mimetic rivalry on a planetary scale: an interview by Henri Tincq', *Le Monde*, 6 November, www.uibk.ac.at/theol/cover/girard/le_monde_interview.html.

Glassner, B. (1999) *The Culture of Fear*. New York: Basic Books.

Glissant, E. (1997) *Poetics of Relation*, trans. B. Wing. Ann Arbor: University of Michigan Press.

Go, S. (1998) 'The Philippines: A look into the migration scenario in the nineties', *Migration and Regional Economic Integration in Asia*. Paris: Organization for Economic Cooperation and Development.

Gordon, M. (2006) 'Living in limbo', *The Age*, 30 September, Insight Section, p. 1.

Graham, S. (2006) 'Cities and the "war on terror"', *International Journal of Urban and Regional Research*, 30(2), pp. 255–76.

Grant, S. (2006) 'GCIM report: defining an "ethical compass" for international migration policy', *International Migration*, 44(1), pp. 13–19.

Grey, S. (2006) *Ghost Plane: The True Story of the CIA Torture Program*. New York: St Martin's Press.

Grosz, E. (1994) *Volatile Bodies*. Sydney: Allen & Unwin.

Groys, B. (2008) *Art Power*. Cambridge, MA: MIT Press.

Grynstejn, M. (1993) 'La frontera/the border: art about the Mexico/US experience', in *La Frontera/The Border: Art about the Mexico/US Experience*. San Diego: Museum of Contemporary Art [exhibition catalogue].

Guattari, F. (1995) *Chaosmosis: An Ethico-Aesthetic Paradigm*, trans. P. Bains and J. Pefanis. Sydney: Power.

Hall, S. (1996a) *Stuart Hall: Critical Dialogues in Cultural Studies*, ed. D. Morley and K.-H. Chen. London: Routledge.

Hall, S. (1996b) 'When was "the post colonial"? Thinking at the limit', in *The Post-Colonial Question*, ed. I. Chambers and L. Curti. London: Routledge.

Handlin, O. (1951) *The Uprooted: The Epic Story of the Great Migrations that Made the American People*. Boston: Little, Brown.

Hannam, K., Sheller, M., and Urry, J. (2006) 'Editorial: mobilities, immobilities and moorings', *Mobilities*, 1(1), pp. 1–22.

Hanru, H. (2002a) 'Event city, Pandora's box', in *P A U S E*, ed. C. Esche, H. Hanru, and S. Wan-kyun. Gwangju, South Korea: Gwangju Biennale Press, p. 31.

Hanru, H. (2002b) *On the Mid-Ground*. Hong Kong: Timezone.

Harding, J. (2001) *The Uninvited: Refugees at the Rich Man's Gate*. London: Profile Books.

Hardt, M., and Negri, A. (2000) *Empire*. Cambridge, MA: Harvard University Press.

Hardt, M., and Negri, A. (2004) *Multitude: War and Democracy in the Age of Empire*. New York: Penguin Press.

Harvey, D. (2009) *Cosmopolitanism and the Geographies of Freedom*. New York: Columbia University Press.

Hassan, I. (1971) *The Dismemberment of Orpheus: Toward a Postmodern Literature*. New York: Oxford University Press.

Hassan, I. (1996) 'Negative capability reclaimed: literature and philosophy *contra* politics', *Philosophy and Literature*, 20(2), pp. 305–24.

Hassan, I. (2008a) 'Postmodernism? A self-interview', *Philosophy and Literature*, 30(1), pp. 223–8.

Hassan, I. (2008b) 'Risk and trust in art and theory', public lecture at the School of Culture and Communication, University of Melbourne, 4 June.

Hayles, K. (1991) *Chaos and Order*. Chicago: University of Chicago Press.

Healy, C. (2008) *Forgetting Aborigines*. Sydney: University of New South Wales Press.

Heater, D. (1996) *World Citizenship and Government: Cosmopolitan Ideas in the History of Western Political Thought*. London: Macmillan.

Helas, P., Lash, S., and Morris, P. (eds) (1996) *Detraditionalization: Critical Reflections on Authority and Identity*. Oxford: Blackwell.

Held, D. (1995) *Democracy and the Global Order: From the Modern State to Cosmopolitan Governance*. Cambridge: Polity.

Henley, J. (2005) 'We hate France and France hates us', *Guardian International*, 9 November, p. 17.

Hess, J. (2006) 'Statelessness and the state: Tibetans, citizenship, and nationalist activism in a transnational world', *International Migration*, 44(1), pp. 79–103.

Heuck, F., Homann, R., and Unverdorben, M. (2007) 'Our goal is mobility X: the federal trade association Schleppen & Schleusen', in *Taking the Matter into Common Hands*, ed. J. Billing, M. Lind and L. Nilsson. London: Black Dog Press, pp. 97–101.

Hlavajova, M., and Mosquera, G. (2004) *Cordially Invited*. Utrecht: BAK.

Hoagland, J. (2001a) 'Terrorists can't be kept in a box', *Washington Post*, 18 November, available at: www.ljworld.com/section/diary_111801/story/73878.

Hoagland, J. (2001b) 'The lifting of the Afghan curtain of horrors should concentrate minds on the consequences of the neglected', *Washington Post*, 17 November, p. 15.

Hobsbawm, E. (1994) *Age of Extremes*. London: Michael Joseph.

Hobsbawm, E., and Ranger, T. (eds) (1983) *The Invention of Tradition*. Cambridge: Cambridge University Press.

Holmes, B. (2007a) 'Do-it-yourself geopolitics', in *Collectivism after Modernism: The Art of Social Imagination after 1945*, ed. B. Stimson and G. Sholette. Minneapolis: University of Minnesota Press.

Holmes, B. (2007b) 'The revenge of the concept: artistic exchanges, networked resistance', in *Art and Social Change*, ed. W. Bradley and C. Esche. London: Tate in association with Afterall, pp. 350–68.

Holmes, B. (2009) *Escape the Overcode: Activist Art in the Control Society.* Eindhoven: Van Abbemuseum.

Hsu, M. (2005) 'Networked cosmopolitanism', in *Knowledge + Dialogue + Exchange*, ed. N. Tsoutas. Sydney: Artspace.

Huspeck, M. (2001) 'Border militarization and the reproduction of migrant labour', *Social Justice*, 28(2), pp. 110–30.

Huyghe, P. (2008) Artist's talk, Sydney Biennale, Museum of Contemporary Art, Sydney, 10 July.

Ivekovic, R. (2005) 'Transborder translating', www.eurozine.com/articles/2005-01-13-ivekovic-en.html.

Jacquard, R. (2002) *In the Name of Osama bin Laden: Global Terrorism and the bin Laden Brotherhood.* Durham, NC: Duke University Press.

Jaukkuri, M. (2001) 'Unfolding perspectives', in *ARS 01: Unfolding Perspectives*, ed. M. Jaukkuri. Helsinki: Museum of Contemporary Art [exhibition catalogue].

Jie, L. (2005) 'Locale and internationale: resituating global networks', in *World Contemporary Art in the Eyes of Asia*, ed. K. Hong-Hee. Gwangju, South Korea: Gwangju Biennale Press.

Johnson, V. (2000) 'Seeing is believing: a brief history of Papunya Tula artists 1971–2000', in *Papunya Tula: Genesis and Genius*, ed. H. Perkins and H. Fink. Sydney: Art Gallery of New South Wales.

Johnstone, S. (ed.) (2008) *The Everyday.* London: Whitechapel Gallery.

Joly, F., Barth, C., Buness, J., and Holmes, B. (ed.) (1997) *Documenta X: Short Guide.* Ostfildern-Ruit: Hatje Cantz.

Jonsson, S. (2010) 'The ideology of universalism', *New Left Review*, 63(May/June).

Julien, I. (2003) 'Créolité' 'Creolizing Vision', in *Créolité and Creolization: Documenta XI, Platform 3*.Ostfildern-Ruit: Hatje Cantz.

Kalra, V., Kaur, R., and Hutnyk, J. (2005) *Diaspora and Hybridity.* London: Sage.

Kanngieser, A. (2008) 'Performative encounter, transformative worlds: creative experiment radical politics, Germany, 2000–2006', PhD thesis, University of Melbourne.

Kant, I. ([1784] 1963) 'Idea for a universal history from a cosmopolitan point of view', in *On History*, trans. L. W. Beck. Indianapolis: Bobbs-Merrill.

Katsiaficas, G. (2006) *The Subversion of Politics.* Edinburgh: AK Press.

Kearney, R. (1988) *The Wake of the Imagination.* Minneapolis: University of Minnesota Press.

Kester, G. (2004) *Conversation Pieces.* Berkeley: University of California Press.

Kester, G. (2006) 'Another turn', *Artforum*, May, p. 22.

Kleinschmidt, H. (2003) *People on the Move.* London: Praeger.

Kleinschmidt, H. (2006a) 'Introduction', in *Migration, Regional Integration and Human Security*, ed. H. Kleinschmidt. Aldershot: Ashgate, pp. 2–8.

Kleinschmidt, H. (2006b) 'Migration and the making of transnational social spaces', public lecture, Australian Centre, University of Melbourne, 12 July.

Kleinschmidt, H. (2006c) 'Migration, regional integration and human security: an overview of research developments', in *Migration, Regional Integration and Human Security*, ed. H. Kleinschmidt. Aldershot: Ashgate, pp. 61–102.

Kofman, E. (2005) 'Citizenship, migration and the reassertion of national identity', *Citizenship Studies*, 9(5), pp. 453–67.

Kopp, H., and Schneider, F. (2003) 'A brief history of the noborder network', http://makeworlds.org/node/29.

Kristeva, J. (1991) *Strangers to Ourselves*, trans. L. Roudiez. New York: Columbia University Press.

Kristeva, J. (1993) *Nations without Nationalism*, trans. L. Roudiez. New York: Columbia University Press.

Lapham, L. (2005) *Gag Rule: On Suppression of Dissent and the Stifling of Democracy*. New York: Penguin.

Larsen, L. B. (1997) 'Superflex: art and biogas', www.superflex.net/texts/super flex_art_and_biogas.

Latour, B. (1993) *We Have Never Been Modern*. New York: Harvester Wheatsheaf.

Latour, B. (2011) 'Some experiments in art and politics', http://e-flux.com/journal/view/217.

Lawrence, C. (2006) *Fear and Politics*. Melbourne: Scribe.

Le Goff, J. (1989) 'Head or heart? The political use of body metaphors in the Middle Ages', in *Fragments for a History of the Human Body*, ed. M. Feher, R. Naddaff and N. Tazi. New York: Zone.

Levitt, P., and de la Dehesa, R. (2003) 'Transnational migration and the redefinition of the state: variations and explanations', *Ethnic and Racial Studies*, 26(4), pp. 587–611.

Levy, J. (2000) *The Multiculturalism of Fear*. Oxford: Oxford University Press.

Lind, M. (2007) 'The collaborative turn,' in *Taking the Matter into Common Hands*, ed. J. Billing, M. Lind and L. Nilsson. London: Black Dog Press, pp. 15–31.

Lippard, L. (1973) *The Dematerialization of the Art Object from 1966 to 1972*. New York: Praeger.

Lippard, L. (1995) 'Escape attempts', in *Reconsidering the Object of Art, 1965–1975*. Los Angeles: MOCA.

Lippard, L. (2007) 'Time capsule', in *Art and Social Change*, ed. W. Bradley and C. Esche. London: Tate in association with Afterall, pp. 408–21.

Lofgren, O. (2002) 'The nationalization of anxiety', in *The Postnational Self*, ed. U. Hedetoft and M. Hjort. Minneapolis: University of Minnesota Press.

Loomba, A. (1998) *Colonialism/Postcolonialism*. London: Routledge.

Lutticken, S. (2009) *Idols of the Market*. New York: Sternberg Press.

Lyotard, J.-F. (1984) *The Postmodern Condition: A Report on Knowledge*, trans. G. Bennington and B. Massumi. Manchester: Manchester University Press.

McCoy, A. (2003) *The Politics of Heroin: CIA Complicity in the Global Drug Trade*. New York: Lawrence Hill.

McEvilley, T. (1991) *Art and Discontent*. New York: Documentext.

McEvilley, T. (2002) 'Documenta 11', *Frieze*, 69(September), pp. 81–5.

MacIntyre A. (1987) 'Relativism, power and philosophy', in *After Philosophy: End or Transformation?*, ed. K. Baynes, J. Bohmen and T. McCarthy. Cambridge, MA: MIT Press.

MacIntyre, A. (1998) *Whose Justice? Which Rationality?*, Notre Dame, IN: University of Notre Dame Press.

Malik, K. (2002) *Man, Beast and Zombie: What Science Can and Cannot Tell Us about Human Nature*. New Brunswick, NJ: Rutgers University Press.

Malkki, L. (1995a) 'National geographic: the rooting of people and the territorialization of national identity among scholars and refugees', *Cultural Anthropology*, 7(1), pp. 24–44.

Malkki, L. (1995b) *Purity and Exile*. Chicago: University of Chicago Press.

Mamdani, M. (2004) *Good Muslim, Bad Muslim: America, the Cold War, and the Roots of Terror*. New York: Pantheon.

Manne, R., with Corlett, D. (2004) 'Sending them home: refugees and the new politics of indifference', *Quarterly Essay*, 13, pp. 1–95.

Marcus, G. E. (1998) *Ethnography through Thick and Thin*. Princeton, NJ: Princeton University Press.

Marcus, G. E. (2006) 'Collaborative imaginations in globalizing systems', lecture delivered at the Institute of Ethnology, Academia Sinica, Taipei, Taiwan, 16–17 September.

Marcus, G. E., and Saka, E. (2006) 'Assemblage', *Theory, Culture & Society* 23(2/3), pp. 101–6.

Marr, D. (2005) 'Odyssey of a lost soul', *Sydney Morning Herald*, 12 February, p. 27.

Martin, J. (1978) *The Migrant Presence*. Sydney: Allen & Unwin.

Martin, S. (2007) 'Critique of relational aesthetics', *Third Text*, 21(4), pp. 369–86.

Massey, D., and Taylor, J. E. (2004) *International Migration*. Oxford: Oxford University Press.

Massey, D., et al. (1998) *Worlds in Motion*. Oxford: Clarendon Press.

Massumi, B. (2006) 'Fear the spectrum said', in *5 Codes: Architecture, Paranoia and Risk in Times of Terror*, ed. G. de Bruyn. Basel: Birkhäuser.

Mbembe, A. (2003) 'Necropolitics', *Public Culture*, 15(1), p. 30.

Meeropol, R. (2005) 'The post 9/11 terrorism investigation and immigration detention', in *America's Disappeared: Detainees, Secret Imprisonment, and the 'War on Terror'*, ed. R. Meeropol. New York: Seven Stories Press.

Melucci, A. (1989) *Nomads of the Present: Social Movements and Individual Needs in Contemporary Society*. London: Radius.

Memmi, A. (2007) *Decolonization and the Decolonized*. Minneapolis: University of Minnesota Press.

Mercer, K. (1994) *Welcome to the Jungle*. New York: Routledge.

Mercer, K. (2005) 'Introduction', in *Cosmopolitan Modernisms*, ed. K. Mercer. London: Institute of International Visual Arts and MIT Press.

Meskimmon, M. (2011) *Contemporary Art and the Cosmopolitan Imagination*. London: Routledge.

Mezzadra, S. (2009) 'Between centre and periphery: the labyrinth of contemporary migration', *Europa*, October, pp. 14–15; available at: www.euroalter.com.

Micklethwait, J., and Wooldridge, A. (2005) *The Right Nation*. New York: Penguin.

Mignolo, W. (1998) 'The many faces of cosmo-polis: border thinking and critical cosmopolitanism', in *Cosmopolitanism*, ed. C. A. Breckenridge. Durham, NC: Duke University Press, pp. 157–88.

Mishani, D., and Smotricz, A. (2005) 'What sort of Frenchmen are they? Interview with Alain Finkielkraut', *Ha'aretz*, 16 November.

Mitchell, W. J. T. (2008) 'Four fundamental concepts of image science', in *Under Pressure*, ed. D. Birnbaum and I. Graw. New York: Sternberg Press.

Mitter, P., and Mercer, K. (2005) 'Reflections on modern art and national identity in colonial India', in *Cosmopolitan Modernisms*, ed. K. Mercer. London: Institute of International Visual Arts and MIT Press.

Montag, W. (1999) *Bodies, Masses and Power*. London: Verso.

Montmann, N. (ed.) (2006) *Art and its Institutions: Current Conflicts, Critiques and Collaborations*. London: Black Dog.

Morphy, H. (1998) *Aboriginal Art*. London: Phaidon.

Mosquera, G. (2003) 'Alien-own/own alien', in *Complex Entanglements: Art, Globalization and Cultural Difference*, ed. N. Papastergiadis. London: Rivers Oram Press, pp. 19–29.

Mosquera, G., and Samos, A. (2004) *Ciudad Multiple City arte>Panamà 2003*. Amsterdam: KIT.

Mouffe, C. (1999) 'Deliberative democracy or agonistic pluralism?', *Social Research*, 66, pp. 745–58.

Mouffe, C. (2009) 'Politics and artistic practices in post-utopian times', in *Meaning Liam Gillick*, ed. M. Szewczyk. London: MIT Press.

Multiplicity (2005) 'Borders: the other side of globalization', in *Empires, Ruins + Networks: The Transcultural Agenda in Art*, ed. S. McQuire and N. Papastergiadis. Melbourne: Melbourne University Press, pp. 169–84.

Murphy, J. (2000) *Imagining the Fifties*. Sydney: UNSW Press.

Nancy, J.-L. (2000) *Being Singular Plural*, trans. R. D. Richardson and A. O'Byrne. Stanford, CA: Stanford University Press.

Nandy, A. (1984) *The Intimate Enemy*. Oxford: Oxford University Press.

Nash, M. (2008) 'Reality in the age of aesthetics', *Frieze*, 114(April), pp. 119–24.

Nava, M. (2007) *Visceral Cosmopolitanism*. Oxford: Berg.

Nederveen Pieterse, J. (2001) 'Hybridity, so what? The anti-hybridity backlash and the riddles of recognition', *Theory, Culture & Society*, 18(2/3), pp. 219–45.

Nederveen Pieterse, J. (2007) *Ethnicities and Global Multiculture*. Lanham, MD: Rowman & Littlefield.

Negri, A. (2008) 'Contemporaneity between modernity and postmodernity', in *Antinomies of Art and Culture*, ed. T. Smith, O. Enwezor and N. Condee. Durham, NC: Duke University Press.

Negri, A. (2009) *Commonwealth*. Cambridge, MA: Harvard University Press.

Nelson, R. (2010) 'Naked fear: a new chapter in the history of anxiety', *antiThesis*, 20, pp. 73–90.

New Museum and Creative Time (2009) *It Is What It Is: Conversations about Iraq*, www.conversationsaboutiraq.org/.

Nussbaum, M. (2001) *Upheavals of Thought: The Intelligence of Emotions*. New York: Routledge.

Oestreich, G. (1982) *Neostoicism and the Early Modern State*, ed. B. Oestreich and H. G. Koenigsberger, trans. D. Mclintock. Cambridge: Cambridge University Press.

Okao, R. (2006) 'Black heart', *Big Issue*, 256 (19 June–4 July), p. 16.

Olshansky, B. (2005) 'What does it mean to be an enemy combatant?' in *America's Disappeared*, ed. R. Meeropol. New York, Seven Stories Press.

Ong, A. (1999) *Flexible Citizenship*. Durham, NC: Duke University Press.

Orta, L. (1999) 'Interview with Hou Hanru', www.studio-orta.com.

Pagden, A. (2000) 'Cosmopolitanism as imperialism', *Constellations*, 7(1), pp. 3–22.

Papadopoulos, D., Stephenson, N., and Tsianos, V. (2008) *Escape Routes*. London: Pluto Press.

Papastergiadis, N. (1998) *Dialogues in the Diaspora*. London: Rivers Oram Press.

Papastergiadis, N. (2000) *The Turbulence of Migration*. Cambridge: Polity.

Papastergiadis, N. (2001) *Metaphor and Tension: Collaboration and its Discontents*. Sydney: Artspace.

Papastergiadis, N. (2003) 'Cultural identity and its boredom, transculturalism and its ecstasy,' in *Complex Entanglements: Art, Globalization and Cultural Difference*, ed. N. Papastergiadis. London: Rivers Oram Press, pp. 156–77.

Papastergiadis, N. (2005) *Spatial Aesthetics: Art, Place and the Everyday*. London: Rivers Oram Press.

Papastergiadis, N. (2006a) 'On being here and still there', *Lida Abdul/Tania Brughera*. Lorraine: FRAC, pp. 54–63 [exhibition catalogue].

Papastergiadis, N. (2006b) 'The invasion complex: the abject other and spaces of violence', *Geographika Annals: Swedish Society for Anthropology and Geography*, 88B(4), pp. 429–42.

Papastergiadis, N. (2006c) 'The meek Michael Riley', in *Michael Riley: Sights Unseen*, ed. B. Croft. Canberra: National Gallery of Australia, pp. 67–73.

Papastergiadis, N. (2007a) 'Art in the age of siege', in *Transnational Lives and the Media: Re-Imagining the Diaspora*, ed. O. Bailey, M. Georgiou and R. Harindranath. New York: Palgrave Macmillan, pp. 52–71.

Papastergiadis, N. (2007b) 'Glimpses of cosmopolitanism in the hospitality of art', *European Journal of Social Theory*, 10(1), pp. 139–52.

Papastergiadis, N. (2007c) 'Hope in white ruins', *Art Monthly Australia*, 199(May), pp. 23–6.

Papastergiadis, N. (2007d) 'The invasion complex: deep historical fears and wide open anxieties', in *White Matters*, ed. S. Petrilli. Rome: Meltemi Editori, pp. 371–91.

Papastergiadis, N. (2007e) 'Nikos Papastergiadis in conversation with Marina Fokidis', *Flash Art*, 39(247), p. 48.

Papastergiadis, N., Riphagen, M., and Andrews, B. (2007) 'Crossed territories: indigenous cosmopolitan', in *Brooke Andrew: Eye to Eye*, ed. G. Barlow. Melbourne: Monash University Art Gallery.

Parekh, B. (2000) *Rethinking Multiculturalism: Cultural Diversity and Political Theory*. Basingstoke: Macmillan.

Parks, L. (2005) *Cultures in Orbit: Satellites and the Televisual*. Durham, NC: Duke University Press.

Parr, M. (2002) *Close the Concentration Camps*, performance at Monash University Museum of Art, Melbourne, 15 June.

Parry, B. (1987) 'Problems in current theories of colonial discourse', *Oxford Literary Review*, 9(1/2), pp. 27–58).

Pavlovic, M. L. (2003) 'Fallout', *Artlink*, 23(1) [curator's statement].

Perkins, H. (2003) 'Parallel universe, other worlds', in *Complex Entanglements: Art, Globalization and Cultural Difference*, ed. N. Papastergiadis. London: Rivers Oram Press.

Phillips, A. (2001) *Houdini's Box: On the Arts of Escape*. London: Faber & Faber.

Phillips, M. (2005) *Londonistan: How Britain is Creating a Terror State Within*. London: Gibson Square.

Phones, A. (2005) 'Remembered racialization: young people and positioning in differential understandings', in *Racialisation: Studies in Theory and Practice*, ed. K. Murji and J. Solomos. Oxford: Oxford University Press.

Pietroiusti, C. (2004) 'The good and righteous work: mechanisms of splitting and paradoxes in relational art', in *Jimmie Durham*. Milan: CHARTA.

Pope, V. (1997) 'Trafficking in women', *US News & World Report*, 7 April.

Portes, A. (1997) 'Immigration theory for a new century: some problems and opportunities', *International Migration Review*, 31(4), pp. 799–825.

Poshynanda, A. (2004) 'Desperately diasporic', in *Over Here: International Perspectives on Art and Culture*, ed. G. Mosquera and J. Fisher. Cambridge, MA: MIT Press.

Poster, M. (2008) 'Global media and culture', *New Literary History*, 39, pp. 685–703.

Pratt, M. L., Wagner, B., Carbonell i Cortés, O., Chesterman, A., and Tymoczko, M. (2010) '*Translation Studies* forum: cultural translation', *Translation Studies*, 3(1), pp. 94–110.

Prigogine, I., and Stengers, I. (1997) *The End of Certainty*. New York: Free Press.

Rabinbach, A. (1990) *The Human Motor*. New York: Basic Books.

Rampton, S., and Stauber, J. (2003) *Weapons of Mass Deception*. New York: Hodder & Stoughton, p. 130.

Rancière, J. (1991) *The Ignorant Schoolmaster*, trans. K. Ross. Stanford, CA: Stanford University Press.

Rancière, J. (2004a) *The Philosopher and his Poor*, trans. J. Dury, C. Oster and A. Parker. Durham, NC: Duke University Press.

Rancière, J. (2004b) *The Politics of Aesthetics*, trans. G. Rockhill. London: Continuum.

Rancière, J. (2006) *Hatred of Democracy*, trans. S. Corcoran. London: Verso.

Rancière, J. (2007a) 'Art of the possible: Fulvia Carnevale and John Kelsey in conversation with Jacques Rancière', *Artforum International*, 45(7), pp. 256–66.

Rancière, J. (2007b) 'The emancipated spectator', *Artforum International*, 45(7), pp. 270–82.

Rancière, J. (2007c) *The Future of the Image*, trans. G. Elliott. London: Verso.

Rancière, J. (2009) *Aesthetics and its Discontents*, trans. S. Corcoran. Cambridge: Polity.

Raunig, G. (2002a) 'A war-machine against the empire: on the precarious nomadism of the PublixTheatreCaravan', trans. L. Rennison, http://eipcp.net/transversal/0902/raunig/en.

Raunig, G. (2002b) 'Transversal multitudes', trans. A. Derieg, http://eipcp.net/transversal/0303/raunig/en.

Raunig, G. (2007) *Art and Revolution: Transversal Activism in the Long Twentieth Century*, trans. A. Derieg. Los Angeles: Semiotext(e).

Raunig, G. (2008) 'What is critique? Suspension and recomposition in textual and social machines', http://eipcp.net/transversal/0808/raunig/en.

Regev, M. (2007) 'Cultural uniqueness and aesthetic cosmopolitanism', *European Journal of Social Theory*, 10(1), pp. 123–38.

Renton, D. (2003) 'Examining the success of the British National Party', *Race and Class*, 45(2), pp. 75–85.

Retort [principally I. Boal, T. J. Clark, J. Mathew and M. Watts] (2005) *Afflicted Powers: Capital and Spectacle in a New Age of War*. London: Verso.

Rice, X. (2007) 'Africa's secret trail of "ghosts"', *Guardian Weekly*, 27 April–3 May, p. 3.

Rich, A. (1986) *Blood, Bread and Poetry: Selected Prose*. New York: W. W. Norton.

Richmond, A. (2002) 'Globalization: implications for immigrants and refugees', *Ethnic and Racial Studies*, 25(5), pp. 707–27.

Ricoeur, P. (2006) *On Translation*. London: Routledge.

Ricoeur, P. (2007) *Reflections on the Just*, trans. D. Pellauer. Chicago: University of Chicago Press.

Robb, A. (2006) 'In support of a formal citizenship text', address to the Jewish National Fund Gold Patron's Lunch, Mercantile Rowing Club, Melbourne, 25 October.

Roberts, T. (2006) 'Dead ends: the spectre of elitism in the zombie film', *Philament*, December, p. 75.

Rogoff, I. (2000) *Terra Infirma: Geography's Visual Culture*. London: Routledge.

Rosenau, J. (1997) *Along the Domestic–Foreign Frontier*. Cambridge: Cambridge University Press.

Rosenau, J. (2003) *Distant Proximities: Dynamics beyond Globalization*. Princeton, NJ: Princeton University Press.

Roy, A. (2004) *Public Power in the Age of Empire*. New York: Seven Stories Press.

Roy, O. (2004) *Globalised Islam: The Search for a New Ummah*. London: Hurst.

Rumford, C. (2008) 'Social policy beyond fear: the globalization of strangeness, the "war on terror", and "spaces of wonder"', *Social Policy and Administration*, 42(6), pp. 630–44.

Said, E. (1993) *Culture and Imperialism*. London: Chatto & Windus.

Sakai, N. (1997) *Translation and Subjectivity*. Minneapolis: University of Minnesota Press.

Salecl, R. (2001) 'The art of war and the war of arts', *European Journal of Social Theory*, 4(1), pp. 81–94.

Santiago, S. (2002) *The Space In-Between*. Durham, NC: Duke University Press.

Sassen, S. (2001) *The Global City*. Rev. edn, Princeton, NJ: Princeton University Press.

Sassen, S. (2006) *Territory, Authority, Rights*. Princeton, NJ: Princeton University Press.

Schneider, C. L. (2007) 'Police power and race riots in Paris,' *Politics and Society*, 35(4), pp. 523–49.

Schofield, J. (2006) *Constructing Place: When Artists and Anthropologists Meet*. Diffusion eBooks, www.diffusion.org.uk.

Seltzer, M. (1992) *Bodies and Machines*. New York: Routledge.

Serres, M. (1982) *Hermes*, trans. J. Harari and D. Bell. Baltimore: Johns Hopkins University Press.

Sholette, G. (2011) *Dark Matter: Art and Politics in the Age of Enterprise Culture*. London: Pluto Press.

Sitas, A. (2001) 'Shadow procession', in *ARS 01: Unfolding Perspectives*, ed. M. Jaukkuri. Helsinki: Museum of Contemporary Art [exhibition catalogue], p. 113.

Sloterdijk, P. (1998) 'Modernity as mobilization', in *Speed: Visions of an Accelerated Age*, ed. J. Millar and M. Schwarz. London: Photographer's Gallery.

Sloterdijk, P. (2006) 'Mobilization of the planet from the spirit of self intensification', *Drama Review*, 50(4), pp. 36–43.

Sloterdijk, P. (2009) *Terror from the Air*, trans. A. Patton and S. Corcoran. Los Angeles: Semiotext(e).

Smithson, R. (2000) 'Cultural confinement', in *The Writings of Robert Smithson*, ed. N. Holt. New York: New York University Press.

Sontag, S. (1986) *On Photography*. Harmondsworth: Penguin.

Sontag, S. (2004) 'Regarding the torture of others', *New York Times*, 24 May.

Spivak, G. (2000) 'Translation as culture', *parallax*, 6(1), pp. 13–24.

Spivak, G. (2002) 'Keynote lecture,' Congress CATH, Translating Class, Altering Hospitality, Leeds, 23 June.

Spivak, G. (2003) *Death of a Discipline*. New York: Columbia University Press.

Spivak, G. (2004a) 'Globalicities: terror and its consequences', *New Centennial Review*, 4(1), pp. 73–94.

Spivak, G. (2004b) 'Terror: a speech after 9-11', *Boundary 2*, 31(2), pp. 81–111.

Sriskandarajak, D., Cooley, L., and Reed, H. (2008) 'Paying their way: the fiscal contribution of immigrants in the UK', available at: www.ippr.org/publications/55/1352/paying-their-way-the-fiscal-contribution-of-immigrants-in-the-uk.

Stalker (n.d.) 'Stalker through the Actual Territories', http://digilander.libero.it/stalkerlab/tarkowsky/manifesto/manifesting.htm.

Stalker, P. (2000) *Workers without Frontiers*. Boulder, CO: Lynne Rienner.

Stengers, I. (1997) *Power and Science*, trans. P. Baines. Minneapolis: University of Minnesota Press.

Stephens, P. (2001) 'Chaos that cannot be tolerated', *Financial Times*, 28 September, p. 21.

Stewart, M. (2007) 'Critique of *Relational Aesthetics*', *Third Text*, 21(4), pp. 369–86.

Stimson, B., and Sholette, G. (eds) (2007) *Collectivism after Modernism: The Art of Social Imagination after 1945*. Minneapolis: University of Minnesota Press.

Summers, D. (2003) *Real Spaces: World Art History and the Rise of Western Modernism*. London: Phaidon Press.

Svendsen, L. (2007) *A Philosophy of Fear*. London: Reaktion Books.

Szerszynski, B., and Urry, J. (2002) 'Cultures of cosmopolitanism', *Sociological Review*, 50(4), pp. 461–81.

Szewczyk, M. (2009) *Meaning Liam Gillick*. London: MIT Press.

Tagg, J. (1992) *Grounds of Dispute: Art History, Cultural Politics and the Discursive Field*. Basingstoke: Macmillan.

Tamir, Y. (1993) *Liberal Nationalism*. Princeton, NJ: Princeton University Press.

Tao Wu, C. (2007) 'Worlds apart: problems of interpreting globalized art', *Third Text*, 21(6), pp. 719–31.

Taylor, C. (1992) *Multiculturalism and the Politics of Recognition*. Princeton, NJ: Princeton University Press.

Thompson, C. (2008) 'Web ushers in age of ambient intimacy', *New York Times*, 8 September, www.nytimes.com/2008/09/08/technology/08iht-07awarenesst.15964570.html.

Thompson, N., and Sholette, G. (eds) (2004) *The Interventionists: Users' Manual for the Creative Disruption of Everyday Life*. North Adams: Massachusetts Museum of Contemporary Art.

Tomlinson, J. (1999) *Globalization and Culture*. Cambridge: Polity.

Torpey, J. (2000) *The Invention of the Passport*. Cambridge: Cambridge University Press.

Touraine, A. (2000) *Can We Live Together?*, trans. D. Macey. Cambridge: Polity.

Touraine, A. (2005) 'Comment on Paris riots', *Berliner Zeitung*, 9 November.

Trumper, E. (2006) 'The view from Howard world', 20 September, http://newmatilda.com.2006/09/20/view-howard-world.

Turner, B. (1992) *Regulating Bodies: Essays in Medical Sociology*. London: Routledge.

Turner, B. (2003) 'Social fluids: metaphors and meanings of society', *Body & Society*, 9(1), pp. 1–10.

Tyler, I. (2006) '"Welcome to Britain": the cultural politics of asylum', *European Journal of Cultural Studies*, 9(2), pp. 185–202.

UNHCR (2008) *2008 Global Trends: Refugees, Asylum-Seekers, Returnees, Internally Displaced and Stateless Persons*, 16 June, www.unhcr.org.

Urry, J. (2000) *Sociology Beyond Societies*. London: Routledge.

Urry, J. (2003) *Global Complexity*. Cambridge: Polity.

Urry, J. (2007) *Mobilities*. Cambridge: Polity.

Urry, J., Hannam, K., and Sheller, M. (2006) 'Editorial: mobilities, immobilities and moorings', *Mobilities*, 1(1), pp. 1–22.

Verhagen, M. (2007) 'Conceptual perspex', *New Left Review*, 46(July/August), pp. 154–60.

Verwoert, J. (2008) 'Living with ghosts: from appropriation to invocation in contemporary art', *Art and Research*, 1(2), www.artandresearch.org.uk/v1n2/pdf/verwoert.pdf.

Virno, P. (1996) 'The ambivalence of disenchantment', in *Radial Thought in Italy*, ed. P. Virno and M. Hardt. Minneapolis: University of Minnesota Press.

Wagner, B. (2010) 'Response to Boris Buden and Stefan Nowotny', *Translation Studies*, Vol. 3, No.1, pp 94-110.

Wallerstein, I. (2003) *The Decline of American Power*. New York: New Press.

Walzer, M. (1989) 'Nation and universe: the Tanner lectures on human values', Brasenose College, Oxford, 1 and 8 May, www.tannerlectures.utah.edu/lectures/documents/walzer90.pdf.

Weber, C. (2005) 'Flying planes can be dangerous', *Millenium: Journal of International Studies*, 31(1), pp. 129–47.

Weber, E. (1976) *Peasants into Frenchmen: The Modernization of Rural France 1870–1914*. Stanford, CA: Stanford University Press.

Welsch, W. (1999) 'Transculturality: the puzzling form of cultures today', in *Spaces of Culture: City, Nation, World*, ed. M. Featherstone and S. Lash. London: Sage.

White, H. (1978) 'The forms of wildness', in *Tropics of Discourse*. Baltimore: Johns Hopkins University Press, pp. 150–82.

Williams, R. (1973) *The Country and the City*. London: Chatto & Windus.

Williams, R. (1983) *Culture and Society*. New York: Columbia University Press.

Wilson, E. (1988) *Hallucinations: Life in the Post-Modern City*. London: Radius.

Wiseman, J. (1998) *Global Nation?* Cambridge: Cambridge University Press.

Wolff J. (1981) *The Social Production of Art*. London: Macmillan.

Wolff, K. (1976) *Surrender and Catch: Experience and Inquiry Today*. Boston: D. Reidel.

Wood, A. (1998) 'Kant's project for perpetual peace', in *Cosmopolitics: Thinking and Feeling beyond the Nation*, ed. P. Cheah and B. Robbins. Minneapolis: University of Minnesota Press.

Wood, R. (1986) *Hollywood: From Vietnam to Reagan*. New York: Columbia University Press.

Young, H. (2001) 'A new kind of war means a new kind of discussion', *The Guardian*, 27 September, p. 22.

Young, R. (1995) *Colonial Desire: Hybridity in Theory, Culture and Race*. London: Routledge.

Zable, A. (2007) 'Australia's very own Devil's Island', *The Age*, 7 September, p. 13.

Zimmerman, M. (ed.) (2003) *The Art Historian: National Institutions and Institutional Practices*. Williamstown, MA: Sterling and Francine Clark Institute.

Žižek, S. (1997) 'Multiculturalism, or the cultural logic of multinational capitalism', *New Left Review*, 225(Sept/Oct), pp. 28–51.

Žižek, S. (2002) *Welcome to the Desert of the Real*. London: Verso.

Žižek, S. (2007a) 'Some politically incorrect reflections on urban violence in Paris and New Orleans and related matters,' in *Urban Politics Now*, ed. BAVO. Rotterdam: NAi.

Žižek, S. (2007b) 'The lesson of Rancière', in J. Rancière, *The Politics of Aesthetics*, trans. G. Rockhill. London: Continuum.

Zlotnik, H. (1998) 'International migration 1965–96: an overview', *Population and Development Review*, 24, pp. 429–6.

Index

5<u>00</u>   Gen 2/16 JD